Richard C. Shimeall

Political Economy of Prophecy

With special reference to its relation to the history of the church, and the civil, military, and ecclesiastical history of the Roman empire, and of its last emperors, the three Napoleons

Richard C. Shimeall

Political Economy of Prophecy
With special reference to its relation to the history of the church, and the civil, military, and ecclesiastical history of the Roman empire, and of its last emperors, the three Napoleons

ISBN/EAN: 9783337244163

Printed in Europe, USA, Canada, Australia, Japan

Cover: Foto ©Suzi / pixelio.de

More available books at **www.hansebooks.com**

THE
POLITICAL ECONOMY OF PROPHECY.

THE FOUR NAPOLEONS.

POLITICAL ECONOMY OF PROPHECY,

WITH SPECIAL REFERENCE TO ITS RELATION TO THE

HISTORY OF THE CHURCH,

AND THE

CIVIL, MILITARY, AND ECCLESIASTICAL HISTORY

OF THE

ROMAN EMPIRE,

AND OF ITS LAST EMPERORS,

THE THREE NAPOLEONS,

WITH AN APPENDIX ON

The Pope's late Encyclical, and the Firman of the Sultan of Turkey,

PROPHETICALLY AND HISTORICALLY DEMONSTRATED.

ILLUSTRATED BY PORTRAITS OF THE NAPOLEONIC FAMILY; A CHART OF
THE COURSE OF EMPIRES; MAPS OF THE HOLY LAND, ETC.

BY THE

REV. R. C. SHIMEALL,

OF THE PRESBYTERY OF NEW YORK.

AUTHOR OF OUR BIBLE CHRONOLOGY, HISTORIC AND PROPHETIC, DEMONSTRATED;
CHRIST'S SECOND COMING—IS IT PRE- OR POST-MILLENNIAL? ETC., ETC.

NEW YORK:
JOHN F. TROW & CO., PUBLISHERS, 50 GREENE STREET.
PHILADELPHIA, POST-OFFICE BOX 1199.
1866.

Entered, according to Act of Congress, in the year 1866, by

R. C. SHIMEALL,

in the Clerk's Office of the District Court of the United States for the Southern District of New York.

JOHN F. TROW & CO.,
PRINTERS, STEREOTYPERS, & ELECTROTYPERS,
50 GREENE STREET, N.Y.

This Volume,

ON THE POLITICAL ECONOMY OF PROPHECY,

IS RESPECTFULLY DEDICATED TO THE

THREE AMERICAN NAPOLEONS;

HIS EXCELLENCY, ANDREW JOHNSON,

PRESIDENT OF THE UNITED STATES;

HON. WILLIAM H. SEWARD,

SECRETARY OF STATE OF THE UNITED STATES;

AND

ULYSSES S. GRANT,

LIEUTENANT-GENERAL OF THE ARMIES OF THE UNITED STATES.

GENTLEMEN:

This volume is dedicated to you collectively, as acknowledgedly the most distinguished and world-renowned in the Executive, Diplomatic, and Military Departments, to whom the Government and best interests of these United States could have been confided. We accord to you, therefore, the rank of the THREE AMERICAN NAPOLEONS, side by side with those memorable personages of that name, who have acted so conspicuous a part in controlling the destinies of the Old World. Inheriting all that is truly great and valuable in their endowments, *without* their detractive characteristics, the American people may well be proud of three such scions of their own native soil.

Though "not a prophet, nor the son of a prophet," yet claiming to hold the position of an *interpreter* of the "POLITICAL ECONOMY OF PROPHECY," as set forth by the inspired seers of the Old and New Testaments; the undersigned, under the shadow of your wings, as the representatives of a great people, is desirous to indicate those "coming events that cast their shadows before;" on the simple principle, that "to be forewarned is to be forearmed" of those "coming events" therein indicated. And that, to the intent that the rulers and the ruled of this great country, may be led to recognize the hand of "THE OMNIPOTENT RULER OF THE UNIVERSE," in controlling alike the destinies of the nations of earth, and of the church of God, amid the upheavings and revolutions—*national, political, civil, social,* and *religious*—that are now shaking to their centre both the Old World and the New.

And, bearing in mind that it is THE LAW OF GOD, and *not* prophecy, that constitutes the rule of human action; to lead them to a preparation to meet "all those things that are coming on the earth;" and to inspire them—despite their ill-deservings—with thanksgiving to God, for the high and glorious destiny still reserved in the Divine purpose for this "LAND OF OVERSHADOWING WINGS."

I have the honor to remain, gentlemen,
  Your obedient and humble servant,
    R. C. SHIMEALL.

CONTENTS.

DEDICATION, ... v. vi.
CONTENTS, ... vii.–xiv.
INTRODUCTION, ... 15–29

POLITICAL ECONOMY OF PROPHECY.

CHAPTER I.

INTRODUCTION.

PROPHETIC BASIS OF THE EXPOSITION, Rev., chap. xvii.—Scope of—Involves the career of the Three Napoleons—Connection with, of the four great Monarchies of the World, the Babylonian, Medo-Persian, Grecian, and Roman—*The Roman Empire*—Its duration—Proof of its *Perpetuated Unity*, . . . 31–48

CHAPTER II.

PROPHETIC HISTORY OF THE ROMAN EMPIRE, CONTINUED.

RECAPITULATION—Seven Forms of the Civil Government of the Roman Empire—Chronology of the *Sixth* Form, the *Imperial*—This the *Gordian Knot* of Expositors—Augustulus—Mr. Elliott and Dr. H. Moore on—Fallacy of—True Chronology of, demonstrated—Eight Proofs of—Result—Further Proofs of the *Territorial and Political Unity* of the Roman Empire—Three arguments in proof that NAPOLEON I. was the *Seventh* Symbolic Head of the Empire, ... 49–64

viii   CONTENTS.

CHAPTER III.

NAPOLEON II. DUKE OF REICHSTADT AND KING OF ITALY—NAPOLEON III., ETC.

RECAPITULATION.—Predicted Short Career of NAPOLEON I.—Exultation of the Crowned Heads of Europe on—NAPOLEON II.—His early Death—Edict of the European Powers against the Napoleonic Family—But, man *proposes*, God *disposes*—the Wound unto death of the Symbolic Seventh *Head* healed in the person of NAPOLEON III., who forms the principal subject of this Exposition—Preliminaries—The FRENCH REVOLUTION between A. D. 1789 and 1848, prepares the way for his Accession to the Throne of the FRANCO-ROMAN EMPIRE—Brief Historic Sketch of—His Escape from the Prison of Ham—Exile in the United States—Müller—Napoleon's Secrets—His darling Idea of forming a UNIVERSAL LATIN DYNASTY, with France as the Head—His extraordinary Career between Dec. 2d, 1848, and Dec. 2d, 1852—Review of the preceding details—THE REVIVAL OF THE SEVENTH AND EIGHTH HEADS—Faber on—Fallacy of—I. The Character and Exploits of the revived Seventh Franco-Roman Emperorship in the person of Louis Napoleon III., AS A PURELY SECULAR POWER—Further Historical Remarks,   .   .   65-81

CHAPTER IV.

LOUIS NAPOLEON III. CONTINUED—THE FUTURE DESTINED SOVEREIGN OF A UNIVERSAL LATIN DYNASTY.

RECAPITULATION—A Startling Announcement—Prophetico-Symbolic *Characteristics* of Louis Napoleon III.—His unprecedented Career to the Present Time—Rev. xiii. 3, 4—First, of the similarity of his Accession to Power with that of his Imperial Uncle—His remarkable Declaration before the National Assembly of France in A. D. 1848—How verified—Appears upon the Stage as the GREAT PACIFICATOR of the Nations—Also as a DESPOT—Illustrated in Seven Particulars,   .   .   .   82-98

CHAPTER V.

LOUIS NAPOLEON III. CONTINUED—SYMBOLIZED BY THE SCARLET COLORED BEAST OF REV. xvii. 1-6, IN UNION WITH THE PAPACY.

EXPOSITION OF THE ABOVE PROPHECY—Its historical application to LOUIS NAPOLEON III.—Preliminaries—Verification of the results of the above union—Oudinot—Archbishop of Paris—His Harlot Rider, the PAPACY, unconscious of his ulterior designs—This Union brings on a *Crisis* in his Career of Destiny—The Bourgeois, the Aristocracy, the Socialists, etc.—Results—Another Fact—The Carbonari of Italy—Republicans—Pius IX., King Charles Albert, and Louis Napoleon III., members of—The Events which grew out of—Expulsion of Pius IX. to Gaeta—Restored by Louis Napoleon III.—Is tried for his *perfidy* by the Carbonari—The matter is compounded—secures Independence to Italy—Napoleon III. has no real love for the Papacy—Is a REPUBLICAN—His Napoleonic *prestige*—Receives Idolatrous Homage—His Star of Destiny in the Ascendant—Comprehensiveness of his Military and Naval Programme as the PACIFICATOR of the Nations—The New York Tribune, etc.
99-114

CHAPTER VI.

LOUIS NAPOLEON III. CONTINUED—THE EIGHTH APOCALYPTICO-SYMBOLIC HEAD OF THE UNIVERSAL LATIN EMPIRE.

INTRODUCTION—Rev. xvii. 8, 10—Fearfully portentous and comprehensive Words!—Objection: Their significancy cannot be known because still *future*—Reply—Another Objection: The *book* mentioned in Rev. v. 1-7 is not the *sealed book* of Daniel—Reply—Fallacy of the argument of *obscurity* of the prophecy, etc.—We of this day have an interest in it—Proof that Louis Napoleon III. is the EIGHTH HEAD of the Apocalyptic Beast—As such, he is designated as the future Leader of the Last Democratic Politico-Antichristian Confederacy of the Nations against the Abrahamic Jewish Race and the Gentile Christian Church, as the last ANTICHRIST—St. Paul's Prophecy, 2 Thess.

ii. 3, 4, and verses 9–12—Also Christ's Prophecy, John v. 43—His "coming" a *personal* one, HUMANITY DEIFIED—Startling Announcement—Hence the *denial* by some writers of a future *personal* Antichrist—Refutation of, ... 115

SECTION I.

THE PROPHETICO-HISTORIC RISE, CAREER, AND DOOM OF THIS GREAT APOCALYPTIC ANTICHRISTIAN POWER.

I.—The *Chronological Period* assigned for the appearance of THE LAST ANTICHRIST—The Spiritual and Ecclesiastico-Political Power of the *Papacy*, and the Civil Power of the *Roman Empire*, were to run a *parallel* course. Compare Dan. vii. 25 with Rev. xiii. 5—The whole period 1,335 years, Dan. vii. 12—Period of the Rise of the PAPACY in A. D. 533—Proof of—Prophetico-Historic Verification of—The Bishop of Versailles and Napoleon III.—Final *Destruction* of the Papacy by the Symbolic "Ten Horns" or "Kings," Rev. xvii. 16, . 115–132

CHAPTER VI. (CONTINUED.)

SECTION II.

LOUIS NAPOLEON III., AS THE HEAD OF THE UNIVERSAL LATIN EMPIRE.

THIS Event still *Future*—Yet nigh at hand—The Harlot-rider still seated on his back—The *Secular* Power of the Popedom nearly annihilated—What is to follow, at variance with the popular views—Five Considerations in proof of the position herein assumed :—

    I. *The Steps which are to immediately precede the Introduction of Louis Napoleon III. upon the stage of action as the Eighth Apocalyptic Head*—Will be preceded by *Miraculous Wonders*—Is warily advancing toward the *acme* of his ambition—Is suspected of an inkling after the POPEDOM—*May* assume it, to effect a change in the functions of the then reigning *Pope* to that of the *False Prophet*, who is to *work Miracles* before him (Rev. xix. 20), as his *own* passport from the *Seventh* to the *Eighth* Headship—Present Aspect of French Affairs favorable to this—Other Facts—The Result.

II.—*His Inauguration, as the Eighth Head, into his Seat of Power, at the hands of the Ten Roman "Horns" or "Kings"*—Certainty of, as derived from the Prophecy, Rev. xvii. 17, "For God hath put it into their hearts," etc.—(Compare Dan. iv. 1-18; 23-25; and chap. vii. 1-8, with 2 Thess. ii. 3, 8, and verse 11)—St. Paul's Prophecy in outline filled up by St. John's respecting the appearance and work of the *Three Unclean Frog Spirits*, Rev. xvi. 13, 14, 16—Exposition of—Meaning of the phrase, "The whole World"—1. Their Origin—2. Extent of the combined Influences of their Miraculous Agencies—3. What we are to understand as denoted by them—4. The Period of their Mission—(Compare Rev. xvi. 12, with verses 13-14)—5. Will culminate in the formation of the LAST DEMOCRATICO-INFIDEL CONFEDERACY—Objection to, on the ground of its alleged impossibility—Reply—Appeal to facts —Most of those now living may witness the things here spoken of—An Appeal, ... 133-149

CHAPTER VI. (CONTINUED.)

SECTION III.

THE POLITICO-HISTORIC MARK, NAME, OR NUMBER (666) OF THE APOCALYPTIC EIGHTH HEAD, QUERE.—DOES IT APPLY TO LOUIS NAPOLEON III.?

INTRODUCTORY REMARKS—The Prophecy, Rev. xiii. 16-18—Furnishes additional evidence that the revived Seventh Head of the Roman Beast, and the Eighth, belong to the *same person*—Distinction between the Power that *confers* and HE who *interprets* said number—Miracles wrought by the former to that end —The *Image* of the Beast, What?—The Mark, etc., imposed as a sign of *Dedication*, etc.—How to be deciphered, or counted— Origin of, illustrated—Zoological Origin of the Eighth Head— The number 666 applied, first, to his ancestry—Illustrated in three particulars—But in order to its *complete fulfilment* must be applied to some ONE MAN—That man, LOUIS NAPOLEON III.—Must be deciphered in the three languages, Latin, Greek, and Hebrew—Illustrations of, with answers to objections, etc.—The great Antichristian Confederacy of which he is the Head—Editorial article from a New York journal on "The Signs of the Times"—Closing Remarks, . . . 150–166

CHAPTER VI. (CONTINUED.)

SECTION IV.

THE PROPHETICO-HISTORIC EXPLOITS OF THE APOCALYPTIC EIGHTH HEAD AND HIS ANTICHRISTIAN CONFEDERACY.

RECAPITULATION—Entrance upon a comparatively *new field* of Scriptural Exegesis—Prophecies relating to the future Restoration of the Jews to Palestine: 167–169

I. FIRST ACT of the Eighth Head, *the restoration of the Jews to their own land*—Has undergone *numerous changes*—PREDICTED ENLARGEMENT AND NEW DIVISION OF, AMONG THE TWELVE TRIBES—First, Successive Geographical Developments of—1. Its first occupancy by the Ten *Heathen Nations*, prior to Abraham's call—Map of—2. From Joshua to the time of the Judges—Map of—3. Canaan as adapted to the period of the Kings—Three Maps; the first adapted to *the Book of Kings*, the second to the *Captivity*, the third to the *time of Christ*—4. The future enlargement of—The new division of—Map of—The Holy Oblation—Illustration of. . . 169–182

The Restoration of Israel will take place in their nationally unconverted State, and in great suffering—Louis Napoleon III. as the Eighth Head the instigator of—Makes a *League* with them to that end—This involves their *allegiance* to him—The Prophet Hosea on—The Jews incorporated with his Confederacy—The Prophet Isaiah on—Astounding effect upon the Nations—AGENCIES employed in their Restoration—Isaiah on, chap. xviii. 1-3—Proof that this Prophecy points to THE UNITED STATES OF AMERICA—Not one of the "*Ten Horns*" of the Roman Empire—Will form *no part* of the Antichristian Confederacy of the Latin Empire—A great and glorious destiny awaits her—Will, nevertheless, be brought under the rod for her national sins—Will form an *alliance* with the EIGHTH HEAD—The Jews will hail him as their MESSIAH—Christ's Prophecy of—The Jews the *wealthiest* nation on earth—When restored, will wipe out the foot-prints of the destroyers of their land—Jeremiah's Prophecy of—Will *rebuild* their Temple—Ezekiel on—Will rapidly rise to national distinction while yet in league with their false Messiah—Ezekiel on—This not the *climax* of their national sin—Ezekiel on, etc. . . 182–210

II. THE SECOND ACT of the Eighth Head—His *desecration* of the Temple—St. Paul on—The *last unparalleled tribulation* of the Jews—Jeremiah, Daniel, and Christ on—Their *revolt* against the false Messiah—This leads to the *last acts* of the Eighth Head, ... 210–212

CHAPTER VI. (CONCLUDED.)

SECTION V.

CONTINUATION OF THE PROPHETICO-HISTORIC EXPLOITS OF THE APOCALYPTIC EIGHTH HEAD AND HIS ANTICHRISTIAN CONFEDERACY—THEIR FINAL DOOM—CONCLUSION.

III. THE THIRD ACT.—Antichrist's *Invasion* of the Holy Land and its Capital, Jerusalem—Gog and Magog Army of Ezekiel—Proof that it is not identical with that of the Apocalypse, chap. xx. 8, 9—Faber on—Reply—This invasion described by Zechariah, chap. xiv. 1, 2. 212–216

IV. THE FOURTH ACT.—Eventuates in "*the Battle of the Great Day of God Almighty*," Rev. xvi. 14—Locality of the Battle-field, ARMAGEDDON—Predicted certain destruction of the Invaders by the VISIBLE PERSONAL APPEARANCE OF CHRIST —Scripture Proofs— 216–223

V. The *final doom of the Last Antichrist and his Magogean Confederacy*—The *result* of the Battle—Are destroyed by the PERSONAL AGENCY of the Lord Jesus Christ—Magnitude of this Confederacy—Number of their Weapons—An Explanation —Conclusion, ... 223

APPENDIX.

I. Prophetical Aspect of the Pope's late "Encyclical,"
II. Prophetical Aspect of the late Firman of the Sultan of Turkey in reference to the Holy City, Jerusalem, . . . 229–258

"The Conclusion of the Whole Matter," 258–280

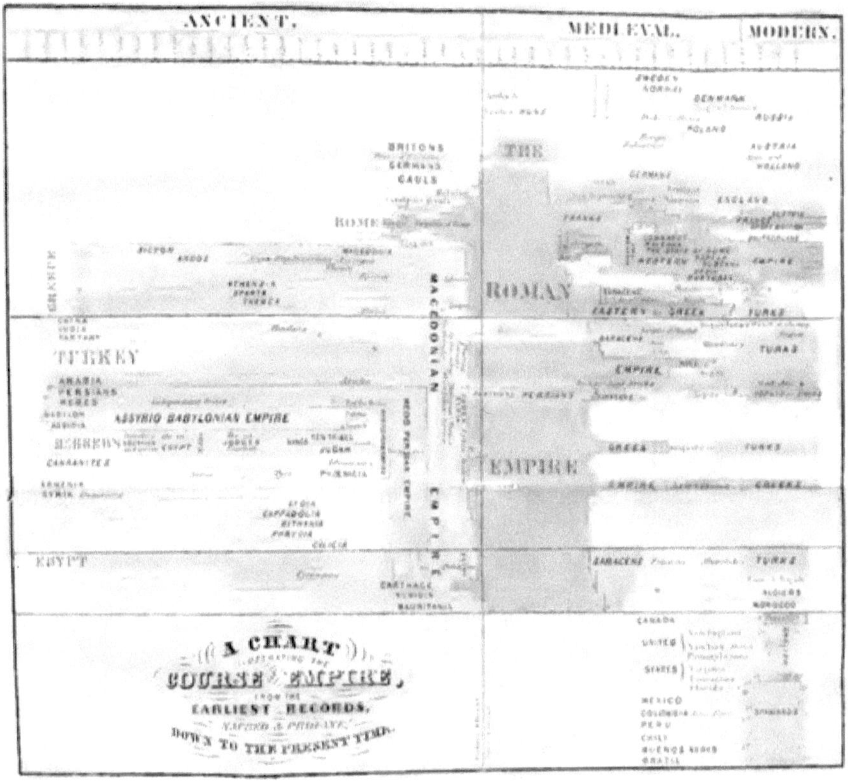
ANCIENT.
MEDIEVAL.
MODERN.
BRITONS
GERMANS
GAULS
ROME
THE
ROMAN
EMPIRE
MACEDONIAN
EMPIRE
GREECE
TURKEY
ARABIA
PERSIANS
MEDES
BABYLON
ASSYRIA
ASSYRIO BABYLONIAN EMPIRE
HEBREWS
CANAANITES
EGYPT
CARTHAGE
NUMIDIA
MAURITANIA
DENMARK
RUSSIA
POLAND
AUSTRIA
HOLLAND
ENGLAND
TURKS
ALGIERS
MOROCCO
CANADA
UNITED STATES
MEXICO
PERU
A CHART
COURSE EMPIRE,
FROM THE
EARLIEST RECORDS,
DOWN TO THE PRESENT TIME.

INTRODUCTION.

It forms no part of the design of this volume, to give an exposition of what appertains to the social, civil, judicial, and ecclesiastical systems of the commonwealth of Israel as enacted by the inspired lawgiver, Moses, between the Exode and the time of Samuel. That system of government was adapted to a union of the Church with the State, and is a matter of history, as constituting the *original theocracy* of Israel.

What we propose in these pages, is, to present a view of "THE POLITICAL ECONOMY OF PROPHECY," as foreshadowing those systems of earthly gentile governments that were to bear rule in the world, subsequently to, and in consequence of, the *abrogation* of the original theocracy by the Israelites under Samuel, onward to the *restoration* of that theocracy by their king, Messiah. It will be found that, during this prolonged interval, those "holy men of God who spake as they were moved by the Holy Ghost," prophetically portrayed the various systems of government of human device to which the Church and people of God, Jewish and Christian, were to be subjected, either as the *punishment* of their sins, or the *trial* of their faith, under and during the dominancy of Gentilism over them.

First. In regard to the *Hebrew, Israelitish,* or *Jewish* nation. Moses, as a prophet, Deut. xxviii. 1-14, gives a summary of the many and great *blessings* that should accrue to Israel as that people whom "God would set on high above all the nations of the earth," *if obedient* to His commands. On the other hand, *if disobedient,* he predicts, in verses 15-68 inclusive, a long catalogue of the most terrific *curses* that could possibly befall any nation. These curses should overtake them while in their own land, not only, but, and especially when, being delivered into the hands of their enemies, "the Lord would scatter them among all people, from the one end of the earth even unto the other; and that there they should serve other gods, which neither they nor their fathers had known, even wood and stone." Among these curses, allusion is made, verse 36, to what would follow *the choice of* "*the king* that they should set over them," viz., that the Lord would bring a nation against them from far, from the end of the earth, as swift as the eagle flieth; a nation whose tongue they should not understand, a nation of fierce countenance, which should not regard the person of the old, nor show favor to the young: and that he should eat the fruit of their cattle, and the fruit of their land, until they should be destroyed." . . Also that he "should besiege them in all their gates, until their high and fenced walls come down, wherein they trusted, throughout all their land, which the Lord their God had given them." And finally, that " they should be left few in number, whereas they were as the stars of heaven for multitude : *because* they would not obey the voice of the Lord their God."

The whole closes with the solemn appeal :—Thus saith the Most High, "See . . . I call heaven and earth to record this day against you, that I have set before you life and death, blessing and cursing : therefore choose life, that both thou and thy seed may live." (Deut. xxx. 19.)

But, alas! Israel chose death, with all its attendant curses. These curses, consequent of their rebellions against God under Moses, commenced with their nomadic wanderings for forty years through the wilderness, and were continued for like causes, during their occupancy of the land of Canaan under the Judges, until the time of the prophet Samuel. But this pious priest, prophet, and judge, had waxen old. Unable longer to bear the weight and responsibilities of his official functions, *the reins of government* were committed to the hands of his two sons, Joel and Abiah.

It is at this point in the history of Israel, when was verified the prophecy of Moses respecting *their choice of a "king."* We read of the two sons of Samuel, that they "walked not in his ways, but turned aside after lucre, and took bribes, and perverted judgment." Whereupon "the elders of Israel came to Samuel unto Ramah, and said **unto him, Behold,** thou art old, and thy sons walk not **in thy ways:** now make **us a king, to** judge us, like all the nations."[1] In vain alike were the protestations, expostulations, and predictions of the venerable prophet as to the *character* of the king of their choice, whose despotic rule and oppression and extortion would make them " cry out **in that day, because of the king whom they** shall have chosen." **They still** persisted in their demand :—" **Nay,** but we will have **a king over us,** that we also may be like all the nations (heathen), and that our king may judge us, and go out and fight our battles."[2]

Now, this conduct of the nation of Israel constituted **the highest act of treason and rebellion against the covenant God** of their fathers. It involved *the abjuration of the original theocracy,* and the substitution in **its place of a system of government** analogous to the *heathen* nations!

God gave them up to their choice. **In answer to** the prayer of Samuel, "the Lord said **unto him, Hearken unto** the voice of the people in all that they say **unto thee: for they have not** rejected thee, *but they have rejected* **me,** *that I should not be king over them.*"[3]

Their error, **however, consisted in their choice of** Saul, the son of Cis, a *Benjamite*, as their **first** king. Whereas the prophecy of Jacob had designated the *tribe of Judah* as the source and centre of the regal power.[4] Hence the anointing of Saul out of a vial,[5] denotive of the *instability* of his short-lived reign. And, although David, **of the tribe of Judah, as his** successor, was anointed out of a horn,[6] the emblem of *permanency;* yet a limit was set to the period **of the Davidic monarchy in** the line of the kings of Judah. A monarchy is not a theocracy. Hence,

---

[1] 1 Sam., viii. 1-5.
[2] *Ibid.,* viii. 10-18; 19, 20.
[3] *Ibid.,* **verses 6, 7.**
[4] Gen., xlix. 10.
[5] 1 Sam. x. 1.
[6] *Ibid.,* xvi. 13.

however the line of kings from David reigned *jus Divinum* (by Divine right), it was to *terminate* at the coming of the "SHILOH."[1] That *covenant* made with David which guaranteed the perpetuity of his throne, therefore, *reached beyond* the royal monarchical line. Accordingly, the Apostle Peter, when addressing his brethren on the day of Pentecost, and "freely speaking to them of the patriarch David," said:—"Therefore, being a prophet, and knowing that God had sworn with an oath to him, that of the fruit of his loins, according to the flesh, HE WOULD RAISE UP CHRIST TO SIT ON HIS THRONE; He, seeing this before, spake of the *resurrection* of Christ, that His soul was not left in hell (ἅδης), neither did his flesh see corruption."[2]

It is, therefore, by and through Christ, as "David's son and Lord,"[3] in *resurrection* power and glory, and by Him alone, that the ORIGINAL THEOCRACY can be restored.

Hence, this event did not transpire at the *first appearing* of the "Shiloh" to Israel. True, the monarchical "sceptre then departed from Judah." Still, the nation, after the example of Israel in the time of Samuel, by their rejection and crucifixion of Him who was "BORN KING OF THE JEWS," furnished the occasion for the *deferment* of the restoration of the previously abjured theocracy. And so, their Messiah, the Lord Jesus Christ, —in analogy to the parabolic nobleman, of whom the "citizens" declared, "we will not have this man to reign over us," and who was driven "into a far country, till he should receive a kingdom and return,"—is now, so to speak, *a king in exile* in the far-off heavens, whither, as "the great High Priest over the house of God," He has gone to *intercede for us*, henceforth expecting, till His enemies be made His footstool; when, being invested of the Father with His *kingly* prerogatives, or, in other words, having "received His kingdom," he will *return the second time* to "build up the tabernacle of David, which is fallen down."

Of this the prophet Daniel speaks, chap. vii. 13, 14:—"I saw in the night visions, and behold, one like the Son of Man came with the clouds of heaven, and came to the ancient of

---

[1] Gen., xlix. 10. [2] Acts ii. 30, 31; Ps. x. 16. [3] Matt., xxii. 41-45.

days, and they brought Him near before Him. *And there was given Him* dominion, and glory, and a kingdom, that all people, and nations, and languages, should serve Him : **His dominion is an everlasting dominion, which shall not pass away, and His kingdom that which shall not be destroyed."** And with this accords the declaration of St. Peter in his address to the *Jews*, Acts iii. 20, 21. **"And he shall send Jesus Christ, which *before* was preached unto you :** whom the heavens must receive *until the times of restitution of all things,* which God hath spoken by the mouth of all His holy prophets since the world began." And so, in regard,

Second. To the *Christian Church.* We now speak of the visible church catholic on earth in her *mixed state,* as constituted of tares and wheat, or the apostate and the true. As it respects the former, the Apostle Paul predicted, Acts xx. 29, 30, that "after his departure should grievous wolves enter in among them, not sparing the flock. Also of their own selves should men arise, speaking perverse things, to draw away disciples after them." This prophecy formed the *basis* of that of 2 Thess. ii. 3, in which he foretells of that "falling away first"—(ἡ ἀποστασία, *the apostasy*), which was finally to culminate in that "revelation of the man of sin and son of perdition," or THE LAST ANTICHRIST; "even him, whose coming is after the working of Satan with all power and signs and lying wonders, and with all deceivableness of unrighteousness in them that perish ; *because* they received not the love of the truth, that they might be saved. And for this cause God shall send them strong delusion, that they should believe a lie," etc. The voice of prophecy also points out, that this apostasy of the nominal church throughout Christendom in its culminated form, is to constitute, out of its subjects, that *last great antichristian confederacy of the nations,* whose appearance upon the prophetical platform is to immediately precede THE SECOND COMING (παρουσίας, personal presence) of the Lord Jesus Christ.

On the other hand, running parallel with the developments of this apostasy, the same voice of prophecy foretells the sufferings of "the faithful in Christ Jesus, called to be saints," as the *trial* of their Christian integrity. Thus Daniel, in reference to the "little horn" of chap. vii. 8, predicts, verse 21, 25, "I beheld, and the same horn *made war* with the saints, and prevailed against them;" and that he "should wear out the saints of the Most High," etc., and to this state of suffering the Apostle Peter alludes, 1 Pet. i. 6, 7,—"Wherein ye greatly rejoice, though now for a season, if need be, ye are in heaviness through manifold temptations; *that the trial of your faith*, being much more precious than of gold which perisheth, though it be tried by fire, might be found unto praise and honor and glory, *at the appearing* of Jesus Christ." These prophecies are in harmony with that of our Lord to his disciples, John xvi. 33, "in the world ye shall have *tribulation;*" and also with that of St. Paul to the believers in Lystra, Iconium, and Antioch, Acts xiv. 22, "that we must through much tribulation enter into the kingdom of God."

The *purpose* of these pages, therefore, is, to show that "all the prophets, from Samuel and those that follow after, as many as have spoken,"[1] have *prophetically* mapped out the rise, career, and final destiny of all those earthly systems of political economy that were to sway their respective sceptres in and over the nations of the world, as *rivals* to that original theocracy established over the commonwealth of Israel; together with the *contemporaneous* vicissitudes and sufferings of the Church and people of God, Jewish and Christian, by and through them, as rods in God's hand, either for the punishment of the apostate or the trial of the faithful; and of the final vengeance which is to overtake them, one and all, as the persecutors of the Lord's chosen people of both classes, in their total subversion, by the *reëstablishment* of that THEOCRATIC GOVERNMENT abjured by Israel in the time of Samuel.

The learned Bossuet and Bishop Porteus have well and truly said of the four prophetic monarchies of Gentilism that were to bear rule in the earth between the *abjuration* and the *restoration* of the theocracy of Israel—the Babylonian, Medo-Persian, Grecian, and Roman—that they "form, as it were, *one vast map of Providential administration*, delineated on so large a scale, and

---

[1] Acts, iii. 24.

marked with such legible characters, that it cannot possibly escape our observation;" and that "*this map has been held up* before the eyes of all nations for the space of nearly three thousand years, to confront the feeble cavils of atheism, and to confirm the *scriptural doctrine of a national Providence.*"

And yet how many, in these "last times," have entirely overlooked the fact, that *in the Bible* is to be found the most extensive and complete system of *political economy* of which the world can boast!

Of the prophecy of Moses, in the xxviiith chapter of Deuteronomy, respecting the numerous curses that should overtake Israel in the event of their disobedience of the Lord's commands, history, both sacred and profane, attests that they have all been *literally* verified, in accordance with the *natural language* in which they are recorded. The same holds true of the prophecy of Samuel in reference to the character, etc., of their first king, Saul, in 1 Sam. viii. 10-18. But it is otherwise with those *subsequent* prophecies, which portray the POLITICAL ECONOMY OF GENTILISM, as adumbrated by the former prophets. In these, natural language, at least for the most part, is exchanged for the *mystical ;* so that the various *anti-theocratic* systems of government that have obtained in the world, and the *anti-Christian* ecclesiastical systems that have prevailed in the nominal church, are revealed by the Holy Spirit under *symbolical* forms. This holds true, more especially, of the things set forth in the books of Daniel and of the Apocalypse, the latter being *synchronical* with, and *expository* of, the former.

It will, however, be shown in the sequel of these pages, that the symbols introduced in these prophecies, being selected from some real objects in nature, either *inanimate*,—as the gold, silver, brass, iron, etc., of the colossal image of Nebuchadnezzar (Dan. chap. ii.),—or *animate*,—as the four rampant beasts of Daniel,—the winged lion, the bear, the four-headed and four-winged leopard, and the nondescript beast, etc.,—are all representative of some corresponding *literal* object, person, event, or thing, which forms the *subject* of the prophecy. Also, that in these symbols, being in numerous instances interpreted by the Holy Spirit who revealed them, we are furnished with *a key* by which to unlock the otherwise hidden meaning of the whole. They hence form, so to speak, A PROPHETICO-HIEROPHANTIC ALPHABET, not in the sense of the mere letters of a foreign tongue, but in the more expansive signification of the objects or events, etc., to which they refer. Or, these prophecies, taken as a whole, may be compared to a dissected map, which, commencing with the larger sections, all the other parts are of comparatively easy adjustment. And, as to the subjects treated of in this volume, we say without hesitation, that every intelligent reader, from his own knowledge of events past and present,— on the admitted principle that history is prophecy verified— will be enabled to decide for himself, as to the *correctness* of the prophetico-historical expositions of the matters signified by them.

And finally. It is specially to be borne in mind, that while those prophecies, which are employed by the Holy Spirit to symbolize the *rival* powers of Gentilism over the suspended theocracy of Israel, extend over the prolonged period from the days of Samuel to the close of " the times of the Gentiles ; " yet are we principally concerned in them, as they point to and centre in the great period of crisis, or that " *consummation of all things* which God hath spoken by the mouth of all his holy prophets since the world began."

The author would now state, that having laid before the church his work entitled " Our Bible Chronology, Sacred and Profane, Historic and Prophetic, critically examined and demonstrated," etc.; and the " Sequel " to it on " Christ's Second Coming, the great Question of the day—is it *pre* or *post*-millennial," etc.; now offers the present volume as what he expects and intends as his last work in book form on prophetical subjects.

The first of these two volumes furnishes all that is essential to a thorough knowledge of the *chronology* of Holy Scripture, on the one hand; and the second of the *doctrine* and *history* relating to the second coming of Christ, on the other. The present volume fills a niche in the department of prophetical exposition, not found in the same form in the others. It furnishes an exhibit of those prophecies which, though spanning a *long interval* of the history of the nations of earth and of the Church of God, Jewish and Gentile, as therein foreshadowed; yet, inasmuch as their concentrated rays, as we have said, centre in and point to THE GREAT PERIOD OF CRISIS in the affairs of both, they will be seen to hold a close relation to the political aspect and the moral and spiritual interests, present and future, of *the age we live in.*

The reader will observe, that the Napoleonic family, and especially the reigning sovereign of the Franco-Roman empire, Louis Napoleon III., occupies a large space in these prophetic expositions. In reference, however, to this last-named personage, the writer wishes it to be distinctly understood, that he does not hold him up to view as " the predestined monarch of the world." There is an essential distinction to be observed between what God *appoints* and what He *permits*. In regard to all the earth-born monarchs and their dynasties, we read that " God, in times past, hath *suffered* all nations to walk *in their own ways.*"[1] As the offshoots of the original USURPER of the earthly " dominion " bequeathed to man in Eden, they are so many *rivals* to HIM—" the woman's seed "—who, as the divinely constituted " Heir of all things," is THE ONLY PREDESTINED MONARCH OF THE WORLD. We are hence to distinguish between " the eternal purpose which God purposed in Christ Jesus our Lord," as the head of that abjured theocracy of Israel which is to be *restored* by Him, and those political systems of human device which He has permitted to obtain among the nations of earth, during and under the usurped dominancy over them of " the god of this world." It is not true, therefore, that any *mere man* will be permitted to attain to the position of " monarch of the world." Louis Napoleon III., by the *sufferance* of Him who is " the Governor " among the apostate nations of Christendom, will rise to a headship over *the short-lived* " *universal Latin empire;*" but that headship *will not* extend over the entire nationalities of earth. The sway of his iron sceptre will not reach the remoter heathen nations, nor will it include these United States. Even in his character and functions as the last Antichrist, though his *influence* and that of his agents will be

---

[1] Acts, xiv. 16.

widespread, yet his **appearance** upon the stage as such, will be restricted more especially to the *Jewish nation in Palestine*. When "he comes to *them* in his own name, him *they* will receive." Though it is said that "power will be given him over all kindreds, and tongues, and nations," and that "all that dwell upon the earth shall wonder after and worship him;" yet this power will extend only to those "whose names *are not* written in the book of life of the Lamb slain from the foundation of the world."[1] Of these latter, a goodly number among all the nationalities, will refuse to "worship his image," or to receive the impress of his "mark, or name, or number of his name in their right hands, or in their foreheads."[2]

Then, as to the *chronology*, in reference to the career of this remarkable man. While it fixes his *introduction* upon the prophetical platform of action at the extermination of the Papacy by the "ten horns" or "kings" of the Latin earth (Rev. xvii. 16), at the close of A. D. 1868, immediately after which "God shall put it into their hearts to give their power and strength and kingdom to him" (Rev. xvii. 13, 17); yet it is not true, as the Rev. M. Baxter, the author of "Louis Napoleon the Destined Monarch of the World," affirms, that it is "foreshown in prophecy" that he will "confirm a covenant with the Jews about, or soon after 1863," etc. This same writer at first fixed upon 1860 or 1861 as *the time* for the confirmation of the above "covenant" with the Jews. But no such covenant has yet (in 1866) been confirmed with them. In fact, this theory is based upon a total misapplication of the prophecy, Dan. ix. 27: "And he shall confirm the covenant with many for one week," etc., meaning *the last* of the seventy prophetic weeks of Daniel, verses 24–27. It is hypothecated of the *lopping off* of the last as a component part of the seventy weeks, and introducing a *long interval* down to the time of the appearance of the last Antichrist, and then *reduplicating* the year-day prophetical numbers, so as to make them apply to the career of the Antichrist on the *literal* day for day principle.

Now, this whole scheme, we maintain, is entirely at variance with the obvious tenor of the prophecy. The whole period of

---

[1] Rev. xiii. 3, 4, 7, 8. [2] *Ibid.*, verses 15, 16, 17.

the seventy weeks is divided into *three distinct parts.* The prophet says, 1st, "Know therefore and understand, that from the going forth of the commandment to restore and to build Jerusalem unto Messiah the Prince, shall be [1.] *seven weeks,*" or 49 years; "and [2.] *threescore and two weeks,*" or 434 years . . . "and [3.], *after* threescore and two weeks," i. e., from the *close* of this last-mentioned period "shall Messiah be *cut off,*" etc. "And he [Jehovah] shall confirm the covenant with many for one week, and *in the midst* of the week he shall cause the sacrifice and the oblation to cease," etc. It is perfectly plain, therefore, that all the above-named events, and none others, are included *within* the "seventy weeks." This prophetical number was given to point out *the time* of the FIRST COMING of Christ, "to finish the transgression, and to make an end of sin, and to make reconciliation for iniquity, and to bring in everlasting righteousness, and to seal up the vision and the prophecy, and to anoint the most Holy." Now, this was all accomplished, first, by the cutting off or *crucifixion* of Messiah "in the midst," or at the expiration of the *first half* of the "one week" of the seventy; and second, by "*the confirmation of the covenant* [Abrahamic] *with many,*" in opening the door of the Gospel to the Gentile nations at the conversion of Cornelius, during the *last half* of said "one week." Then it was, that Jehovah "caused the sacrifice and the oblation to cease," by the "one offering of Christ for the sins of the people," so that "there remaineth no more sacrifice for sin."

But, in addition to, and reaching beyond these seventy weeks, the prophet says:—"*And the people of the prince that shall come* shall destroy the city and the sanctuary,"—which was literally fulfilled by the invasion of Judea and the destruction of Jerusalem and the temple at the hand of the Roman general Titus and his army in A. D. 70. Then he says: "And the *end* thereof shall be with a flood, and *unto the end of the war* desolations are determined. . . And for the overspreading of abominations he [the prince] shall make it desolate, *even until the consummation,* and, that determined, shall be poured upon the desolate," or the desolator.

Thus we see that a *prolonged season* of trouble and suffering was marked out for the Jewish nation and the Christian Church, from *the close* of the above "seventy weeks," onward to the final overthrow of the last Antichrist. This prolonged season of tribulation commenced with the *subversion* of the Jewish nation and polity in A. D. 70. It was continued *by the war* waged by the "little horn" of the Papacy against the saints of the Most High. And it will reach its culminating point under *the last Antichrist*, with whose destruction it will end *at the time of* the "consummation."

We do not claim for the above the merit of a critical exegesis of the above passage. Had our space allowed it, such a process would have been found to confirm the plain, commonsense exposition which we have given of it. Our blessed Lord, in His last great prophecy, Matt. xxiv., Mark xiii., and Luke xxi., most minutely *fills up* the above prolonged interval of events, from the destruction of Jerusalem to the close of "*the times of the Gentiles.*" In regard to the commencement and close respectively of the three periods into which Daniel divides the "seventy weeks," we must refer the reader to "Our Bible Chronology" for their historic verification. And so of the *year-day* prophetical numbers connected with the events which *follow* the close of the "seventy weeks" down to the "consummation." All these prophetical dates, we maintain, run out at A. D. 1868. We are then ushered into *a short unchronological period*—"that generation which shall not pass away, *until all shall be fulfilled*" as pointed out by prophecy in reference to the career of the *last Antichrist*. And *the fact* that these events are furnished with *no dates* by which to determine when they begin and end, formed the ground of our Lord's prophecy when speaking of *the time* of His second appearing, when "every eye shall see Him, and they also which pierced Him," etc. :—" Of that day and hour *no man maketh known*, no, not the angels in heaven, neither the Son, but the Father."

We deferentially submit, therefore, that the theory of a *re-duplication* of the year-day prophetical numbers, by a series of corresponding literal days, and then applying them to a determination of the *exact time*, even to half a month, etc., of the confirmation of the so-called covenant which he is to make with the Jews; and also of the *visible* second coming of Christ, is neither authorized by Scripture nor supported by fact. It is a vain speculation, and the endless intricacies into which it is involved, only tend to bewilder and confound inquiry, and create hostility to prophetical investigations, the evidence of which is to be seen in the repeated shiftings of the date for the making the above covenant, as proposed by the writer alluded to.

But we have said that this theory is based upon a total misapprehension of the prophecy in Dan. ix. 27, respecting the "*covenant*" there spoken of. In addition, therefore, to what we have already offered in proof, we now add, that it arises from a confounding of said covenant with the "*league*" spoken of in Dan. xi. 23. This subject, however, being fully laid open in the sequel of these pages, it would be superfluous in this place to enter further into the matter. We have felt called upon thus to *disabuse* a momentously important subject of prophetical interpretation, from the injurious effects to which the above and similar perversions of its real significancy exposes it.

We now pass to observe, that the *chronology* of the prophecies introduced into this volume, as applied to the commencement and close of the career of the POLITICAL SYSTEMS respectively that have obtained in the world, demonstrate, as shown in the sequel, that they have nearly run their course. He who hath said: "I will overturn, overturn, overturn it; and it shall be no more, until He come whose right it is.; *and I will give it Him;*"[1] is "nigh at hand, even at the doors." This prophecy has reference to the removal of the crown from the head of Zedekiah, and the vacancy in the royal line of David, which, however, should be restored when the "sceptre" should be given into Christ's hands, whose true right it should be to reign. And although, as we have seen, the *exercise* of that right has been and still is suspended, yet Jehovah hath sworn unto David, that to HIM who is his "root and offspring," even Jesus, as the "KING OF KINGS AND LORD OF LORDS," shall be given UNIVERSAL EMPIRE, and that God will remove every obstacle and impediment, until it be accomplished. Aye, the doom of *every earthly dynasty*, as now constituted, whether

[1] Ezek., xxi. 27.

autocratic, despotic, monarchical, or democratic; and *every false system of religion,* whether Heathen, Pagan, Papal, Mohammetan, Judaic, or nominally Protestant, is unalterably fixed. The *destruction* of those powers that have so long " destroyed the earth " hastens on apace. In the present agitations, and upheavings, and revolutions among empires and kingdoms and states, we have the evidence that God is " *now* shaking not only the earth but heaven, that those things which cannot be shaken may remain." The REDEMPTION of " the whole creation," which for near 6,000 years has been " groaning and travailing in pain together until now," is near. Those of Christ's faithful ones, whether numbered among the departed martyr " souls under the altar," or " who are alive and remain unto the coming of the Lord," but yet are " groaning within themselves, waiting for the adoption, to wit, *the redemption of the body,*" shall soon be gathered into the " one fold under the one shepherd." And soon " the DELIVERER shall come to Zion, and shall turn away ungodliness from Jacob."

We write for the benefit of all who admit the authenticity and *plenary* inspiration of Holy Scripture; and we affectionately and earnestly entreat, that they give earnest heed to the things which " the Spirit of Christ that was in the prophets " hath spoken, " lest at any time they should let them slip." We appeal to " all, of every name, who love our Lord Jesus Christ in sincerity and truth," that they forget not that " THE HEAVENS DO RULE;" that " GOD IS THE GOVERNOR AMONG THE NATIONS;" and that, " according to the eternal purpose which he hath purposed in Christ Jesus our Lord " as the divinely constituted " heir of all things," every of the *rival* forms of existing governments must pass away, and give place to the establishment of that THEOCRATIC " KINGDOM which cannot be moved."

And we appeal especially to those to whom has been " committed a dispensation of the Gospel " as the " ambassadors of Christ," that if, in their view, we have presented in these pages anything *not* in accordance with " the mind of the Spirit," *that they point it out.* If, on the other hand, we have, as we claim, *demonstrated* the true application of the symbolic prophecies to the momentous things " signified " by the prophets who announced them, *they do confess it*, and unite in their efforts to spread the light among the people. We would say to them in all sincerity—" Dearly beloved in the Lord," we have all slept long enough. Let each one of us, therefore, join in the cry, " Watchmen, what of the night ? Watchmen, what of the night ?" The response of the " watchmen " is, " The morning cometh, and also the night." But, as in the order of nature, so here, the " night " *precedes* the " morning." Yea, " darkness *now* covers the earth, and gross darkness the people."[1] " If, then, ye will inquire, inquire ye : return, come."[2] Come to THE LIGHT of the " more sure word of prophecy, to which we all do well that we take heed, as unto a light which shineth *in a dark place*."[3] Let us " search the Scriptures *daily*, whether these things are so."[4] In the view of the approaching " sword " of the Divine vengeance now being suspended over the guilty nations of earth and the apostate of the nominal church, let us read and ponder over Ezekiel's description of the doom of the *unfaithful*, and the deliverance of the *faithful* " watchmen."[5] It has its *analogy* in the ministry of *the present day*.

R. C. S.

NEW YORK, *January*, 1866.

[1] Isa., lx. 1.
[2] Ezek., xxi. 12.
[3] 2 Pet., i. 19.
[4] Acts, ii. 46.
[5] Ezek., iii. 16-21.

POLITICAL ECONOMY OF PROPHECY.

CHAPTER I.

PRELIMINARY.

THE FOUR GREAT GENTILE MONARCHIES—THE ROMAN EMPIRE.

"AND here is the mind which hath wisdom. The seven heads which thou sawest are seven mountains, on which the woman sitteth. And there are seven kings: five are fallen, and one is, and the other is not yet come; and when he is come he must continue a short space. And the beast that was, and is not, and yet is (verse 8), even he is the eighth, and is of the seven, and goeth into perdition. And the ten horns which thou sawest are ten kings, which have received no kingdoms as yet, but receive power as kings one hour with the beast. . . These (ten kings) shall hate the whore, and shall make her desolate and naked, and shall eat her flesh, and burn her with fire. For God hath put it in their hearts to fulfil His will, and to agree, and give their kingdom unto the beast, until the word of God shall be fulfilled. . . These (ten kings) shall make war with the Lamb, and the Lamb shall overcome them: for He is the Lord of lords, and King of kings: and they that are with Him are called, and chosen, and faithful." (Rev. xvii. 9–12; 16, 17; and verse 14).

"THE testimony of Jesus is the spirit of prophecy."[1] "All things which were written in the law of Moses, and in the prophets, and in the psalms," were written "concern-

---

[1] Rev. xix. 10.

ing Christ,"[1] who is declared to be "the Alpha and Omega, the first and the last, who *was*, and *is*, and *is to come*,"[2] or "THE COMING ONE." Hence the derivation of that "more sure word of prophecy" to which we are admonished to "take heed as unto a light which shineth in a dark place, until the day dawn, and the Day-Star arise in our hearts."[3]

Prophecy is history *anticipated*. History is prophecy *verified*.

Prophecy takes within its scope the mighty conflict that was to be waged between the promised seed of the woman, THE LORD JESUS CHRIST, as the divinely constituted "Heir of all things,"[4] and THE SATANIC USURPER of His royal prerogatives in the earth and over man; from the catastrophe of the fall in Eden, onward to the final "restitution of all things which God hath spoken by the mouth of all His holy prophets since the world began."[5] These are the "*things*" concerning which the old prophets are said to have "inquired and searched diligently as to WHAT," i. e., of the events predicted, "and *what manner of time* the spirit of Christ which was in them did signify, when it (rather He) testified beforehand the sufferings of Christ, and the glory that should follow."[6]

But, while prophecy is an *unveiling* of the "eternal purpose of God which He purposed in Christ Jesus our Lord,"[7] spanning, as it does, the entire period already indicated, each successive link in its gradual developments of the past from the beginning, like the polar star to the mariner in mid-ocean, points to the great period of crisis, in which all are to be headed up. The inter-

---

[1] Luke xxiv. 44. [2] Rev. i. 8. [3] 2 Pet. i. 19.
[4] Heb. i. 2. [5] Acts iii. 21. [6] 1 Pet. i. 11.
[7] Eph. iii. 2.

vening events of prophecy, therefore, as forming the *integral parts* of the whole, are interesting to us only as landmarks to guide us to a right apprehension and appreciation of this great period of crisis. This, I am sure the reader will agree with me, holds signally true, if the evidence can be furnished in the sequel of the subject in hand, that WE are they who stand upon the very threshold of this impending crisis.

Without further delay, then, we observe, that the prophecies of Holy Scripture, either directly or indirectly, relate, first, to *the vicissitudes and sufferings* of the church and people of God, Patriarchal, Jewish, and Christian. Second. To the *cotemporaneous rise and succession* of those Gentile nations, by whom they were to be persecuted and oppressed. And third, to the *final destruction* of these Gentile nations, and the establishment of the Church, first in her Millennial, and finally in her eternal state of blessedness. They hence comprehend all that is embraced in the great scheme of human redemption as founded on the first promise to man, "THE SEED OF THE WOMAN shall bruise the serpent's head," as the meet penalty of the "serpent's bruising His heel."

It forms no part of our present design, however, to enter upon an exposition of this vast field of prophecy in detail. We have now to do, for the most part, with an exposition and application of the prophecy quoted from the Apocalypse in reference to the Four Great Gentile Monarchies, and particularly the last, the Roman, and its last rulers, the FIRST THREE NAPOLEONS, as emperors of the Franco-Roman empire. We repeat, for the most part. For while—as will be shown in the sequel—this trio of Napoleons form the *main subject* of the things signified in the symbolic imagery of this wonderful prophecy, it embraces the *entire period* allotted to the history of that empire, from its commencement. It will be necessary, however, first, to take note of those *pre-existing* empires, of which the Roman constituted the *fourth* in the order of succession. A glance at these, in connection with the last, will lead to the discovery of the important fact, overlooked by many in these last times, that *in the Bible* is to be found the most extensive and perfect system of Political Economy of which the world can boast. Indeed, it may be said that the laws of every nation throughout the civilized world, political, judicial, civil, social, and ecclesiastical, in one form or another are borrowed from and are permeated by the *principles* of jurisprudence scattered through the pages of this inspired universal text-book.

Let us direct attention, first, to

THE FOUR GREAT GENTILE MONARCHIES OF EARTH.

These were all *prophetically* foreshadowed in the two wonderful visions of Nebuchadnezzar and of Daniel, and of the series of visions revealed to St. John in the Apocalypse. In the dreams of Nebuchadnezzar there stood before him *a colossal metallic "Image,* whose brightness was excellent, and the form thereof terrible," his " head being of fine gold, his breast and arms of silver, his belly and his thighs of brass, and his legs of iron, with the feet part of iron and part of clay."[1] To remove all doubt from the mind that these four compartments of this colossal Image denoted the FOUR GENTILE MONARCHIES that for a long time were to bear rule in the earth,—viz., the Assyrio-Babylonian, the Medo-Persian, the Grecian, and the Roman—of the *first three* the Holy Spirit inter-

[1] Dan. ii. 31-33.

prets and applies the "head of gold" of the Image, (Dan. i. 1), to the first empire, the BABYLONIAN, of which Nebuchadnezzar was " king," with unlimited autocratical power. This empire took its rise in A. M. 3520, B. C. 612, and reached down to B. C. 538, a period of seventy-four years. It was succeeded by the MEDO-PERSIAN empire, denoted by the " breast and arms of silver " of the image. By comparing Daniel v. 1, 2, and verses 28, 30, 31, with chapter vi. 1, it will be seen that Belshazzar, the son of Nebuchadnezzar, succeeded him as king of Babylon. But it was to this profane, debauched and dissolute king that the prophet Daniel, in his interpretation of the mysterious handwriting on the wall of his palace, said: "God hath numbered *thy* kingdom, and finished it;" and "*thy* kingdom is divided *and* given to the Medes and Persians." This empire began its course in A. M. 3594, B. C. 538, and continued down to B. C. 331, a period of 207 years. It was followed by the GRÆCO-MACEDONIAN empire, symbolized by the " belly and thighs of brass " of the image.

It is here in place to introduce the corresponding vision of Daniel, chapter vii., to that of the image. The symbols in this vision are changed, from the four metallic and clay compositions of the image, into that of " FOUR GREAT BEASTS, which came up from the sea, diverse one from another." "The first was like a lion, and had eagle's wings," and symbolized the *Babylonian* empire. The " second was like a bear, having three ribs in its mouth," and denoted the *Medo-Persian* empire. The " third was like a leopard, with four heads and four wings upon the back of it," representing the *Græco-Macedonian* empire. But this third power is also described by the prophet in the eighth chapter, under the symbol of a " *he-goat*," with a " great horn," etc. (Verses

5, 8.) We introduce this change in the symbolic imagery denoting the Græco-Macedonian empire from the leopard to that of the he-goat, for the reason that under this last named symbol, the Holy Spirit by the prophet tells us, (verse 21), that "the rough goat is the king of *Grecia;* and the great horn that is between his eyes is the first king," i. e., Alexander the Great. This empire took its rise in A. M. 3801, B. C. 331, and continued down to B. C. 168, a period of one hundred and sixty-three years, and was succeeded by

THE ROMAN EMPIRE.

This, as the *fourth* in the series of the great ruling Gentile monarchies, is that which is now more especially to engage our thoughts. It is symbolized by the two "legs of iron, and the feet and ten toes, part of iron and part of clay" of the image, and the corresponding symbol in the vision of Daniel of a "*beast, dreadful and terrible, and strong exceedingly,* having great iron teeth; and it devoured and brake in pieces, and stamped the residue with the feet of it; and it was diverse from all the beasts that were before it, and it had ten horns." To this the prophet adds concerning this nondescript beast: "I considered the horns, and behold, there came up among them *another little horn,* before whom there were *three* of the first horns plucked up by the roots; and, behold, in this horn were eyes like the eyes of a man, and a mouth speaking great things; . . whose look was more stout than his fellows." The prophet continues: "I beheld, and the same horn made war with the saints, and prevailed against them. . . And he shall speak great words against the Most High, and shall wear out the saints of the Most High, and think to change times and laws: and they shall be given into his hand until a time, and times, and the dividing of time." Daniel further says: "I beheld, because of the voice of the great words which the *horn* spake: I beheld, even till the *beast* was slain, and his body destroyed, and given to the burning flame. As concerning the *rest of the beasts*," i. e., the ten horns, "they had their *dominion* taken away; yet their *lives were prolonged* for a season and a time," or "*until* the Ancient of Days came, and judgment was given to the saints of the Most High; and the time came that the saints possessed the kingdom." For, adds the prophet, "The judgment shall sit, and they shall take away his dominion," i. e., the *ten principalities* of the "ten horns" or "kings," so long under vassalage to the "little horn," "to consume and to destroy it unto the end." This consummated, and *immediately following* this destruction both of "the beast" and the "little horn" with his ten kingdoms; in the order of succession, the prophet says:

"I saw in the night visions, and, behold, ONE LIKE THE SON OF MAN CAME WITH THE CLOUDS OF HEAVEN, and came to the Ancient of Days, and they brought Him near before Him. And there was given Him dominion, and glory, and a kingdom, that all people, nations, and languages, should serve Him. His dominion is an everlasting dominion, which shall not pass away, and His kingdom that which shall not be destroyed."[1]

It is also in place here to note the *special agency* by which the destruction of the Roman civil and ecclesiastico-political powers, together with all the other forms of antichristianism, is to be effected. Daniel, in his interpretation of Nebuchadnezzar's dream, said: "Thou sawest till that A STONE was cut out of the mountain

[1] See Daniel, chap. vii.

without hands, which smote the image upon his feet that were of iron and clay, and brake them in pieces. *Then was the iron, the clay, the brass, the silver, and the gold, broken in pieces together*, and became like the chaff of the summer threshing-floors ; and the wind carried them away, that no place was found for them: and THE STONE THAT SMOTE THE IMAGE BECAME A GREAT MOUNTAIN, AND FILLED THE WHOLE EARTH." [1]

And finally, to show that no other kingdom is to come in *between* the overthrow of the four Gentile monarchies denoted by the symbols of the colossal image and the mountain kingdom of the "Stone," Daniel says : " *In the days of these kings* shall the God of heaven set up a kingdom which shall never be destroyed: and the kingdom shall not be left to other people, but it *shall break in pieces and consume all* these kingdoms, and it shall stand for ever." [2]

What a picture is here presented to our view, as foreshadowed in the *prophetico-historic* origin, character, exploits, and final doom of this stupendous Roman power, and of the final triumphs over her of the REGENERATED NATIONALITIES, both Jewish and Christian!

Nor must we overlook the fact of the relation which she sustains to the other *three powers*, the Babylonian, Medo-Persian, and Grecian. They are to be taken collectively, as forming so many agents, as "*rods*" in God's hand for the chastisement of the Jewish and Christian apostasies, on the one hand, and as the trial of the faith and constancy of the faithful people of God during a long period, on the other.

This period is designated in the New Testament, Luke xxi. 24, and Rom. xi. 25, as

---

[1] Dan. ii. 34, 35. [2] Dan. ii. 44.

"THE TIMES OF THE GENTILES."

The interpretation of the apocalyptic prophecy relatively to the ROMAN EMPIRE now in hand, involves the necessity of determining *the length* of these "times of the Gentiles." In order to this, we must go back to the period of the "*seven times*" chastisement of Israel and Judah on account of their sins, as predicted by Moses, Levit. xxvi., and by Daniel, chap. iv., which, being given, not in common time, but as a prophetical or mystical date, must be deciphered according to the laws of interpretation of the *symbols* of prophecy, thus:—as the term "time," etc., when used as a prophetical number,[1] denotes a year of 360 lunar days, and "*each day*" is to be taken "for a *year*,"[2] the "seven times" or seven years give us a total of 2,520 years.

But the question is, can we determine from Scripture the exact date for the *commencement* of this period? To settle this point, we have only to refer to the joint prophecies of the *captivities* of Israel and Judah, as announced by Hosea and Isaiah. Hosea, thus: "And the pride of *Israel* (the ten tribes) doth testify to his face: therefore shall Israel and Ephraim (the principal of the ten tribes) fall into captivity: *Judah* (the other division) shall also fall *with them*."[3] On the other hand, Isaiah pointed out *the very time* when these captivities should take place: "and within *threescore and five years* Ephraim shall be broken, that it shall not be a people."[4]

Now, this *last* prophecy was made in the 2d year of the 16 of Ahaz's reign over Israel, A. M. 3377. The above 65 years is made up of the 14 from the 2d year of

[1] Dan. vii. 25. [2] Ezek. iv. 1-8.
[3] Hosea, v. 5. [4] Is. vii. 8.

Ahaz, and the 29 years' intervening reign of Hezekiah, down to the 22d of Manasseh, A. M. 3441, when the captivity of *Ephraim*, or the ten tribes, took place under Esarhaddan (the same with Asnappar, Ezra iv. 2, 10) king of Assyria; and, *the same year*, having caught *Manasseh*, king of Judah, hid in a thicket, he bound him in chains and carried him a captive to Babylon.¹ But Manasseh, having repented of his sins, was *restored* to his kingdom for 39 years down to A. M. 3480; while the *nation*, not having repented of their idolatry, etc., during that interval, the above " seven times " or 2,520 years commence from that date.

Take the following in proof: " Manasseh *hath made* Judah to sin with his idols: therefore, thus saith the Lord God of Israel, behold, *I am bringing* (i. e., by the personal captivity of their king) such evil upon Jerusalem and Judah, that whosoever heareth it, both their ears shall tingle."² The meaning here is, that the unrepenting nation of Judah was punished for those idolatrous practices which Manasseh, their king, *had instigated*, consisting of a loss to them of their national independence, and of which his captivity was but the *prelude*. We have only to add, that while *Israel*, or the ten tribes, from the time of their captivity under Esarhaddan, have never recovered their national independence; so *Judah*, since A. M. 3480, have remained subjugated to the dominancy of Gentilism over them. This, therefore, constitutes *the whole period* called " the times of the Gentiles," which, commencing B. C. 652, end in A. D. 1868, thus: 652 + 1868 = 2,520. Add to A. M. 3480, the " seven times or 2,520 years, and it gives the preordained 6,000

¹ Compare 2 Kings xvii. 24, with Ezra iv. 2, 10; and 2 Chron. xxxiii. 11.
² 2 Kings xxi. 12.

years from the creation and fall, down to the close of " the times of the Gentiles."[1]

We now observe that, of this period, *the much larger portion* was allotted in the purpose of the Great Lawgiver, God, to the career of the ROMAN EMPIRE. The first three of the four great Gentile monarchies—the Babylonian, Medo-Persian, and Grecian—commencing, as has been shown, in A. M. 3520, and ending in A. M. 3964, embraced an interval of only 444 years. On the other hand, the Roman Empire, which (as every school-boy knows) was founded by Romulus A. M. 3379, B. C. 753, came to maturity A. M. 3964, B. C. 168, the *final* stroke in its course of conquests consisting of the subversion of Egypt in A. M. 4101, B. C. 31. And, although this empire is not specially designated *by name* either in the visions of Nebuchadnezzar or of Daniel, yet, that it *immediately succeeded* that of the Grecian divided empire, as denoted by the four heads of the leopard, is evident from the facts following: first, that both Cæsar and Augustus were titles of the Roman emperors immediately before the first coming of Christ. Second. That Judea, being *tributary* to the prefecture of Syria when Christ was upon earth, the chief priests of the Jewish Sanhedrin declared, " We have no king but *Cæsar*."[2] Third. That our blessed Lord Himself enforced upon all the injunction, " Render therefore unto *Cæsar* the things which be Cæsar's,"[3] etc. And finally, fourth. That the chief priests and Pharisees, apprehending the powerful influence which might accrue to Christ from the astounding miracles wrought by Him before the people, said, " If we let HIM alone, all men will believe on Him; and the *Romans* shall come, and take away both our place and nation."[4]

[1] See on this " Our Bible Chronology," etc., ch. vi. sec. 1, pp. 79-82.
[2] John xix. 15. [3] Matt. xxii. 21. [4] John xi. 48.

It results, then, that the ROMAN EMPIRE, which was founded A. M. 3379, B. C. 753, and 101 years before the commencement of the mystical "seven times" or 2,520 years of "the times of the Gentiles," did not attain to its position as the mistress of nations, till the conquest of Egypt, 722 years after, in A. M. 4101,[1] B. C. 31.

And yet—as will be shown in the sequel—we have revealed to us the generally unrecognized fact, that, THE PROPHETICO-HISTORIC POLITICAL ECONOMY OF THE BIBLE reaches back to its very *commencement*, and extends forward to the *last year* of its close.

In order, however, to a proper understanding of the subject before us, we must premise,

First. That in tracing the *numerous mutations* signified by the symbolic imagery which depict the rise, exploits, and destiny of the four ruling monarchies of earth, the first thing to be noticed is, that the vision of the four wild beasts of Daniel, chap. vii., were given to explain *more fully*, the things denoted in Nebuchadnezzar's vision of the metallic colossal image of chap. ii.; while the corresponding synchronical symbols of the same monarchies in the Apocalypse, not only present them under *additionally new phases*, but furnish us with a complete exposition of the otherwise obscure imagery of the others. We observe,

Second. That the *difference* between the subjects treated of in Daniel and in the Apocalypse relatively to these monarchies, is, that the former prophet presents to

---

[1] It will doubtless occur to the reader, that this date, A. M. 4101, varies materially from the current chronology adopted from Archbishop Usher in our English Bible. It is, however, founded upon a correction of the *discrepancy* between 1 Kings vi. 1, and Acts xiii. 17-22, on the period between the Exode and the 4th year of Solomon; for the adjustment and proof of which, the reader is referred to "Our Bible Chronology, critically examined and demonstrated," etc. (See Index.)

our view the *supremacy of Gentilism* from the time of Nebuchadnezzar, down to their overthrow by the Messianic "stone," as connected with the destiny of his own beloved nation, THE JEWS; whereas St. John, in addition to this, unfolds the dominancy of the *same* Gentile powers, as linked with and tracking the long course of ecclesiastical corruption under the present dispensation, with especial reference to *the apostasy of Christendom;* while at the same time he carries us through, and transports us *beyond,* the close of the millennial era, to the final issues of the saved and the lost.

Third. Another remark, and one of special importance, as more immediately connected with the subject in hand, is the evidence, both in the Book of Daniel and of the Apocalypse,

OF THE CONTINUANCE, DOWN TO THE PRESENT DAY,

of these four Gentile monarchies, and particularly that of the ROMAN, *subsequently* to its dismemberment into two parts, the west and the east, which occurred between A. D. 307 and A. D. 408, as symbolized by the two legs of iron of the colossal image; and also its subdivision into the following TEN PRINCIPALITIES, as denoted by the "ten toes" of the image, and the "ten horns" of the nondescript beast, viz.: 1, *Lombardy;* 2, *Ravenna;* 3, *the State of Rome;* 4, *Naples;* 5, *Tuscany;* 6, *France;* 7, *Austria;* 8, *Spain;* 9, *Portugal;* and 10, *Great Britain;* an event which transpired in A. D. 531, consequent of the invasion of the empire by the barbarous hordes from the north. The same holds true also of the eleventh, or Roman "little horn," which sprang up "among the ten horns."[1]

[1] Dan. vii. 8.

On this subject of the PERPETUATED UNITY of these four empires, Daniel, in speaking of the smiting of the colossal metallic image by the Messianic stone, says: "*Then* was the iron, the clay, the brass, the silver, and the gold, *broken to pieces together*,"[1] etc. Of course, the monarchies denoted by these symbols, if "broken in pieces together," must all have been present to receive the blow! In other words, *at the time* of the smiting, the image must stand *intact* in all its parts! Accordingly, in further confirmation of this, the prophet affirms that it is "*in the days of these kings* that the God of heaven shall set up a kingdom," etc. But, if "in the days of these kings," it follows that they must all be in existence at the time of the setting up of said kingdom.

But to this it is objected, that the four monarchies here spoken of *have long since passed away*, leaving nought behind them but the historic records of their former power, magnificence, and territorial extent. *If* this be so, then, all we have to say is, that there is swept away the entire fabric of the prophetic word, and Christianity is left without a shield of defence against the bold and blasphemous taunt of the infidel, "Where is the promise of Christ's coming?" We submit, therefore, the following, as a solution of this historic problem :—

Originally, the *first* of the above-named monarchies, in its geographical territory, population, and government, was Babylonish. Under the *second* dynasty, the territory and population of Babylon were annexed, and the government of the two were made Medo-Persian. Under the *third*, in like manner, the territory and population of Medo-Persia were annexed, and the government of the three was merged into that of Greece. And under

[1] Dan. ii. 34, 35.

the *fourth*, the territory and population of Greece were annexed to Rome, and the whole became Roman.

These, therefore, form what, for the sake of distinction, is termed THE PLATFORM OF THE PROPHETICAL EARTH. Nationally and politically, this platform has attained to its present dimensions by the process of *successive annexations* of the one to the other, retaining, *throughout*, their national, political, and ecclesiastical characteristics—as signalized by the various imagery which denote them—as so may "*rods*" in the hand of God for the chastisement of the APOSTATE CHURCH, Jewish and Christian.

Undeniably, therefore, the prophetic colossal image of Nebuchadnezzar *now exists intact in all its parts*—gold, silver, brass, iron, and clay; or the same, as symbolized by the four corresponding beasts of Daniel—the lion, the bear, the leopard with four heads, and the nondescript beast, inclusive of the principalities denoted by the "ten toes" of the image, and the "ten horns" of the BEAST, together with the *eleventh* little horn.

To this we now add another "little horn," *distinct* from the preceding, as introduced upon the prophetic stage at a later period, and of a different nationality, political and religious characteristics, and exploits and destiny. We here refer to the "rough he-goat," with a "notable horn between his eyes," which, being broken and giving place to four others, "out of one of them came up *another little horn*, which waxed exceeding great,"[1] etc.

Now, these FOUR MONARCHIES, as is attested by history both sacred and profane, *began* their course on the great river Euphrates, whereon stood Nineveh, the capi-

[1] Dan. viii. 5-12.

tal of Assyria, with Babylon on the Tigris. From these two cities *proceeded* that stupendous power, the Assyrio-Babylonian, which destroyed the national existence of the ten tribes of Israel, and finally brought the two tribes of Judah and Benjamin into captivity. And it is notorious, that both these ancient capitals, Nineveh and Babylon, with the countries which they ruled, have now, for eight centuries, down to the present day, been under the dominion of the TURCO-MOHAMMEDAN " little horn " of the rough goat. So there always has been, and still is, a kingdom of Persia. On the other hand, the Grecian leopard, Alexander, added to the territory of the great image that very portion of Greece which, *in our times*, has risen out of oppression and political death into the state of an independent kingdom, such as it was when it first came on the prophetical stage. And finally, we have the Romans, still subsisting in the ten kingdoms of modern western Europe, to wit: Lombardy, Ravenna, Italy, Naples, Tuscany, France, Austria, Spain, Portugal, and Great Britain.

Turn we now to the Apocalypse. Here, also, we find the nondescript or " GREAT BEAST " of Daniel, in both his *civil* and *ecclesiastico-political* characteristics, occupies, as we shall show, the *last*, and by far the *longest period* allotted to the prophetico-historic metamorphoses of Gentilism, *as made up of all* the four despotic monarchies denoted by the four metallic and beast-like symbols. In proof, take the following peculiar structure of the hierophantic imagery of St. John on this point. He says: " And *the beast* which I saw "—he is here speaking of the fourth or ROMAN POWER—" And *the beast* which I saw, was like a leopard " (*Greece*), " and his feet as the feet of a bear " (*Medo-Persia*), " and his mouth as the mouth of a lion " (*Babylon*), etc. Hence, the *swiftness* which marked the conquests of the Grecian leopard; the *weight* of Medo-Persian oppression; and the *majesty* of Babylonian greatness, are all here found to *coexist* in this fourth great and terrible empire, the Roman, as *the special form* in which it was revealed to him.

It follows, therefore, that the four rampant beasts of Daniel, and the corresponding metallic colossal image of Nebuchadnezzar, *at this very moment*, remain intact in all their parts. It is true that they have been subjected, through the lapse of past ages, to several transmutations, and have undergone various modifications. Nevertheless, through *all* these changes, their *original* metallic and beastly identity of character and work, have been preserved, and still exist in THE ROMAN POWER. And more: they will so continue to exist, till the predestined time shall come for the *smiting* of the colossal image, or, which is the same thing, the *destruction* of the Roman beast, together with all other antichristian antagonisms, civil, political, and religious—and there are others besides this—by the MESSIANIC " STONE."

We submit, therefore, that we have demonstrated in the light of the prophetico-historic word, and the concurrent facts of profane history, *first*, the rise and succession of the four great ruling monarchies of earth; and *second*, of their national, territorial, and political unity, as all having been merged, through the process of annexation of one to the other, into that of the Roman Empire.

But these facts, as we have said, are simply *preliminary* to an exposition and application of the symbolic imagery of the passage from the Apocalypse. That they point us, not exclusively—for they take a wide range—but specially, to those world-renowned personages, THE

FIRST THREE NAPOLEONS, and particularly the last, LOUIS NAPOLEON III., as emperors of the present Franco-Roman empire, it will be our business to show in what is immediately to follow.

CHAPTER II.

PROPHETIC HISTORY OF THE ROMAN EMPIRE, CONTINUED,
—NAPOLEON I.

As we have seen, the symbolic imagery in the prophetico-historic account of the four ruling monarchies of Gentilism during "the times of the Gentiles," was not exhausted in the preceding pages. What has been offered thus far respecting the rise, etc., of these successive monarchies, was designed merely as *preliminary* to what is to follow. We have remarked that the visions of Daniel, chapters vii. and viii., were given to explain more fully the things represented in Nebuchadnezzar's vision of the metallic colossal image of chap. ii.; while those revealed to St. John in the Apocalypse, so far as they relate to the same monarchies, present them to view under phases not brought to light in either of the others. Not, indeed, that these latter symbols, taken as a whole, relate equally to each of those monarchies separately. Rather, they are more especially designed as *expository* of the history of the ROMAN DOMINION in its *various mutations*, from the period of its rise to its final overthrow, a synopsis of which is furnished to our hand in the notable and much litigated passage now under consideration.

Unless we greatly err, the *internal structure* of this prophecy will show, incontrovertibly, the misconceptions and consequent misapplications of the symbols contained in this passage to the things signified, on the part of a large class of modern popular expositors. It will be seen that they have all originated from their failure to recognize the cardinal prophetico-historic fact, as already shown, of the successive merging of these four monarchies into *one;* and that one constituting the STUPENDOUS ROMAN POWER, both in its civil and ecclesiastico-political aspects. For, with this fact before us, we are furnished with an infallible test of the applicability of the symbols in the passage under review, so far as they relate to the history of this power, from the beginning, not only, but to the appearance upon the stage of the FIRST THREE NAPOLEONS, as the last emperors of the MODERN FRANCO-ROMAN EMPIRE.

Without further preliminaries, therefore, we shall introduce the reader at once to St. John's description of the " seven-headed scarlet-colored beast having ten horns," denotive of the *civil* or *political* power of Rome ; and on which is seated the " woman arrayed in scarlet color, and decked with gold and precious stones and pearls,". etc., Rev. xvii., 1–4, descriptive of the *ecclesiastico-political* character of the same power.

Take, then, the following particulars, detailed by the prophet respecting this "beast."

I. "The seven heads," he tells us, "*are seven mountains,*"[1] etc. And so history certifies that ancient Rome, founded by Romulus B. C. 753, was built on *seven hills*— Mounts Palatinus, Capitolinus, Quirilinus, Qiminalus, Esquilinus, Cælius, and Aventinus. Then the prophet adds,

---

[1] Rev. xvii. 9.

II. That these "seven mountains" are those "*on which the woman sitteth*,"[1] etc. That is, they constituted the *territorial seat* occupied by this "woman." She still holds her seat there, as the capital of the Roman empire. But, in the next place,

III. St. John, having stated that "the seven heads are seven mountains," further explains: "*and there are seven kings*," which kings, being symbolized by the "seven heads" of the "beast," denote that the Roman empire, from the time of its foundation to its final overthrow, was to pass through SEVEN DISTINCT FORMS OF GOVERNMENT, each of which should emanate from, and retain their seat in, the seven-hilled city of Rome as their capital.

Now, of these symbolic "*seven heads*," or forms of government of the Roman beast, the apostle says: "And there are SEVEN KINGS; *five are fallen*, and *one is*, and the other *is not yet come:* and when he cometh, he must continue *a short space.*" Then comes the next part of the prophecy, to wit: "And the beast that *was*, and *is not*, and *yet is* (verse 8), even he is the EIGHTH, and is *of the seven*, and goeth into perdition."[2]

We here repeat, that these symbols were employed by the Holy Spirit to denote the *successive* prophetico-historic mutations of the Roman *civil* power, through *a long period of time*. Their application to the things signified is intended to remind us,

FIRST, OF THE ORIGIN, UNIVERSAL EXTENT, AND POLITICAL POWER OF THE ROMAN EMPIRE.

Once, as all know, it "*was*." Then, second, in its

---

[1] Rev. xvii. 9.   [2] Rev. xvii. 10, 11.

original consolidated govermental form, it ceased to be, or "*was not.*" But, third, it was destined to undergo a *revivification.* "One of the seven heads," we are informed, Rev. xiii., 3, " was *wounded unto death,*" but, " his deadly wound was *healed.*"

It is quite superfluous to remark that the very phraseology employed in this prophecy denotes that the " seven heads " of this Roman beast were characterized by *diversity* in the exercise of their respective political functions. Otherwise, on the hypothesis that the government of the empire symbolized by the beast was uniformly the same during its entire existence, *one " head"* would have sufficed to represent it. Our business, therefore, is to search out and apply the facts of history, in adaptation to this *septiform* symbolic imagery as descriptive of the governments of the empire. Unless this can be done, the symbolic imagery of this prophecy will remain an inexplicable enigma.

1. Of the phrase respecting these " seven heads," "*five are fallen.*" History attests that, of the seven forms of government of the Roman empire, the first was *regal.* This form extended from the foundation of the empire, from B. C. 753 to B. C. 509, a period of 244 years. Then followed an interregnum of 11 years. The second was a *dictatorship,* which began B. C. 498, and ended in 47 years, B. C. 451. This administration was founded in necessity, and was invested with unlimited power. The third consisted of a *decemvirate,* which commenced B. C. 451, and reached down to the time of Appius Claudius, in A. D. 60, in all 511 years. It consisted of officers or magistrates who held their power in succession for two years. The fourth was a *consulate,* which continued only a short period from the time of Appius Claudius, and was invested with sovereign authority for one year. And the fifth

was a *triumvirate*, which lasted about 50 years, down to B. C. 31. It was constituted of a coalition of three men, in the government of the empire.

These "*five*" forms of government, we now observe, had all exercised their respective powers over Rome, and had ceased to be, *prior* to the period when the Apocalypse was written, viz., in A. D. 96. It is to them, therefore, that St. John refers, when he says, "five are fallen." But,

2. The apostle adds, "*and one is.*" This was the sixth form of government—the *Roman imperial*. This form of the civil polity of Rome, we shall now proceed to show, was *long-lived*. It spanned the whole period from B. C. 31, to A. D. 1804. This statement regarding the prolonged existence of the sixth headship of the empire, forms the Gordian knot of modern prophetical expositors. Hence the various theories which have been proposed by them, in the interpretation of this hierophantic discourse of the angel sent by Jesus to St. John, to "show unto him the things which must be *hereafter*."[1]

Now, of these theories, many writers have proceeded on the hypothesis that the Roman emperorship, which all concede was the *sixth head* in the time of St. John, ended with the deposition of Augustulus in A. D. 476 or 479, and that, consequently, the *seventh* and *eighth* heads were to be discovered in the *Papacy*.[2] Mr. Elliot, on the other hand, in his Horæ Apocalypticæ, adopting the same general principle of interpretation, makes Augustulus the sixth head, and his successor, Diocletian, to be the *short-lived seventh* head, which was slain by the sword

[1] Rev. iv. 1. See also chap. i. 1.
[2] We are indebted to the Rev. Mr. Faber's work, "Napoleon III. the man of Prophecy," for the historic proof of the territorial and gubernatorial unity of the Roman empire.

of Constantine the Great.¹ While Dr. H. Moore, in his Synopsis Prophetica, on the ground that all the first six heads were pagan, would make the short-lived seventh head to constitute the line of Christian kings *before* they relapsed into Pagano-Christianism; and the eighth head to be the same line of emperors *after* that period.

To these speculations, we have simply to say, that while we have nothing to object to the *principle* that we are to look for the rise of the seventh head of the Roman beast at or about the time of the *extinction* of the sixth head, yet we cannot but express our surprise, that any otherwise reputable writers should have adopted such variant and conflicting theories on the subject in hand, and especially those of them which involve the gross incongruity of making a *spiritual* power, *e. g.*, the papacy, to be the head of a declared *secular* empire. This will appear from the fact of the evident violence committed by these theorists to the import of the symbolic imagery of these apocalyptic representations, when viewed as a whole.

We shall assume, therefore, as indispensable to a determination of "the mind of the spirit" as to the things signified by these symbols, the following :—

First. We must ascertain the *true chronological position* of the sixth and seventh heads in the series. And,

Second. We must determine the *relation* of the seventh to the eighth head.

As preliminary to an exposition of this important prophecy, the following stand-points will be found to furnish us with the principles of interpretation which are to guide us in the application of the symbolic imagery to the things signified.

[1] Horæ Apoc. iii. pp. 103-103, 2d ed.

1. The first is this : That the great seven-headed scarlet-colored beast, with his characteristic multiform badges of the Babylonian *lion*, and the Medo-Persian *bear*, and the Macedonian *leopard*, borrowed from the well-known vision of Daniel, figure the EASTERN platform of the Roman empire: while the ten horns of the great nondescript beast, describe the WESTERN platform, *after* it had been divided and occupied by the ten Gothic nations. The conformation of this curiously-devised symbol, therefore, exhibits the Roman empire, not as confined to the west, but as encircling in its vast territorial extent both the west and the east, and thus constituting ONE EMPIRE, of which the city of Rome, built on the seven hills (or "mountains") of the Apocalypse, was the *metropolis*. It follows from this,

2. That as the seven-headed scarlet-colored beast, as symbolic of the Roman power, represent the *seven secular* forms of government signified by them; so the "beast itself," with its *united* "characteristics of the Babylonian lion and the Medo-Persian bear and the Macedonian leopard, all concur in exhibiting the *territorial* Roman empire, and the presiding Roman *emperorship*, as each being A STRICT UNIT." Hence, "the imperial head, which the angel declares to have been in existence when he conversed with St. John, however administered, or wherever locally seated,"—i. e., whether in the west or east, or extending his sceptre over both—"is *the head*, either gubernatively, or feudally, or reputedly, of the legally ONE EMPIRE IN ITS FULL ENTIRETY; while the ten horns [of the "great beast"] describe the western platform, *after* it had been divided and occupied by the *ten Gothic nations*."

It is, therefore, on this broad principle of the territorial unity of the empire, both west and east; and the governmental unity of the emperorship only that the *septiform* governments depicted in the prophecy before us can be truthfully interpreted and applied to the things denoted by them. On this common principle, all other theories, like those already noticed, vanish away like the baseless fabric of a vision. It will be found to prove demonstrably, that *no other* form of government appeared in the Roman empire, *intermediate* of the long interval which we have assigned between the *sixth* head of the beast, B. C. 31, and the appearance upon the prophetical stage of the *seventh* head in A. D. 1804, a period of 1835 years.

It is scarcely necessary to add, that we rely upon and adopt this broad principle of interpretation, as demonstrative of the application of the symbolic *seventh* and *eighth* heads in this prophecy, as pointing to the FIRST THREE NAPOLEONS, as emperors of the Franco-Roman empire.

But this by the way. We now return to several other stand-points. The next in order is,

3. That the seventh head *had not yet come*, when St. John penned this vision.

4. That when it appeared, it was to occupy a place in the Roman empire analogous to that of the *sixth* head, as the emperorship of Rome.

5. That this seventh head was to be *short-lived*.

6. That after being *wounded to death*, its deadly wound was to be *healed*.

7. That when restored to life, it was to emerge *out of the sea*. And finally,

8. That out of this resuscitated seventh head as a *secular* power, was to spring forth an EIGHTH head, possessed of the characteristics of an APOSTATE DEMOCRATICO-RELIGIOUS HEAD, to whom the " ten horns " or " kings "

of the "beast" Roman, with *one mind*, will give their power, and strength, and kingdom; and this, in conformity with the singular compound formation of the symbolic imagery as a *double type*—"The beast that was, and is not, and yet is: even HE is the EIGHTH, and is OF *the seven*." In other words, by the use of this double type, the Holy Spirit clearly distinguishes between the *two* headships, the seventh, which receives the deadly wound, being resuscitated in its *secular* form; while the eighth, being *of* the seventh, emerges from it, and *as* the eighth head, is *changed* in its character from a merely secular, to that of an *apostatic democratico-religious power*. It will hence result from this:

1st. That the period assigned to the *sixth* imperial head of the Roman beast as a secular power, must include the *whole interval* from B.C. 31, down to the time of the appearance upon the prophetical stage of the EIGHTH head, which is at the point where the secular power of the revived seventh head *ceases*, as such, to exist. And,

2d. That the Papacy, whatever its characteristics as *an* Antichrist—and that it is such we fully concede,—could not have constituted either the seventh head, which is a *purely secular* power; nor the eighth head, which, when it appears as the great apostatic democratico-religious power, "exalting itself *above all* that is called God" either in heaven or in earth,—which the Papacy never has done or will do,—will constitute, preëminently, THE ANTICHRIST.

We shall now proceed to a historic verification of the statements assumed in the preceding stand-points, by a return to a consideration,

I. *Of the chronological position* of the sixth and seventh heads in the series. Here we are to observe, in the first place, that *three* of the predicted characteristics of the *seventh* head are clearly defined.

1. In contrast with its long-lived predecessor, the *sixth* head, it was to "*continue but a short space.*"

2. Unlike *five* out of the six heads which preceded it, that are declared simply to have "fallen," this seventh head was to be *politically slain* by the sword of military violence. Yet,

3. It was at length to be revivified from this political death, by the *healing* of its deadly wound.

It is here to be observed, that Rev. xiii., 3, does not specify *which one* of the seven heads of the beast was to be "wounded unto death." To determine this point, we are dependent on chap. xvii., 10. There we learn, that "*five*" out of the seven heads had simply "fallen" *before* St. John's time.

We now refer you to the following facts, in proof that the existing sixth head of St. John's time fell, "by the *renunciation* of the ancient throne and dignity of the Roman emperorship," when the *last* Roman emperor, Francis, thus expressed himself, in A. D. 1806:

> "Being convinced of the impossibility of discharging any longer the duties which the imperial throne imposed upon us, we owe it to our principles to *abdicate a crown* which could have no value in our eyes when we were unable to discharge its duties and deserve the confidence of the princes electors of the empire. Therefore it is, that, considering the bonds which unite us to the empire as dissolved by the confederation of the Rhine, *we renounce the imperial crown*, and, by these presents, absolve the electors, princes, and states, members of the supreme tribunal, and other magistrates, from the duties which unite them to us *as their legal chief.*"[1]

It follows from this, that the *seventh* head, which was

---

[1] Alison's History of Europe, vol. v., p. 600. See Faber's Napoleon III., pp. 44, 45. Appleton, 1859.

to be " wounded to death," and to be again resuscitated, was *still future.*

If, then, it can be historically demonstrated, that this sword-slain seventh head appeared in the *French emperorship*, as constituted in the person of NAPOLEON I., in A. D. 1804; and that, after a short-lived existence, being *slain* by the sword of military violence, it was again *revived* in the person of LOUIS NAPOLEON III., in A. D. 1852; it will be fair to infer, that all the predicted characteristics, save those peculiar to the same personage as the still future EIGHTH HEAD, have been, and are being verified in that perpetuated power.

As already stated, we see that the curiously-devised symbol of the great seven-headed beast *from the sea*, with its characteristic badges of the Babylonian lion and the Medo-Persian bear and the Grecian leopard, denoted the Roman empire in its greatest territorial extent west and east, as constituting ONE EMPIRE under the administration of its *sixth* head.

Now, this symbolic representation will be found to exactly correspond with the principle of the ROMAN LAW, which is, "that the territorial Roman empire and the gubernative Roman emperorship were, each alike, A UNIT. Hence, whatever number of personal emperors, either in the west or east, might govern the one Roman empire; and however that one empire might be gubernatively arranged in point of division; still, those *personal* emperors and that *territorial* empire were, each alike, deemed ONE, and in Roman law were never held to have departed from the principle of UNITY.

"A want of attention to this vital principle,"—a principle, as the sequel will disclose, involving the most stupendous issues to the church of God, to the nations of earth, Jewish and Gentile, and to every individual of these "last times"—"a want of attention," we repeat, "to this vital principle," lies at the root of all the failures to identify the *seventh* and *eighth* heads in this prophecy, and to assign to them their proper chronological position in "the great drama of the world!"

We will now proceed, "through a series of historical facts, to trace the *political* course of that [sixth] Roman head, which the angel declared to be in actual existence" when St. John wrote.

"The ONE universal Roman empire was governed by a *single individual*, from the time of Augustus to Dioclesian, who, to meet the necessity of the case, so modelled the constitution that four persons—the two elder with the title of Augusti, and the two junior with the title of Cæsars—were *simultaneously* emperors of the Romans. The empire, nevertheless, retained its legal UNITY. Each emperor was regarded as supreme in his own province, and their joint edicts were recognized as authoritative by all. Even the *division* of the empire into west and east, did not disturb this theory of UNITY, which continued to exist to the very last. This quadruple arrangement of Dioclesian, however, by the transfer of the seat of government from Rome in the west to Constantinople in the east, was exchanged for that of a single individual, from the time of Constantine to Theodosius. On the death of this latter monarch, the empire was permanently divided into *west* and *east*, and his two sons, Arcadius and Honorius, were each emperor of the Romans, and so continued, in the line of their successors, down to the extinction of the *eastern* half of the ONE empire in A. D. 1453," by the valor of the Turks.

On the other hand, when the *western* half of the one empire fell by the deposition of Augustulus in A. D. 476 or 479, the Gothic tribes, by whom it was partitioned into ten sovereignties in A. D. 531,[1] still adhered to the principle of territorial unity; so that, from this period to the time of Charlemagne in A. D. 800, no military chieftain, either in or out of Italy, ventured to assume the imperial title. The fallen western branch, however, being *restored* by Charlemagne, again placed the government of the UNITED empire in the hands of two individuals, each bearing the style and admitted rank of emperor of the Romans.

But, from A. D. 1453, " no more than a *single Roman emperorship* remained: and, in the breaking up of the vast dominions of Charlemagne, its seat was transferred from France to Germany; which, with its feudatory Italian appendages, and the broken Gallican kingdoms of Burgundy and Arles, was henceforth styled "THE HOLY ROMAN EMPIRE." Meanwhile, its chief, whose paramount claim of princely authority (well shadowed out by its three ecclesiastical electors being respectively denominated the chancellors of Italy, and Germany, and France) extended to the whole empire, always bore the title of emperor of the Romans, and was always deemed the Kaisar, and thus the official successor and representative of Augustus, as the *first* in the line of personal monarchs of this *sixth* imperial head, and of whom, as already stated, Francis, by his abdication of its imperial prerogatives, was the *last*.

Now, the terms of the prophecy before us require that, with the extinction of the *sixth* head of the " beast" as a Roman polity, the *seventh* should " start into existence either simultaneously with its fall, or immediately before its fall, and thus intrusively causing its fall." Otherwise, " we shall have the zoölogical anomaly of a

---

[1] See p. 43.

wild beast continuing to live without having any living head."

Turn, now, to historical facts. " Just two years before the fall of this *sixth* head, in the person of the Roman emperor Francis, which was in A. D. 1806, started up a NEW POLITY, which, under the title of the EMPEROR OF THE FRENCH, was actually master of Rome and Italy, both of which were soon after *annexed* to its already ample dominions—a circumstance necessary to the character of a ROMAN HEAD,—the prophetic symbols of the seven heads of the "beast" representing both the *seven hills* of Rome, and the *seven polities* which should govern the empire.

NAPOLEON I.

And do you ask, *Who was this master of Rome and Italy?* None other, we reply, than that " Little French Corporal," born in Ajaccio, the capital of Corsica, in France, a little island in the Mediterranean, and who, as the veriest tyro in history knows, subsequently became the French emperor, NAPOLEON I. Yes, he it was who, commencing his wonderful career of conquests in A. D. 1804, soon subjugated all Europe, with the exception of Great Britain and Russia, to his despotic sway.

The *polity* of the sixth and seventh heads of the beast is substantially the same, the difference between the two arising from the change of title—that of emperor of the *Roman*, for the emperor of the *Franco-Roman* empire.

But there is another prophetical mark, which was to signalize this seventh headship of the " beast." It was to be *short-lived*, caused by " a wound unto death." If, then, it can be historically shown, that this feature of the prophecy was *verified* in the political and military career

of the first Napoleon, in a sense in which it will apply to
no other man, it must decide the question of the Franco-
Roman emperorship in favor of Napoleon I., as constituting the *seventh head* of the apocalyptic "beast."

First, then : Three circumstances, for a time, seemed
to *militate against* a verification of this mark, in its application to this world-renowned man : the first, the unprecedented strides of his military conquests ; the second, the apparent stability of his rapidly growing power ;
and the third, the prospect of its perpetuity by the birth
of a son, the Duke of Reichstadt, when in the strength
and vigor of his life. But, behold ! This *seventh* head
of the Franco-Roman empire, in the very midst of those
unparalleled triumphs which struck terror to the heart
of all Europe, after the very short period of *eleven years*
from A. D. 1804, having been severely though not mortally wounded in the war of 1814, the following year *was
finally slain* by the sword of military violence ! The
famous battle of Waterloo tells the story ! Defeated by
the valorous arms of the British lion, he is transported to
the desolate, sea-girt island of St. Helena, the humbled
exile of his most implacable foe, where, after a short interval of ignominous suffering, he dies !

We deferentially submit, therefore, that we have historically demonstrated the true chronological positions of
the *sixth* and *seventh* heads of the ROMAN POLITY, as
designated in this prophecy, after an interval extending
from B. C. 31 to A. D. 1804, a period of 1,835 years, as
founded, on the one hand, upon the uninterrupted *territorial unity* of the empire, and on the other, upon the
equally uninterrupted *governmental unity* of the emperorship.

The next subject will treat of the *relation* to Napoleon
I., of the other two members of the great Napoleonic

family, viz., Napoleon II., Duke of Reichstadt, and Napoleon III., as symbolically depicted in this prophecy.

It will be found that the importance and interest of this subject will increase as we advance.

CHAPTER III.

NAPOLEON II., DUKE OF REICHSTADT, AND KING OF ITALY—LOUIS NAPOLEON III.—RECAPITULATION.

WE have, in the preceding pages, historically demonstrated the true chronological positions of the *sixth* and *seventh* Heads of the ROMAN POLITY, as designated in this remarkable prophecy after the lapse of 1,835 years, from B. C. 31 to A. D. 1804. This, as we have seen, is founded upon that great principle of the old Roman Law, which established the uninterrupted territorial unity of the empire through all its changes during that period, and also the equally uninterrupted governmental unity of the emperorship. Hence the historic verification, in accordance with the terms of the prophecy, of the succession of the seventh to that of the sixth Head in the person of *Napoleon the I.*, in A. D. 1804, as emperor of the Franco-Roman empire.

So also of the application of the prophecy respecting this seventh Head, that " when he cometh, he must continue *a short space.*"[1] The career of Napoleon I., it was shown, lasted only eleven years, from A. D. 1804 to 1815, when he received his death-wound at the hand of the British lion on the battle-field of Waterloo.

[1] Rev. xvii. 10.

We now observe, that the defeat of the Napoleonic forces, followed by the imprisonment of this terrific Franco-Roman "Beast" in the sea-girt island of St. Helena, caused all the crowned heads of Europe and of the world to *exult* over the downfall of him who had been proclaimed emperor of France and King of Italy, as a successor of the Cæsars.

NAPOLEON II., THE DUKE OF REICHSTADT.

The history of NAPOLEON THE SECOND is a brief one. Although Napoleon the First abdicated his throne in favor of his son, the hopes of France were buried in his grave before he had attained to manhood.

On the other hand, the so-called "Holy Alliance," in A. D. 1815, had decreed that *no Bonaparte* should ever again rule over France. Indeed, it was the general belief that this seventh Franco-Roman emperorship had disappeared forever from the prophetic stage; a belief too that seemed to be reasonably confirmed by the early death of the Duke of Reichstadt. Besides, the *original* dynastic head of the empire, having dragged out a few short years of miserable existence in his solitary exile, lay slumbering, as it were, in the depths of the sea! In the most emphatic sense, therefore, it may be said of this seventh Beastly Head, as in the symbolic phraseology of this prophecy, that it "*was;*" and, also, after "continuing a short space," that it "*is not.*"

But man *proposes*—God *disposes*. Human decrees cannot defeat the purposes of Him who is "the governor among the nations."[1] The same angel who said of this seventh Head of the Franco-Roman emperorship, that it

---

[1] Ps. xxii. 28.

"was" and "is not," also declared of it, that though it should receive "a wound unto death," yet that its "*deadly wound was healed.*" (Rev. xiii. 3.) The meaning is, that the *same* Franco-Roman Dynasty that was thought to have been forever exterminated, should be again *revived*.

Here we must premise that the *healing* of the death-wound of this seventh Head must coincide with his restoration to a NEW TERM of political existence. So also, a coincidence must exist between the *mode* of introduction upon the prophetical platform of the sixth and seventh Heads. As St. John beheld, retrospectively, the ascent of the sixth Roman Head out of the *troubled sea ;*[1] so the then future seventh Head, in acquiring its new existence, was to emerge out of the oceanic sea (ἄβυσσος, *abyss*), or "bottomless pit"[2] of revolutionary violence.

We now proceed, as in the other case, to demonstrate the *revival* of the defunct seventh Franco-Roman emperorship, in the person of the present ruling sovereign of France, namely:

LOUIS NAPOLEON THE THIRD.

This brings us to a consideration of the more direct and immediate purpose of these prophetico-historical expositions. The reader will be enabled the more confidently to sit in judgment and pass sentence upon what we have to offer on this subject, from the fact that we are now to speak of that world-renowned personage, whose name, especially since A. D. 1848, having flourished in the columns of both foreign and home daily and weekly journals, secular and religious, has become as familiar to him as "household words."

---

[1] Rev. xiii. 1.   [2] Ib. xvii. 7, 8.

To proceed. To say nothing of the long series of events connected with the civil or political and military affairs of the Roman empire, inclusive of those which resulted in its division into the West and the East at the opening of the fourth century, onward to the ERA OF THE FRENCH REVOLUTION towards the close of the seventeenth, as depicted in the prophetico-historic symbols of the first six apocalyptic trumpets; we remark, that with the seventh commenced that period of revolutionary changes, both *political* and *religious*, which, beginning with France, convulsed every throne throughout continental Europe. As "signs of the times," these commotions of the symbolic *abyss* portended the arrival of the period for the accomplishment of the prophecy relatively to the *resuscitation of the seventh* Franco-Roman emperorship. They are symbolized by the *first five* out of the seven apocalyptic "vials" or "last plagues," all of which are included under the Seventh Trumpet.

We have said, that as the seven-headed scarlet-colored beast arose out of the "*sea*" of popular commotions, so there must be a correspondence between *it* and the circumstances which should mark the introduction upon the prophetic stage of the *revived seventh* Franco-Roman Head. Accordingly, after the lapse of about sixty years; that is, from the commencement of the French Revolution in A. D. 1789, down to A. D. 1848—to quote from the columns of one of our secular journals—" the casket was *fished up out of the sea*, and is again in power, to the astonishment of all the parties of the 'Holy Alliance.' " A pretty fair though undesigned exposition this, of the predicted revival of the *defunct* Franco-Roman Headship. We here allude to the extraordinary course which marked the progress of Louis Napoleon as an exile, until, out of the revolutionary elements of France he was elevated to the throne of that empire as he who, being "OF *the seventh*," is the veritable revived secular Roman Emperor.

We have spoken of Louis Napoleon as an exile. While in this country, whither he fled and found refuge from the prison walls of Ham, he had for his companion and counsellor a certain Mr. Müller, from whom, through an intimate friend of his, a correspondent in one of the secular issues of New York, dated September 5, 1863, was informed "that the dream of Louis Napoleon's whole life was his *accession* to the throne of France ; and that such was his aptitude for reverie, and facility for speculative development, that he had three large volumes filled with his plans for attaining the grand aim of his ambition." These volumes, according to Mr. Müller's statements, contain a series of remarkable *Napoleonic secrets*, which run through the pages of this imperial programme. We shall have occasion to refer to these more at large in the sequel. Suffice it now to say, that they all are made to bear upon carrying out Louis Napoleon's darling idea of founding a UNIVERSAL DYNASTY, of which the *Latin* race is to compose the body, and *France* the Head. We now, however, confine ourself to his *secret* plans, formed when in this country some twenty years ago, to grasp the sceptre of the *Franco-Roman* emperorship.

"The attempt to take France with about sixty followers, in the steamboat City of Edinburgh, *was distinctly marked out* in these volumes. The calculation was, that the electric fire which always runs in the veins of the French, and which is known as ' Glory,' would burst into a universal glow at the watchword of ' Napoleon !' while the counter view and calculation of defeat were contained in a marginal note, to the effect, that should he fail, the conviction that he was an easily-handled, soft-brained fool, would make him only the more eligible with the scheming sharpers of European politics as a *future* candidate. It was to help this latter calculation entirely that the performance of the tame eagle was thrown in. The eagle," said Müller, " will catch the fools, if we succeed; it will catch the sharpers if we lose. In playing for the minds of men we must never forget the two divisions of society." This latter calculation was undoubtedly justified by the manner in which the intriguing leaders in French politics afterward seized upon Louis Napoleon, almost by common consent, as their candidate for the position of PRINCE PRESIDENT. "They thought that they had the man of the *tame eagle*," said Müller, " but they got nothing better than the *Corsican wolf*." [1]

This last phraseology deserves a passing remark. Who can fail to detect the striking resemblance between those two figures of speech—" the tame eagle " and " the Corsican wolf"—as applied by Müller to this extraordinary man, and those two apocalyptic symbols in the thirteenth chapter of Revelation, of a " beast which had *two horns like a lamb*," but who " *spake as a dragon*," and which, as we shall presently see, point us to the same man!

See now the exact verification of this astounding prophetic foresight of Louis Napoleon as "THE MAN OF DESTINY"—a term which he has always appropriated to him-

[1] Müller did not go back to Europe with Louis Napoleon; but he confidently expected to be sent for as soon as his protégé should arrive at power. When, however, he found himself neglected, nay, forgotten by his aspiring pupil in the grand dazzle of events, which always buzz and sparkle around a throne, he sunk into a deep dejection, and died in obscurity and poverty in Howard street, New York, in A. D. 1853, about one year after Napoleon became Emperor of France.

self—in the historic events following. The continued revolutionary upheavings which immediately followed the "reign of terror" in France, like the restless billows of the perturbed and agitated "sea," fully prepared the nation for the *first step* towards Louis Napoleon's darling idea of founding a UNIVERSAL LATIN DYNASTY.

"December 10, 1848. Louis Napoleon is voted into a professedly *constitutional Presidentship* by 6,000,000 suffrages.

"December 2, 1851. He violently dissolves the factious assembly, which were preparing his ruin, and which were meditating a return to all the murderous atrocities of Jacobinism; and then, throwing off the old Bourbon tyranny of the unprincipled metropolis, he boldly appeals to the nation at large.

"December 20, 1851. He is voted into an *absolute Dictatorship*, still under the name of a Presidentship, by about 7,000,000 suffrages.

"November 4, 1852. He accepts the *Senatus Consultum* proposed to be laid before the people. It runs thus: The nation wishes the reëstablishment of the imperial dignity in the person of Louis Napoleon, with hereditary succession in his direct legitimate or adopted line; and gives him the right to regulate the order of succession to the throne in the Bonaparte family.

"November 21 and 22, 1852. The nation votes a *Revival of the French emperorship* in the person of Louis Napoleon the Third, by about 8,000,000 suffrages! And, finally:

"December 1, 1852. The votes of the nation are examined and ratified by the Senate, and are then submitted to the President for his acceptance. And he *formally accepts* the imperial dignity at the hands of the nation, their wish being expressed by an almost unanimous vote in the affirmative. While,

"December 2, 1852, THE REVIVAL OF THE FRANCO-ROMAN EMPERORSHIP is proclaimed in Paris, and three days after throughout the provinces."

It is worthy of notice, in this connection, that one of the banners that graced the entrance of Louis Napoleon into Paris on his return from his tour through France—the express object of which was to *prepare the way* for the proclamation of the empire—bore the following significant inscription: "The UNCLE that *was*—the NEPHEW that *is*." Thus using, though unconsciously to themselves, *the very words* in which these prophetico-historic events respecting them were given!

RECAPITULATION.

Let us now briefly survey the ground over which we have already passed. We submit that we have scripturally and historically demonstrated,

I. The rise, successively, of the four great symbolical monarchies of Gentilism—the Babylonian, Medo-Persian, Grecian, and Roman—that were to bear rule in the earth during the prolonged period of the mystical "seven times," or 2,520 years, predicted by Moses in Leviticus, chapter xxvi., called in the New Testament "THE TIMES OF THE GENTILES."

II. The territorial and governmental UNITY of the Roman empire, pagan and Christian, political and religious, during the whole stage of its existence, from B. C. 31 down to the present time, as symbolized by the seven mountains of Rome as the capital of the empire, and the seven forms of polity through which it was to pass, as denoted by the *seven Heads* of the fourth nondescript beast.

III. That *five* forms of the Roman Polity had "fallen" prior to the time when St. John wrote, which was in A. D. 96, the *sixth* Head, the imperial, being the one existing in his day, and which commenced from B. C. 31; and that the empire, though divided into two parts, the West and the East; and though subject to great and important changes and modifications in both branches; yet continuing to retain its territorial and political and ecclesiastical UNITY intact, and merging into itself the other three preceding monarchies on the principle of *annexation;* so when the Messianic "stone cut out of the mountain without hands,"—or which is the same thing, when " One like the son of man shall come in the clouds of heaven " to *smite* the colossal metallic image on the ten toes; or, which is the same thing, to destroy the four rampant beasts, together with the ten horns of the last of the four,—ALL will be found to be present in their entirety, to receive the omnipotent blow! Particularly in reference to the *last* one of these four monarchies, the ROMAN, as we have seen, although the imperial sceptre, just before the rise of the papacy in A. D. 533, had fallen *in the West* by the deposition of Augustulus in A. D. 476 or 479, it still continued *in the East* till A. D. 1453. Also that *before* it became extinct in the East, it had been revived in the West by Charlemagne in A. D. 800, and continued *unbroken* in the emperors of Germany or Austria till overthrown—

IV. By the *seventh* Franco-Roman emperorship in the person of NAPOLEON I. This emperorship, we have shown, having been originally established in A. D. 1804, was mortally wounded by the sword of military violence by the hand of the British lion, on the battle-field of

Waterloo, in A. D. 1815, but again revived in A. D. 1852, in the person of the reigning Franco-Roman emperor, LOUIS NAPOLEON III.

We have not, however, exhausted the revelations of the prophetico-historic oracle relatively to this *revived seventh* Franco-Roman Head.

OF THE SEVENTH AND EIGHTH HEADS.

On this subject we observe that, while we acknowledge our indebtedness to a recently published tract from the pen of the late Rev. Geo. Stanley Faber, under the title of "Napoleon III. the Man of Prophecy," for aid in our remarks on the territorial and governmental unity of the Roman empire; yet we must beg to dissent from his statements in regard to the *seventh* and EIGHTH Heads of this prophecy. Thus, on page 54, speaking of the *healing* of the mortal wound of the seventh head of the beast, this learned writer says: " it experienced an extraordinary revival, and enters upon a new course of existence, *apparently* as an eighth Head, but *really* as the restored seventh," etc. And again. On page 33 he says: " the prophecy again and again declares that the symbol [representative of the Roman beast] had *only seven* heads, and never mentions an EIGHTH Head," etc.

But to this we reply that the prophecy before us, which treats of this *same* Roman Beast, *does* make mention of an "eighth," which is declared to be "OF *the seven*." Wherefore, then, we ask, introduce this "eighth," if it is *identical* with the "seventh Head" in its revived form? On such an hypothesis is not the introduction of this symbol into the prophecy altogether superfluous? —a circumstance which could not otherwise than detract from the infinite wisdom of the Holy Spirit who revealed it!

Now, we agree with Mr. Faber, in rejecting the theory of Mr. Elliott and others that the characteristic marks answerable to the eighth Head are found in the PAPACY. But we also think that *he* equally errs when he insists that *all* the symbolic imagery in this part of the prophecy are met in the *revived seventh* Head as a merely secular power. It is true, as this writer says, page 59, that "the *healing* of the mortal wound [of the seventh Head] coincides with the symbol's restoration to a *new term* of political existence." But it is not true that the eighth Head does not form a power *beyond* and *distinct* from the seventh revived Head. Look again at the angel's account of these Heads. He speaks first of "the Beast that *was*," viz.: the Franco-Roman or *seventh Head* dynasty in the person of NAPOLEON I. Then, second, he says of it that it "*is not*." This is the same with the dynasty of the First Napoleon as *overthrown* by the sword of military violence, and as thought to have been forever exterminated by the early death of NAPOLEON II., in whose favor his father had abdicated the throne of France. And, finally, he adds, respecting this same dynasty, third, "*and yet is*."[1] That is, the dynasty as *revived* in the person of NAPOLEON III. Clearly, therefore, all these statements speak of and are strictly confined to the symbolic history of the *seventh* Head. Then is introduced, fourth, *another phase* in this prophecy. The angel says: "even he," *i. e.* the revived seventh Head, Napoleon III., "is the EIGHTH, and is OF *the seven*."

Here, then, observe: the angel does not say, as Mr.

---

[1] Rev. xvii. 8.

Faber affirms, that "he is *one* of the seven," as though the "eighth" was *included in* them as such; but as it is in the Greek—ἐκ τῶν ἑπτά ἐστι, that is, he is "*out of* or *from* the seventh," as denoting *origin* or *source;* as we find in Matt. i. 3—ἐκ τῆς θαμαρ, "*out of* Thamar."

It would be quite superfluous to a scholar of general history, to prove the *genealogical relationship* of the first and second Napoleons as UNCLE and NEPHEW. Still it may not be out of place to state, that Charles Louis Napoleon III. is the third son of Louis Napoleon, king of Holland, and of Hortense Eugénie, daughter of the Empress Josephine, first wife of Napoleon I., by her first husband, the Viscount de Beauharnais. He was born in Paris, at the palace of the Tuilleries, April 20, 1808. His father, Louis, was the fourth in age of the brothers of the emperor; but Napoleon I., by the imperial edicts of 1804 and 1805, *set aside* the usual order of descent, and declared the *succession* to the imperial crown to lie in the family of his brother Louis. Louis Napoleon III. was the *first* prince born under the imperial rule in the direct line of succession; and his birth was announced in consequence throughout the empire by discharges of artillery and other solemnities. At his baptism in 1810, his sponsors were the emperor and Empress Maria Louisa. Until the *abdication* of Napoleon I., with whom Hortense was always in great favor, she resided in Paris. While Napoleon I. was at Elba, Louis Bonaparte, her husband, instituted a suit in the court of Paris to have her sons removed from their mother's charge and restored to him; but the emperor's return put a stop to the proceedings, and henceforth the children remained under the charge of their mother. At the great assemblage on the Champ de Mai, Napoleon I. presented his nephew, Louis Napoleon, then seven years of age, to the soldiers and to the deputies, and the scene is said to have left a deep impression on the memory and the imagination of the boy. After the battle of Waterloo, Hortense and her sons attended Napoleon I. in his retirement at Malmaison. The scholastic education of Louis Napoleon was conducted under the direction of M. Lebas. In 1830, Louis Napoleon being refused by Louis Philippe, "the citizen king," to return to France as a common soldier in the national army, he and his brother retired to Tuscany, and at once united themselves with the Italian revolutionary army, in which, in 1831, they both took an active part in the insurrectionary movements of that year. His brother, however, died at Pesora, a victim to fatigue and anxiety in 1831, and his elder brother in infancy. In 1832, the only son of Napoleon I., now known as Napoleon II., but then as the Duke of Reichstadt, also died. Louis Napoleon had thus become, according to the imperial decree of 1804, the *immediate successor* to the emperor.

Thenceforward, the restoration of the empire and the Napoleonic dynasty in *his* person became the predominating idea of his life. To this end he published his "Political Reviews," in which the *necessity* of the Emperor to the State is assumed throughout, as the sole means of uniting *republicanism* with the genius and the requirements of the French people. And in 1839 he published his famous "*Idées Napoléoniennes*," a remarkable illustration of the intensity of his own grand thoughts, as connected with the conception of a future UNIVERSAL LATIN EMPIRE.

We now proceed to demonstrate, agreeably to the tenor of this remarkable prophecy when taken as a whole, that the circumstance of the revived seventh head being also accounted as an eighth, arises from the fact of the *mutation* which it is destined to undergo, to wit, that of its passing from its state or condition as a *merely secular* power, such as it now is, to the possession and exercise of *absolute apostatico-democratic religious* functions. The purpose of the Holy Spirit in the previous apocalyptic revelations concerning this seven-headed sea-beast as the *last* of the four monarchies of Gentilism, was, to instruct His people as to what concerned them as connected with and effected by the character and exploits of the revived seventh head, not only; but more especially when, having run its course as a mere secular power, it should give place for the introduction upon the prophetical platform of a more stupendous and terrific power under an EIGHTH HEAD, which should be "OF *the seven*."

In treating, therefore, of this eighth headship, which is *still future*, and which will stand forth (not as *one* of the heads of the beast, for their number is limited to *seven* only, but) *as entirely separate and distinct from and independently of it;* much care will be required in the interpretation and application of the symbolic imagery in which its *whole complex career* is portrayed. We shall here find that the terms of the prophecy imply, as already intimated, that there is an essential distinction between the *functions* of the revived seventh, and those of the eighth headship. Accordingly, the Holy Spirit will be found to have furnished us with a class of symbols explanatory of its *complex characteristics*, as such. The difficulty here will be, to discriminate between those symbols which relate to the *secular powers* of the revived seventh head, as contradistinguished from those of the still future eighth headship, as an *apostatico-political and ecclesiastical or religious power*. Let us take a view of them separately. And may that "wisdom which is from above," so guide our thoughts in the elucidation of the subject in hand, as to enable us clearly to discover " the mind of the spirit " who has revealed them!

I. THE CHARACTER AND EXPLOITS OF THE REVIVED SEVENTH FRANCO-ROMAN EMPERORSHIP, IN THE PERSON OF LOUIS NAPOLEON III., AS A PURELY SECULAR POWER.

St. John, we submit, furnishes us, Rev. xiii. 11, 12, with a full-drawn portrait of the present ruler of France, in the following apocalyptic imagery :—" And I beheld another beast coming *up out of the earth:* and he had *two horns like a lamb,* and he *spake as a dragon*"—the exact prototype of Mr. Müller's " tame eagle " and " Corsican wolf." " And he exerciseth all the power of the *first beast before him,*" namely, Napoleon I., " and causeth the earth and them that dwell therein to *worship* the first beast, whose deadly wound was healed."

It is here to be noted that this beast is said to " come up out of the earth ; " whereas, in analogy to the seven-headed and ten-horned beast from the sea, Rev. xiii. 1, he is said to " ascend out of the bottomless pit," or abyss, Rev. xvii. 8. The question, therefore, is, how are these statements to be reconciled with their *joint application* to the revived seventh head ? The explanation is, that the term " *earth,*" in this prophecy, out of which this beast is said to come up, refers to the *preëxisting territorial* limits of the Roman world; while the terms " *sea* " and " *bottomless pit* " or abyss, are used to denote the *national and political revolutions* which brought both upon the stage.

That the " beast" here described refers to the *revived seventh* Franco-Roman emperorship in the person of

Louis Napoleon III. will, we submit, appear from the following *prophetico-historic characteristics* of this wonderful man, when compared with the symbols in which it is draped—a "beast" represented as coming up out of the earth in the pretended *innocency* of the lamb, and in the pretended *power* of "the Lamb of God:" for he is described as having "two horns like a lamb." And further, he is declared, at the same time, to display all the *arrogance* and *fierceness* of the "dragon."

Viewed in all its aspects, none others that flourish in the annals of profane history, will at all compare with THE FAMILY OF THE NAPOLEONS. The senior of the race, Napoleon I., emerging from the little, obscure Mediterranean island of Corsica, in a few short years eclipses the glory of all the mighty warriors who had preceded him, both by the brilliancy of his genius and the valor of his arms. His tragical end on the sea-girt island of St. Helena corresponds with his beginning. After his decease, those who swayed the sceptre of his once extensive and powerful dynasty, rapidly pass away from off the stage. First, his son, the Duke of Reichstadt and king of Italy, is laid in an early grave. Then the Bourbon, Charles the Tenth, disappears. And after the revolution in A. D. 1830, "the citizen king," Louis Philippe, ruled France for eighteen years, when a sudden popular outbreak drove him from his throne on the 2d of March, 1848, and he flees to England to escape an ignominious death. Meanwhile, modern history is marked with no event of more portentous significance than the *escape* of Louis Napoleon from the fortress of Ham, May 25th, 1846, after an imprisonment of six years. In no other individual do the same extremes meet of human *degradation* and *exaltation*. Having wandered in this country as an almost penniless exile for two years, on the 27th of August,

1848 (the very year that Louis Philippe was driven from his throne), returning to France, he is elected to the FRENCH ASSEMBLY; and on the 20th of December following, he is chosen president of it for *three years*. On the 13th of November, 1851, by a "*coup de main*," effected at the cost of several thousands of lives and the exile of others, that presidency is extended to *ten years*. Still one step remained to be taken, ere he could meet the condition of the apocalyptic symbol which designated him as the *revived seventh secular* head of the Franco-Roman dynasty, the darlingly-cherished Napoleonic idea of his life! But of this in the next chapter.

CHAPTER IV.

LOUIS NAPOLEON, CONTINUED—THE FUTURE DESTINED SOVEREIGN OF A UNIVERSAL LATIN DYNASTY, ETC.

WE have now traced the prophetico-historic career of Louis Napoleon III., from the time of his escape from the fortress of Ham, May 25th, 1846, within the walls of which he had been confined as a prisoner of state under Louis Philippe for six years, and have followed him as an almost penniless wanderer in the United States for two years; when, returning back to France, in the short interval which elapsed between August 27, 1848, and November 21, and 22, 1852, we found him, by successive strides, wading through a sea of human blood and other atrocities, to his seat on the throne of the Franco-Roman empire. It will be found, therefore, both interesting and instructive, to devote such further space as the momentous subject in hand may require, to a contemplation of what *the same prophetico-political* text-book reveals, regarding this wonderful personage, in connection with his complex characteristics, as the *revived seventh secular headship* of the Franco-Roman polity, and of his still future predestined EIGHTH HEADSHIP over a universal Latin dynasty.

Yes, we repeat:

LOUIS NAPOLEON III., THE PREDESTINED SOVEREIGN OF A UNIVERSAL LATIN DYNASTY.

Does this announcement startle the reader? And yet, methinks, he is ready to concede the truthfulness of the application of the prophecy under review, so far as connected with the subject in hand down to the point just alluded to. With the assurance, then, that "*the half* has not been told him," and begging him to bear in mind that we are not drawing our arguments and facts from the political legerdemain of worldly diplomatic cabinets and statesmen, but from the *inspired* statute-book of HIM who sits enthroned as " the governor among the nations ; " I ask his further indulgence and a suspension of his judgment, until we shall have reached the issue.

As we are still engaged with the *secular power* of this revived seventh imperial headship of France, it will be most appropriate to consider,

I. What the inspired prophetic oracles reveal of *the peculiarities of his character, both intellectual and moral.* Now, in the Apocalypse, St. John, speaking of this revived seventh head, says of him, that " he *deceiveth* them that dwell on the earth,"[1] etc. So the prophet Daniel, describing this same power, calls it " *a vile person* " (*i. e.*, one despised), " to whom they shall not give the honor of the kingdom ; but he shall come in *peaceably*," as denoted by the apocalyptic " beast with *two horns like a lamb*,"[2] " and obtain the kingdom by *flatteries*." Moreover, as a " king," he " shall do *according to his will*,"[3] and he " *shall exalt himself above every god*," etc.

[1] Rev. xiii. 14.   [2] *Ibid.* xiii. 11.   [3] Dan. xi. 36.

We have seen that in the three large volumes in which were recorded the Napoleonic secrets, written while in exile, their imperial author prognosticated that the conviction would obtain among men " that he was an easily-handled, soft-brained fool." And so it was. For, " before Napoleon III. obtained the emperorship, he was so despised on account of his obscurity, that there was scarcely a man in the world upon whom more contemptuous epithets and opinions were passed than upon him." He was supposed to be without understanding, an idiotic dreamer, as short of brains as he was of friends and means. Such an estimate, however, of his intellectual imbecility and personal meanness, scarcely comports with those *prophetic characteristics* above ascribed to him. Rather, they would indicate that one of his prominent characteristics would be that of " impenetrability, inscrutability, reticence, cunning, secret craftiness, and a sphinx-like inflexibility of countenance;" all of which intellectual attributes are implied in and are essential to, one who was to obtain imperial power against a world of opposing obstacles "*peaceably*," and by "*flatteries*." Hence it cannot fail to strike the mind how well these attributes apply to a man of whom a personal friend of his, who laboriously attempted an analysis of his character, has said: " Frigidly affable, and repulsively polite, he avoided either offence or familiarity, but seemed instinctively to coil up his nature from observation. In phrase and demeanor all that became his birth, still the man was perfectly inaccessible. There was much of peculiarity, much of contrast; abstract yet vigilant, inquisitive in everything, but studiously incommunicative; diligent in acquiring all men's knowledge, retentive of his own; cold and impassive, but full of latent energy; cautious in decision, but, having decided, prompt, rapid, and impetuous. Almost intuitive in grasping opportunity or detecting weakness; improved by study, steeled by adversity, disciplined for every vicissitude of fortune, he has inestimable qualifications for his own position. . . Marvellous as his character appears at present, it is, in my judgment, *as yet very partially developed.*" This we shall see more fully in the sequel. He adds: " The *reserve*, however, in which Napoleon habitually shrouds himself, may not now be violated. Few can see, in the taciturn recluse, the talents, the attainments, and accomplishments which he undoubtedly possesses."[1] Madden also confirms this well-drawn portrait, where he says that " This *man-mystery*, the depth of whose duplicity no Œdipus has yet sounded, is a problem even to those who surround him. I watched his pale, corpse-like, imperturbable features, not many months since, for a period of three hours. I saw eighty thousand men before him, and I never saw a change in his countenance or an expression in his look, which would enable the bystander to say whether he was pleased or otherwise at the stirring scene that was passing before him, on the very spot where Louis XVI. was put to death. He did not speak to those around him, except at very long intervals, and then with an air of nonchalance, of ennui, and eternal occupation with self." " Dark, mysterious, impenetrable, inscrutable in his designs," says another writer,[2] " concealing every passion of his heart within the innermost depths of his soul; of great personal courage and inflexible will, conjoined with cool deliberation and consummate prudence; entirely devoid, apparently, of any real religion or moral principle,"—" *a vile person:* "—" impelled, guided, protected, as he announces himself to be, by his uncle's

---

[1] Phillips on Napoleon III.   [2] The author of Armageddon.

shade; with the subtlety of that 'more subtle than any beast of the field,' he has hitherto defeated all his opponents, and reached *by craft* a pinnacle which his uncle could only attain *by the sword*. Striking not until his quarry be certain, or never uncoiling himself to seize his prey until sure of his victim; daily increasing in power and influence over the nations, and bringing the eyes of an astonished world to contrast with wonder his past and present career: all in relation to him seems to be after a *superhuman* working that none can fathom."

But it is predicted of him,

That "*he shall have power over the treasures of gold and silver.*"[1] And it is a marvellous fact, that Napoleon III. has not only succeeded in securing all the money requisite for the extraordinary cost of carrying on his government and vast improvements, but in the years 1855, '56, and '57, he coined more gold than both England and the United States together!

If, then, all these incomparable intellectual and moral characteristics and resources of power, are found to stand out in bold relief as developed in the prophetico-historic career of Napoleon III.; those of this day—in the executive, judicial, legislative, and other departments of state, general and sectional, *and especially the clergy*—will incur a most fearful responsibility before God, *by a neglect* to study the character and watch the portentous movements of such a man. Simply reminding the reader of what the historian, Alison, has said of him, that "the *idea of a destiny*, and his having a mission to perform, was throughout a fixed one in Napoleon's mind;" and that "no disasters shook his confidence in his star, or his

---

[1] Dan. xi. 43.

belief in the *ultimate* fulfilment of his destiny," let us pass on to a brief review,

II. Of his unprecedented career from its commencement to the present time.

It will be well, however, to premise by way of preparing the mind for what is to follow, that, in comparison with others of the world's mightiest warriors, "Alexander, Cæsar, and the first Napoleon, were men of limited views. Their circle of empire fell far within the circle of the globe. Alexander wept for new worlds to conquer, but he never approached to the circumvallation even of the world on which he lived. Their ambition and their powers were limited by a Divine decree, *because* their destiny was not that of universal empire. But there is ONE MAN who is destined for universal empire, a man whom raw beginners fancy to be identical with the *Pope;* but whom all but raw beginners know to be the *supplanter* of the Pope." This one man is symbolically depicted in Rev. xiii. 3, 4. As soon as the seventh wounded head of the beast is healed, he *reappears* in the form of the *revived seventh* head, after whom it is said " all the world wandered; " and that " they worshipped the dragon," " which is the Devil and Satan,"[1] " that *gave power* " unto this revived seventh head of the " beast ; " and also that they " *worshipped* " him, saying, " Who is like unto the beast ? who is able to make war with him ? " And so, as an English writer, the Rev. R. Purdon, says : " Wonderful to tell, after all our ' balance of power;' after all our ' holy alliances;' after all our ' march of intellect ;' we see ONE MAN rising to universal

[1] Compare Rev. xii. 9, with chap. xx. 2.

empire, and that man the head of the *Napoleonic race*— a just judgment upon our pride and malignity! One man is throwing a girdle round the globe. One man has forged a chain of iron; he has connected the links, and holds the extremities in his hand. Every separate link acts upon the other, and when one link is moved, all will move along with it. There is no limit to his power but the limits of the globe! Less brilliant than Alexander or Cæsar, he is more subtle, more patient, and by far more ambitious. As the *last*, so he aspires to be the *greatest* of monarchs, and takes in within his grasp regions of the earth whose very existence was unknown to Cæsar and Alexander. . . What concerns us [at present] is, not the person, but the power; and we cannot deny that A POWER is now rising in the world which threatens universal dominion, and which no man is able to counteract. Every nation in Europe is occupied at home— Russia with her serfs; Austria with Venetia and Hungary; Prussia with the Germanic question; England with her public debt and cruel taxation; France alone is free to act, . . and she alone is prepared at every point. The Napoleonic race is master of the age!"

Strong language this. Is it true? We answer, with a slight modification, which will be pointed out in the proper place, that it is true. It may help to decide this question by taking a cursory view,

FIRST, of the similarity of his accession to power with that of his imperial uncle. We have seen how the Napoleonic "little corporal," emerging from the obscure island of Corsica, rapidly rose at the point of the sword to the highest grade of military distinction. Advancing in his conquests on the right hand and on the left, he at length wrested from the emperor of Austria his Italian dominions. With this achievement he graced his triumphal entry into Milan, May 26, 1805, by placing upon his own head the imperial iron crown of Charlemagne, pronouncing at the same time the historical words: " Dio me la diede ; guai a chi la tocca!" That is—" God has given it me; beware of touching it." In the year A. D. 1808, he took possession of Rome; and, in exchange for Pope Pius VII.'s bull of excommunication that had been fulminated against him, Napoleon I. demanded his surrender of all *temporal* sovereignty, on refusal of which the refractory Pope was banished as an exile into Savonia, in Lombardy. Following his coronation, as above, at Milan, in which, by the way, was verified the *first* condition of the prophecy relating to the seventh imperial Franco-Roman emperorship, most of the nations of Europe, including Rome as the metropolis of the territorial domain of the *first six* heads of the united empire, were numbered among his conquests; so that at Dresden, before he set out for Moscow on his Russian campaign, in A. D. 1812, nearly all the crowned heads of the old world—the emperor and empress of Austria; the kings of Prussia, Saxony, Naples, Bavaria, Wurtemburg, and Westphalia ; together with the elector of Baden and a host of princes of inferior grade—met to do him homage as THE CHIEF of a great empire !

Turn now to NAPOLEON III. We have already spoken of him as the revived seventh head of the Franco-Roman empire. We have also stated that this revival occurred in the person of one who was looked upon as a mere restless trifler or rash adventurer, whose attempt with a few devoted followers at Boulogne to subvert the citizen governmentship of Louis Philippe brought him only a contemptuous imprisonment in the fortress of Ham, the same year, A. D. 1840, that the corpse of his uncle, in accordance with his dying request, was exhumed and brought back to France in so much triumph!

One would suppose that such a contrast in the tragical incident which marked the fortunes of the "*uncle*" and "*nephew*" were sufficient to crush out forever the last spark of ambition enkindled by the latter's dream of attaining to "universal empire." But so far from it, two years after his escape from his six years' imprisonment, in the same year of Louis Philippe's flight from France, in A. D. 1848, he returns from his exile, and, being elected as one of the representatives in that legislative Babel, the National Assembly, in his proclamation in connection with the Boulogne affair, he said: "I feel behind me the shade of the emperor, which impels me forward. I will not stop till I have regained the sword of Austerlitz, and replaced the nations under our standards."

In further confirmation of this, Dr. Leask, of Scotland, in his *Rainbow*, for September last (1865), notices a recent publication in England, the manuscript of which was written five years ago, in which Napoleon III. is set forth as most seriously scheming the entire conquest of Europe and of the world. The following extract is given as having been one of the utterances of the great adventurer before he came into power:

"When all the world is nearly in my hands, I'll bring it all to bear against *Great Britain*. She is all scattered. I concentrated. Everywhere her commerce shall be attacked, her colonies invaded, her seaports stormed. Electric wires shall flash my orders at a given moment, rise in all climes, and *crush Great Britain*. She shall go down, and I will reign supreme throughout the world. Builder and arbiter of my own fortune! Happier than Napoleon's son, and greater; greater than he himself! I will transcend his glory! *Never name shall be like my* name!* The image of all glory shall be my image! I, the great reality, *like unto God*, my power universal. But soft—I dream—I am but a captive now! Well, well, all's one for that! I'll let time shape; and then—an end. Now to my studies!"

"Thus," says the writer, "he sat him down. He knew not it is writ: 'This matter is by a decree of the watchers, and the demand by the word of the Holy One; to the extent that the living may know that THE MOST HIGH RULETH IN THE KINGDOM OF MEN, and giveth it to whomsoever He will, and setteth up over it *the basest of men.*'" (Dan. iv. 17).[1]

Now, we would submit with deference, as argued from the facts of the past, that it is not difficult to anticipate—certainly that it is not beyond the bounds of possibility—from the present condition of the world, and Louis Napoleon's position in it, that it would not take any great length of time to fulfil *in him* the words of the prophet, in which it is said (Rev. xiii. 7) that "*power was given him* (and mark, he is speaking of the revived seventh head of the Roman beast when merged into that of his eighth headship) *over all kindreds, and tongues, and nations!*"

We repeat, then, that the rapid ascension to power and dominion of the now ruling emperor of France has startled the world, and his influence and authority are augmenting still in all quarters of the globe. He is at this moment the most daring, the most ambitious, the most powerful, and the most dangerous man on earth! Aye, and the more so, because the rulers, and statesmen, and politicians, and the clergy and people of Protestant nations *will not believe it!* And yet who will, who can

---

[1] Prophetic Times. Phila., Dec., 1865.

deny that the Crimean war put him at the head of European affairs? His interference in the war of Austria and Sardinia shows with what a controlling hand he is competent to dispose of the *disputes* of nations. His annexation of Savoy and Nice to France is another illustration of his growing preëminence and independence of the old combinations of Europe. The recent war with China, and the French occupation of Syria, have planted his power in Asia. Turkey lies crouching at his feet. The north of Africa is his. He has planted his foot in MEXICO, and that in *defiance* of all the newspaper blustering about the "*Monroe doctrine.*" Let American politicians, statesmen, and diplomatists mark this! *Quære*. Will the government of the United States go to war with France in support of the integrity of the Monroe doctrine against the monarchical encroachments of that power in Mexico? From the time of MAXIMILIAN'S arrival in that devoted country, notwithstanding the numerous assurances that his expulsion from his throne was a mere question of time—which assurances have been apparently confirmed by the reported *successes* of the Liberals against the imperial army—the writer has uniformly persisted in expressing the confident belief that this *Austrian protégé* of the French emperor would be left undisturbed so far as *the United States Government* is concerned. And he must confess that this belief is not a little strengthened by the appearance of an editorial article in "*the New York Sun*" of December 26, 1865, under the following head:

CAN WE AFFORD TO FIGHT FOR MEXICO?

The spirit of the President's message, the action of Congress, and the temper of the people in respect to the Mexican question, leaves no room for doubt concerning the antipathy of the United States toward the monarchical usurpation in Mexico. As a nation, we cherish the doctrine that monarchy should not be permitted to extend its power upon this continent, and we are naturally jealous of every encroachment upon liberty and republican government. Unfortunately, this principle was disrespected and infringed at a time when we were powerless to uphold and protect it. Taking advantage of our civil conflict, the hated institution of monarchy established itself upon our southwestern border, and as we emerge from the war of the rebellion, exhausted and impoverished, we see the government of a despot striving to crush out liberty in a neighboring republic. We are indignant, even belligerent at this cowardly outrage, and we have the *will* to teach the usurper and his backers a lesson that they would never forget. This being the case, what should we do? Napoleon and Maximilian know how warmly we cherish the Monroe doctrine; they know that we never would have permitted their aggression upon Mexico had not the hands of the government been tied by civil war. Therefore they have determined to ignore the great principle which we have upheld for nearly fifty years, and the question becomes narrowed down to this point: Shall we attempt the expulsion of Maximilian by force, and thus incur an inevitable war with France, possibly allied with Austria? On making a cursory examination of this question, we see that the nation is already satiated with war, and to a great extent exhausted, impoverished, and prostrated by the desperate civil contest which has just ended. Every dollar of money, and every strong arm are now needed, as they were never needed before, to repair, restore and replenish. We know that it is only by the strictest frugality, and the closest husbanding of our resources, that we can recover the waste of the last five years; and experience has given us an idea of what another war would cost. Can we afford it? Would it be prudent in the present condition of the country to inaugurate a war with a first-class military power, for the sake of a cherished principle? Or would it not be more prudent, more in accordance with discretion and good policy, to be less precipitate in our vindication of the Monroe doctrine—to patiently abide our time and wait until we can strike a blow for Mexico without the risk of bringing upon our country ruinous financial disaster?

But to proceed. Napoleon III. is now virtually the ruler of Rome. You will soon see that he will have the *Jews* completely enlisted in his favor. It has been recently announced that Napoleon III. has declared himself *emperor of Algeria*. In his recent visit to that country, "in reply to an address made to a Jewish rabbi of that country, the emperor said: '*Soon, I hope, the Algerian Israelites will be French citizens.*' Since then the members of the Israelitish consistory of Oran have addressed their brethren of Algeria, congratulating them on 'the ineffable happiness' vouchsafed to them in those 'august words,' and urging them to accept the offer, with all the conditions imposed by '*that noble name,*' NAPOLEON III. They say: 'You are aware that to the Israelite the law of the state has the force of a *religious* law. Henceforward French, after your struggles for so many ages, the eternal hearer of your tears and prayers, *the greatest and justest of princes* has opened to you the finest country in the world. Its laws will be your laws, as its destinies have been your destinies.' This may serve to indicate what sort of impression is being made upon a large portion of the *Jewish* mind with respect to Napoleon and his disposition and capacity to do for that remarkable people.' " [1] Palestine seems as if preparing to open her gates to receive him. Jerusalem, the Holy City, is at this moment stirring throughout its desolations under the influence of his power. The same holds true of Greece, the succession to whose throne is at his disposal. It remains to be seen what will be the result of his chameleon-like interference and manœuvring with the affairs of these United States.

We now proceed to observe, as confirmatory of what is here indicated, that the year following Napoleon's "*coup de main,*" on the anniversary of the great battle of Austerlitz, December 2, 1852, he, after the example of

[1] Prophetic Times.

his uncle, ASSUMED THE OLD ROMAN TITLE OF EMPEROR. Soon after this, he was acknowledged as such by all the crowned heads of Europe, notwithstanding that they, at the Congress of Vienna, in A. D. 1815, entered into a treaty, as already stated, *that no member of the Napoleon family should ever again reign in France!* And who will deny that, since his inauguration as emperor of the French, he has reached to a pitch of power the greatest and most absolute in the world? Why, his subjects make it their boast, that in *one year* from December, 1852, he has been personally acknowledged in his IMPERIAL character by the queen of England, the emperor of Russia—neither of whose monarchs paid that honor to Napoleon I.,—also by the kings of Prussia, Bavaria, Belgium, and Wurtemberg, the queen of Greece, the prince of Nassau, and the grand dukes of Baden-Baden, and of Saxe-Cobourg.

SECOND. But let us now consider more directly the applicability of the symbols employed by the Holy Spirit in Rev. xiii. 11, 12, in illustration of his *secular* character and functions, as the revived seventh head of the French nation.

1. It is notorious that Napoleon III., on ascending the throne of France, appeared before the world in the character of "THE GREAT PACIFICATOR," following out the new Napoleonic "idea." Hence his announcement to the nations—"L'Empire, c'est la paix"—"*The Empire is peace!*" How much in resemblance this to "the beast from the earth having *two horns like a lamb!*" How like Mr. Müller's "tame eagle!" We ask, therefore, was it chance, suppose you, or was it a verification of this part of the above prophecy, which led to his adoption and use of the above-named axiom? Did ever potentate before him thus attempt to *counterfeit* this in-

effable attribute of "the Lamb of God" as "THE PRINCE OF PEACE?" But,

2. Take a glance, now, at the exercise of the secular power of this "beast like a lamb," viewed in connection with that other feature of his character, as indicated by the words of the prophet,—"*he spake as a dragon.*" We have, in this symbol, a representation of the authority exercised by this revived seventh Franco-Roman headship in the affairs of Europe, since his accession to power. The following facts will be found in point:

(1.) In 1849, an insurrection occurred at Rome, in the midst of which the holy pontiff, Pius IX., flees as an exile for safety to Gaeta. But Napoleon III. sends to Rome a large body of so-called French republican (!) troops to quell the rebels, restore the Pope to his throne, and protect the government of the papal states; thus demonstrating that the "*life*" of the papal "little horn" only subsists by the sufferance of this arbiter of its fate. Again,

(2.) In 1854, King Otho of Greece is made to succumb to the demands of his imperial majesty, on the ground of his agency in quelling a local disturbance in his dominions, from which time *Greece* has remained entirely under his sovereign control.

(3.) The same holds true of Napoleon's connection with the *Russian* war. Here too he is preëminent. For although his British ally, after the fall of Sebastopol, in August 10, 1855 (which followed the capture, by the French, of the famous Malakoff fortress), was anxious to continue the war; yet, from motives of state policy, this renowned "pacificator" resolved upon "peace," leaving no alternative to England but that of unconditional submission! Accordingly, peace was consummated at the Tuilleries in April, 1856, and the Crimean campaign, commenced ostensibly to maintain the integrity of the *Turkish empire*, as the only preservative of the "*balance of power*" in Europe, has been made greatly to accelerate the ascent of his "star of destiny."

(4.) So of the *Neufchatel* trouble in 1856, between Switzerland and Prussia. Whilst the mediation of England, Austria, and America combined, failed utterly to restore peace, one word from the French emperor, and the sword was sheathed!

(5.) The same preëminence of the Napoleonic policy is maintained against Turkey and England on the question of the *Danubian principalities*, Moldavia and Wallachia, he favoring their union under a single head; they, of an election by each power of a separate head. But, a lamb-like visit of his majesty to Queen Victoria in the Isle of Wight, prevails at once to nullify the elections, thus, without doubt, preparing the way in the end to place some dependant of his own choice, as king or governor of those provinces.

(6.) We might also mention the potency of his mediation between *England* and *Persia* in 1857, and the advancement of his own interests thereby; for it left Herat, about which the war commenced, still in the hands of the enemy; while England, after a vast expenditure both of blood and treasure, is forced quietly to submit to a treaty made by Napoleon with the Persian court on his own account! And finally,

(7.) From that period onward, and especially since the humiliation of *Austria* at his hand on the battle-field of Italy, the valor of his arms, the formidable dimensions of his military and naval forces—for it is declared on reliable authority, that in one month he can place in the field two million disciplined men, while he is possessed of a fleet the most powerful in the world, with one ex-

5

ception (that of the United States), and which he is engaged in rendering sevenfold stronger by the addition of powerful iron-clads of his own invention—his incomparable statesmanship as displayed in carrying out the treaty of peace at Villafranca, and the deeply mysterious oscillations of his policy with the courts of Turin, Vienna, Rome, England, and the United States, by which he holds at bay, and confounds the most astute diplomacy of all the cabinets of both hemispheres, together with the unparalleled brilliancy of his unchecked career, have rendered him thus far the ruling spirit of the destinies of Europe and of the world!

CHAPTER V.

LOUIS NAPOLEON III., CONTINUED—SYMBOLIZED BY THE SCARLET-COLORED BEAST OF REV. XVII. 1–6, IN UNION WITH THE PAPACY, ETC.

HAVING presented to view those prophetico-historic incidents connected with the extraordinary career of Napoleon III., during the short interval that elapsed between his escape from the fortress of Ham in A. D. 1846, and his recognition by all the crowned heads of Europe as the *revived seventh secular* head of the Franco-Roman empire in A. D. 1853; it is pertinent now to bring to your notice the SPECIAL AGENCY revealed by the Holy Spirit, which was employed in raising him to a pitch of power the most absolute and unprecedented in the world. To this end, we point you to Rev. xvii. 1, where the angel, addressing St. John, says: "Come hither, and I will show thee the judgment of the great whore that sitteth upon many waters," etc. . . And St. John says: "I saw a woman sit upon a scarlet-colored beast, full of names of blasphemy, having seven heads and ten horns."

The "woman" in this prophecy, is the same with the sun-clad woman of Rev. xii. 1, now an apostate, upon whose forehead a name was written, MYSTERY, BABYLON THE GREAT, THE MOTHER OF HARLOTS AND ABOMINA-

TIONS OF THE EARTH" (verse 5), or, "the great whore, with whom the kings of the earth have committed fornication, and who has made the inhabitants of the earth drunk with the wine of her fornication" (verse 2). All the best Protestant writers concur in interpreting these symbols to denote the PAPACY, by whose corruptions of the primitive doctrines and polity and ordinances of Christianity, the kings of the earth and their subjects have been seduced into the sin of spiritual fornication. Hence her "sitting upon *many waters*," is interpreted by the angel, verse 15, to represent "peoples, and multitudes, and nations, and tongues," or the population of the Roman empire over whom she presides.

On the other hand, the "scarlet-colored beast, *full of names of blasphemy*, having seven heads and ten horns," is the same with the "beast" which St. John saw "rise up out of the sea," Rev. xii. 3, and chap. xiii. 1. This is evident from the *various mutations* through which this "beast" has passed, from his first introduction upon the prophetical stage.

First, we see him with "seven crowns upon his *heads*," chap. xii. 3, denotive, as we have said (see chap. xvii. 10), of the *seven forms of government* through which the empire was to pass from its first foundation to its final overthrow.[1] But, as these forms of the Roman polity each differed from the other, the mutations of which we now speak relate partly to Rome under its Pagan, and partly under its Christianized state. In this aspect, the *pagan* period of the crowned-head history of the empire extended from its foundation, B. C. 31, down to its extermination under Constantine in A. D. 323, and onward to the division of the empire into ten principalities

---

[1] See pages 52-55.

by the Gothic tribes in A. D. 532; when, these tribes having conformed to that system of corrupt Christianity consequent of the union of church and state under Constantine, upon the elevation of John II., the patriarch of Rome, as UNIVERSAL BISHOP by the edict of Justinian in A. D. 533; Second, the "crowns" were removed from the "seven heads" to the "*ten horns*" of the beast, while upon *his* "*heads*" was inscribed "the name of blasphemy." The empire, therefore, symbolized by the *body* of this "beast from the sea," under its first six heads, or forms of government, passes through its successive *religious stages*, pagan, pagano-christian, and ecclesiastico-political—which last consisted of an addition of the temporal to the spiritual power of the popedom, or *the union of the mitre with the sword*, by the donation of Pepin to the Pope of the Exarchate and Pentapolis in A. D. 756—down to the appearance upon the stage of the same beast,

Third, as the "scarlet-colored beast, *full of names of blasphemy*, having seven heads and ten horns." Now, of the "beast," or Roman body politic under this form of its development, we must note, first, the transfer of "the name of blasphemy" from the seven heads to "*the entire body*," which is said to be "full of," or covered all over with, "the names of blasphemy!" signifying thereby, that the *apostasy* of the "woman" or the "great whore," as the symbol of the Papacy, and of which the "scarlet-colored beast" is the secular head, had at length attained its *culminating point*. Our second remark is, that the phrase, "scarlet-colored," which now distinguishes the "beast," denotes the exercise of unlimited and unscrupulous power in the accomplishment of its ends. And third, its appearance with its "ten horns" *uncrowned*, represents the termination of *all* the septiform systems of the

Roman polity, with the head who now wields the seventh form, which is identical with the "beast from the earth having two horns like a lamb," but who "speaks like a dragon."

Now, then, for *the point* to which these expositions conduct us. St. John tells us that he "saw a woman sit upon a scarlet-colored beast," etc. Or,

THE "SCARLET-COLORED BEAST," BEARING UPON HIS BACK A HARLOT RIDER!

Is there, then, anything in the prophetico-historic relations of Napoleon III. to and with the Papacy, at all analogous to the above symbolic imagery?

This is the question. And it is one of momentous import. But we must premise, even at the expense of a partial repetition, in order to clear the way before us, that NAPOLEON I., having assumed to be the successor of the Cæsars, and being proclaimed emperor of France and king of Italy, verified that he was the seventh head of the Roman beast:—"it *was*." But soon, "it *is not*," for it was to "continue but a short space," and the world supposed that it had disappeared forever. Not so the purpose of the great Lawgiver and Arbiter of nations. "Its deadly wound was *healed*." Ere forty years had passed away, this seventh head *reappears* "out of the bottomless pit" or abyss, to the wonder of the world! Not, observe, as a separate and distinct dynasty from the other. It is the same that "was," then "is not," and "yet is." Aye, it is the "uncle" that "*was*," the "nephew" that "*is*,"—NAPOLEON III.

We remark in the next place, in this connection, that the vastness of the Franco-Roman empire, territorially, politically, commercially, and financially, together with the unprecedented prosperity and glory that surround her under the guidance of the present revived seventh head, is founded upon the *prestige* which is derived from the preceding one, and that it is not unlike it in its general features.

And yet, it is to be observed, that an essentially different *animus* characterizes the revived, in contrast with the defunct head. Napoleon I. ruled by *coercion*, which his subjects *repelled*. Napoleon III. sways the masses by *conciliation*, through *universal suffrage*. The reason is obvious. The uncle had nothing to expect from the Roman hierarchy; the nephew, everything.

Hence, in ascending from the abyss of poverty and ignominy, one of the very first acts of the *revived* Napoleonic headship was, to permit the papal harlot to take her seat upon his back! The circumstances were these: —a revolution in Rome, to which we have already adverted,[1] had *expelled* the Pope, Pius IX., from the papal throne, the pontiff having fled for safety to Gaeta, with no ability in himself to recover his lost dominions. But, by a coalition between the emperor, as the eldest son of the church, and the Pope, each becomes a help to the other. This coalition involved two things: first, Napoleon III. was to *reinstate* the Pope at Rome. And second, Pius IX. was to raise Napoleon to IMPERIAL POWER. In the accomplishment of the first, the "scarlet-colored beast" sends his republican army to Italy, and the Pope is restored. At *this point it is, that the papal harlot mounts upon the back of the beast.*

And so, the "*judgment*" of the "great whore," that had begun to take effect by the pouring out of the vials of the Almighty's wrath upon her between A. D. 1789

---

[1] See page 96.

and 1793, and which had recommenced by the above expulsion of the papal power from Rome, is for the time arrested. The French general Oudinot, sent by Napoleon to Rome in 1849 to quell the republican insurrection in that city, having consummated that mission, received a deputation of church dignitaries of high order, who came to thank him for the " important services " he had rendered the church. Oudinot, in his reply, said :

"I thank you, in the name of France and the army, for your good wishes. For my part, I am proud of having defended the *military* honor of France, and reëstablished order. I am equally delighted to have it in my power to serve *the church* and you, gentlemen, who must have suffered so severely during the evil days through which you have passed. The army, gentlemen, and the clergy, are the *two great powers* called to save society. United by the same tie that consolidates our power; united by discipline, it is only from the *religious* sentiment and the respect for authority, that society can derive its strength and salvation."

So, also, the Archbishop of Paris, at the great fête held after Napoleon had *reinstated* the Pope, in the presence of eighty thousand soldiers and six hundred priests, surrounding the altar in the Champ de Mars, exclaimed:

"Astonishing circumstance! . . . *the church*, which preaches peace to all . . . the church has always had abundant benedictions for the *soldier*, for his arms, and for his standards. The explanation of THIS 'MYSTERY' is not difficult. It is the meaning of this solemnity, at once *military* and *religious!*"

Here, then, the fact stands out distinct, that the " mother of harlots and abominations of the earth," with her clergy, could not save themselves from the "*judgment*" that had commenced, as already stated, in 1789, and that they took refuge in Napoleon's power as president of the French Assembly, to rescue them from the "severe sufferings" of this thrice-repeated draught from the cup of Jehovah's wrath! The "woman and the beast of scarlet color united!" the *religious* and *military* character of which, the Archbishop of Paris unconsciously denominates a "MYSTERY:" aye, and such a mystery as makes any church, be it papal or protestant, a "harlot!"

So also—as the sequel has shown—the papal "harlot"-rider of this "scarlet-colored beast," knew but little of those *ulterior* purposes which lay concealed beneath the external "material aid" vouchsafed her at his hand. She saw not that his ambition for personal aggrandizement was the all-inspiring *motive* which induced his intervention in her behalf; and that, having used her to that end, he would despoil her of the last remaining shred of her *secular* power.

But, at the period of which we now speak, the need-be for a *reciprocity* of kindly offices, was about equally balanced. Napoleon had fulfilled his part of the contract toward the Pope and holy church. It now remained for the latter to fulfil theirs. It was a time of CRISIS in Napoleon's career of "destiny!" On the one hand, the anti-papal or republican revolutions of 1830 and 1848 were composed of the middling classes, called *bourgeois*, who, associating religion and the priests with the aristocracy, had attempted to throw off the papal yoke as antagonistic to liberty. On the other hand were the socialists, who denounced all religion as a farce, property a robbery, and marriage an infamous institution, the modern archetypes of the spiritualists of our day. Then there was a third class, the priests and the aristocracy, who, had they possessed the power, stood ready to restore the Bourbon dynasty.

Now, amid this whirlpool of national commotion,

while the priests and the aristocracy were for the restoration of the imperial power, the infidel extravagances of the socialists alarmed and staggered the bourgeois. It was this latter circumstance, therefore, that formed the *turning-point* at which Louis Napoleon could seize the reins of the empire. What does he do? Just this. He *conciliates* the priests, by restoring the Pope. This secures their coöperation, and through them, he gains the assent of the aristocracy, who, with the bourgeois, preferred a NAPOLEONIC DYNASTY to the anarchy of socialism. Accordingly, when the time arrived, the clergy of France went in a body for Louis Napoleon as EMPEROR OF FRANCE! They exhorted the faithful to vote for him, and though the election took place on the Sabbath, they led the people to the polls, bearing the banner of the cross before them!

Thus, then, through these combined agencies, the *revived seventh* Napoleonic head of the Franco-Roman empire "*is.*" It has been "fished up from the casket of the abyss to the astonishment of the world," and is seen as the "scarlet-colored beast" with "two horns like a lamb, and speaking as a dragon"—Müller's "tame eagle" joined with the "Corsican wolf"—and the "great harlot," papal Rome, "sitting upon his back!"

So far, therefore, we submit, the fulfilment of this prophecy, as it respects the *seventh slain* and *revived* headship of the Franco-Roman empire, is perfect in all its parts.

There is, however, another fact in this connection, in close alliance with the *future* destiny of this wonderful man, Louis Napoleon III., which calls for special remark, inasmuch as it holds an intimate relation to the prophetico-historical developments of his *complex career* as the revived seventh and eighth headships. The fact here alluded to has reference to one important feature of his *political* character, as developed in his alliance with Italian affairs, as that upon which is dependent his *transfer* from his present *seventh* to his EIGHTH headship. In bringing out this fact, we ask:

What evidence have we that the Italians, in ridding themselves thus far of the *temporal* power of the popedom, have placed themselves under the monarchy of Victor Emanuel from choice! So far from it, the fact in regard to them is, that throughout the entire peninsula they are at heart REPUBLICAN. There is, in Italy, a secret society called the *Carboari*, which has for its object the overthrow of despotism in Europe. This organization is one of great power. A European correspondent of one of the New York journals, in referring to it in 1858, says:

"Immediately after the French Revolution of 1830, there were a series of outbreaks throughout the Roman territory. They were the work of the Carbonari," etc. To this he adds, "This society never forgives a renegade member." He also states that the present Pope (Pius IX.) and the late King Charles Albert, are active members of it.

And so, while, in the establishment of a constitutional monarchy in Piedmont, Victor Emanuel has achieved what his royal father failed to accomplish, and which success, as we shall see, was the work of the *Carbonari;* Pius IX., who disappointed their hopes in completing the reforms with which he commenced his pontificate, is by them *expelled from Rome!*

But this same writer informs us, that,

"In the Roman legation, the present emperor [of France, Louis Napoleon III.] and his brother, who died during the insurrection, were actively engaged," and that "they were both sworn members of the Carbonari."

How, then, it may be asked, could Louis Napoleon *reconcile* the obligations growing out of his relationship to this society of republicans, with his restoration of the Pope to Rome? He could not: and for this act of *perfidy* on his part, Louis Napoleon was tried by the chiefs of the society, was formally condemned to death, and received notice of the doom to which he was consigned. This is the *real secret* of all those murderous attempts of Italians on the Emperor's life. The assassin Orsini, who was beheaded in France in 1858, was only seeking to carry out the decree of the chiefs of the Carbonari, of which he was one. Thousands of others were prepared to fall as martyrs in the same cause. And yet, LOUIS NAPOLEON LIVES!

Now, how is this to be accounted for? The *primary cause*, we reply, was, that his fall would have defeated a most important feature in the unfulfilled prophetic destiny which had been marked out for him. Hence, under the overruling providence of the Most High, the *secondary* cause was, that the Carbonari, having resolved to rid themselves of the papal yoke, compounded the matter with the Emperor, by absolving him from the death-penalty, *on the condition that he would give liberty to Italy!* The compromise was a fearful one. Napoleon must *fight* for Italian liberty, or he must *die!* Of the two alternatives, he chose the former. The result is before us. If, at this time (August, 1865), we except Rome and Venice, ALL ITALY IS FREE. Aye, and by the concession of Europe and the world, the possession of that freedom by Italy, either directly or indirectly, is the fruit of the Imperial pledge to the Carbonari.

Nor are we to infer from the *existing union* of this revived seventh Franco-Roman head with the harlot-rider that bestrides his back, or any of the *acts* of either as growing out of that anomalous relation, that Napoleon III. has any *love* to the papal power, spiritual or temporal, only so far as it may be made to subserve his ambitious designs in the ultimate establishment of A LATIN UNIVERSAL DYNASTY. For, in following out his "Napoleonic Idea" as "the GREAT PACIFICATOR," one would suppose that he had, by his restoration of the Pope to Rome, overlooked his membership with the Italian Carbonari, or that he had forgotten the peril to which he would expose himself by that act; yet it is clear that he *did not* forget that he was "THE MAN OF DESTINY." In a word, we mean to say, that, despite the continual oscillations which have marked the *policy* of this strange man, in mind and in heart he is a REPUBLICAN. It is upon this political theory that he relies to bear him onward to the highest pinnacle of his gigantic aspirations. This conviction is fastening itself upon the minds of thinking men on both sides of the Atlantic more and more every day. We are not surprised, therefore, to find the following statement from a "correspondent" of the *N. Y. Tribune*, May 6, 1859. He says of Napoleon III.:

"His popularity in Italy and France is unbounded, in spite of the opposition of the Orleanist and Legitimist, and the moneyed world. . . The *Republicans* admit, that the Emperor is now, for once, just and generous. Should he remain true to his proclamation," *i. e.*, in regard to his liberation of Italy from the Austrian yoke—"it will be a great step toward the reconciliation of liberal France. Nobody can guess his future plans, but he tries to surround himself with men of *liberal* principles, and arouses hopes of a better future."

Since 1859, whatever may be said of his draconic utterances, or his acts as the "Corsican wolf," yet his character as the "GREAT PACIFICATOR"—the "beast with two horns like a lamb,"—has decidedly predominated. This may be gathered from his advice to the Bourbon king, Francis Joseph II., to flee from Gaeta; his removal of the French naval fleet from that port; the proposal of his government, with that of others, that Austria should cede Venice to Victor Emanuel, for a consideration; and the recent grant of enlarged liberty to the French press, etc., etc.

Again. We have spoken of the *prestige* of Napoleon III. Take the following incident in illustration. Soon after his humiliation of Austria, on the battle-field of Italy, he was actually rendered an object of *idolatrous homage.* Yes, it is a fact, that, in view of the valor of his arms, and his incomparable statesmanship as displayed in carrying out the treaty of peace at Villafranca, the Italians of Florence, infatuated by the glory which had signalized his career, put in circulation the following *parody* on the apostle's creed:

"*Suffered* under the Orleans, reviled, arrested, imprisoned. *Descended* from the fortress of Ham, thence resuscitated from civil death.

"*Rose* to the presidency of the French Republic; *sits* upon the throne of NAPOLEON THE GREAT.

"From thence has come to judge the *living* Italians and the *dead* Austrians.

"*I believe* in the constitutional reign of Victor Emanuel, in the Holy Italian League, in the return of all emigrants, and in the life of brotherhood eternal."

More than this. From the pulpit of the church of Notre Dame in Paris, this very man has been already proclaimed *a greater than Jesus Christ!* And so far from his having rebuked the fanatical zeal of his admirers, and spurned such "blasphemy," Napoleon listened to the above paraphrase on the apostle's creed when addressed to him with the greatest pleasure, and actually rewarded his Parisian pulpit eulogist with the presentation of a valuable gold snuff-box!

What, then, may we not expect of him ere *the close* of his career? We shall see.

We now observe that, impelled onward under the influence of this unbridled ambition and lust of power, it is undeniable that this Napoleonic "star of destiny" is *now* in the ascendant. This, we submit, is evident from the results which have followed, since his *union with his harlot rider*. It will be interesting to take a bird's-eye glance at the *comprehensiveness* of this grand programme of his military and naval schemes.

" We see ONE MAN, all-powerful and all-accomplished, completing the circumvallation of the globe. While he is perfecting his armaments, he is equally perfecting his lines. Beginning at Rome and Paris—the centres of empire—he is drawing a cordon round the world. France, Savoy, the Alps, Rome, Italy, Corsica, Sicily, Tunis, Greece, Ionia, Syria, Egypt. He crosses the Isthmus and enters the Red Sea. Abyssinia, Madagascar, Bourbon, Cochin, Cambodia, China,[1] follow next. He then plunges into the depths of the Southern ocean, and grasps New Caledonia and Tahiti. He crosses right through the Southern ocean, and ascends in latitude to Guiana, the French West Indies, Mexico, etc. He then crosses the Atlantic, and arrives at home, after the completion of a circle of twenty-five thousand miles. He then throws out his connecting lines, and draws in Spain and Morocco on the south; Denmark, Sweden, and Holland

---

[1] The French government has always been desirous of extending its power in the East. Hence the Cochin-China expedition. They are not, however, idle in China itself, where one province, that of Honan, containing a population of *fourteen millions*, is said to be anxious to place itself under *French* "protection."

on the north. He traverses the zones of the earth, from the south temperate zone to the arctic circle. Along this vast circumference, every spot that we have named is subject to his influence—some by *strict alliance*, some by *fear*, some as *provinces* of his empire, and ALL BY INTEREST. He calls to his aid the master passions of the human breast, ambition and revenge; and holds to each its object until his own objects have been gained. In this immense circle each point is so arranged as to support the other. He disposes his alliances with military precision, and by strategic rules. Every position he has seized upon commands some vital point. Savoy commands Italy; Egypt commands the highway to the East; his American alliances command the British possessions; Spain commands the Straits; Denmark the Baltic; New Caledonia is the outwork against Australia. Observe the military skill of these arrangements. There is nothing isolated, nothing left unsupported. And at each of these points he has a military or naval force, either his own or his allies', ready at a signal to coöperate with the next. Are these things merely accidental? Are they a childish display of power? They are parts of one vast scheme, the object of which is UNIVERSAL EMPIRE! . . And this grand and comprehensive scheme is so arranged, that no one of his allies shall be able to overshadow him, nor will any one at any single point be stronger than himself. He has their COÖPERATION, while he precludes their COMBINATION. The aggregate of his allies is greater than that of France; yet France is stronger than any one of them at any determined point; so that he carries out with nations the military principles of the first Napoleon when dealing with armies."[1]

---

[1] Napoleon III. and his schemes, by Rev. R. Purdon, of England.

And we now add, that this stupendous scheme of universal empire is but the exponent of his great "*Napoleonic Idea*" as "the Pacificator of nations." And, taken in connection with the fact of his *republican* character and policy as a member of the Italian Carbonari, when he shall have accomplished his purposes as growing out of his present alliances with the papacy and other powers; the way will be prepared for the display of those prophetico-historic events, preparatory to his *transfer* from the revived secular seventh, to that of his politico-religious EIGHTH HEADSHIP.

And finally, how far he is *proximately* removed from that consummation of the prophecy respecting him, may be inferred from the following editorial in the "*New York Tribune*" of August 9, 1865:

"The time has passed when Paris exercised the 'power to lead the will of a mighty nation, or to crown or discrown monarchs.' Those who read the lessons of *the recent elections* properly, will see in the results the rebellion of the *reactionary* party in France against centralization of Paris and Parisian influence. We have never particularly fancied the French emperor. . . We may call him a step from *Bourbonism* to *Republicanism*. . . If the European powers had permitted the First Napoleon to work his way, France would have been in a proper condition for freedom long ago. *That work the present Napoleon is doing.* The centralization of power under the Bourbons made Paris the embodiment of French political thought. . . We never had much confidence in Paris. Her *Republicanism* is like the foam of her own champagne—pleasant, creamy, effervescing, but ephemeral and transitory. . . No great city has the right to speak a nation's thought, nor to aggrandize the political power of the people. . . If New York had been to America what Paris is to France, this republic would have pronounced for Davis as President in 1861, and our liberties would have ended as rapidly as the liberties of France in the memorable days of December.

The policy of Napoleon has been *to restrain Paris and rest his power on the people*. He appeals to the pride of the people as the *heir of a great name*, and he protects and fosters their interests. . . Before we can have true liberty in France, the people must escape from the thraldom of Paris. *Their only escape is in Napoleon,* and so long as he remains on his good behavior, they trust him and vote for him and keep his throne intact. So long as his people stand by and sustain him, he can afford to leave Paris to his gendarmes and secret policemen, his architects and painters. This course of treatment will finally bring good results. Napoleon, in spite of himself, is making the people of France more and more *self-dependent* and prepared for liberty. Every blow at the political pretensions of Paris strengthens Lyons, Marseilles, and Toulon. When the time comes for the next rising in behalf of liberty, it will not be confined to the Boulevards and Faubourgs. FRANCE HAS SHOWN THAT SHE HAS MEN CAPABLE OF OVERTHROWING EMPIRES AND CHANGING DYNASTIES. She has never yet shown the power of self-government. We live in the hope that that power is coming to her, and the recent election shows that our hope is being *realized.*"

Aye, Mr. Editor, and that *coming power* is nearer realization than their or your philosophy dreams of. And, *when* it comes, you will better understand the so-called "*good results*" of the NAPOLEONIC RULE!

But of this in our next chapter.

CHAPTER VI.

LOUIS NAPOLEON III. CONTINUED—THE EIGHTH APOCALYPTIC SYMBOLIC HEAD OF THE UNIVERSAL LATIN EMPIRE, OR THE LAST ANTICHRIST.

SECTION I.

THE PROPHETICO-HISTORIC RISE, CAREER, AND FINAL DOOM OF THIS GREAT APOCALYPTIC ANTICHRISTIAN POWER.

We now proceed to treat of the EIGHTH APOCALYPTIC HEAD. The prophet says (Rev. xvii. 8–10):

"And the beast that *was*, and *is not*, and *yet is*, even he is the EIGHTH, and is *of* the seven, and goeth into perdition."

Fearfully portentous and comprehensive words! "Why?" perhaps you will say, "as they relate to the *future*, what can we know of their significancy?" The answer is, "Nothing, IF the Apocalypse, like the visions of Daniel, were commanded when written to be '*closed up and sealed*.'"[1] But, so far from this, even the sealing of the visions of that book was not designed to be perpetual. It was only to be "closed up *till the time of the end*."[2] And though the length of that period was not chrono-

---

[1] Dan. xii. 8, 9.   [2] Ib. v. 9.

logically designated by "the Father, who hath put the times or seasons in his own power;"[1] yet we know that the Danielic "closed" book was *opened* at the penning of the Apocalypse by St. John on the isle of Patmos in A. D. 96. Its very name imports the *uncovering* or laying open of things previously hidden. And so in chapter v. 1–7, we read that the apostle " saw in the right hand of Him that sat upon the throne *a book*, written within and on the back side, *sealed with seven seals*. And he wept much, because no man in heaven or earth or under the earth was able to open the book or to look thereon." But "one of the elders said unto him, Weep not: behold, in the midst of the throne, etc., stood a Lamb as it had been slain," even "THE LION OF THE TRIBE OF JUDAH, THE ROOT OF DAVID: and He came, and took the book out of the right hand of Him who sat upon the throne, and *prevailed* to open the book, and to *loose* the seven seals thereof!"

If to this it be objected, that the "book" here spoken of *is not* the book of Daniel, inasmuch as that book is not said to have been "sealed with seven seals," we reply, that the number "seven," in Scripture, is generally used to denote perfection, and in this place denotes the completeness with which the *prior* secret things in that "book" *are now laid open*. Hence, as we have said— and this is conceded by all expositors—that the symbolic imagery of the Apocalypse, though more full, and set forth in hierophantic drapery differing in form from that of Daniel, is nevertheless *synchronic with* and *expository of*, the things contained in that book. Accordingly it is declared to be "The revelation of Jesus Christ, which God gave unto Him, to show unto His servants things

---

[1] Acts i. 6, 7.

which must shortly come to pass; and HE sent and *signified* it by His angel unto His servant John."¹ And hence the benediction—"Blessed is he that readeth, and they that hear the words of this prophecy, and keep those things which are written therein: for the time is at hand."²

We must therefore insist, that all who, under whatever pretext, talk of the obscurity and unintelligibleness of this book in justification of their neglect to *study* its contents, virtually ignore it as a part of God's inspired word, even that "more sure word of prophecy" to which St. Peter declares that "we all do well *to take heed*, as unto a light which shineth in a dark place."³ It is to "*take away from* the words of the book of this prophecy," the which, "if any man" do, that tremendous penalty will surely follow: "God shall take away *his part* out of the book of life, and out of the holy city, and from the things which are written in this book."⁴ And so of those who, to support a favorite theory, by their false glosses or interpretations "*shall add unto* these things, God shall add unto him *the plagues* that are written in this book."⁵

But to return to the subject in hand. We have said that "prophecy is history anticipated." Also, that "history is prophecy verified." And, you are ready to concede the exposition and application of prophecy to any event or series of events as true, when their *fulfilment* can be shown to have been demonstrated by authentic history; while, in regard to unfulfilled prophecy, you demur. It is presumption, you think, to venture on this ground. But we deferentially ask: If a prophecy of a

---

¹ Rev. i. 1.   ² *Ibid.* v. 3.   ³ 2 Pet. i. 19.
⁴ Rev. xxii. 19.   ⁵ *Ibid.* v. 18.

certain event or person or country cannot be understood *before* it is fulfilled, how are we to know *when*, in *whom*, or *where* it is fulfilled? To defer, therefore, its interpretation until it is historically verified, by leaving those who are interested in it in ignorance of its meaning and intent, it passes by unheeded, because unrecognized by them. Hence the lamentation of Jesus over the Jewish nation, consequent of their having *overlooked* all those prophecies of the Old Testament which pointed Him out to them as their Messiah:—"If thou hadst known, even thou, in this thy day, the things which belong unto thy peace: but now they are hid from thine eyes!"[1] That judicial blindness of mind followed, which resulted in their rejection and crucifixion of the Son of God! And so also our Lord's reproof of His own disciples, for their *neglect to* "*take heed*" to those prophecies which announced his resurrection and future kingdom, etc. "Oh fools, and slow of heart to believe all that the prophets have spoken concerning me."[2] No, "history is prophecy verified," only in the sense that it is a *record* of it. And yet we hear it constantly reiterated from the pulpit, that "prophecy can only be understood when it is *fulfilled*." Than which, no greater and more fatally ruinous Satanic delusion was ever palmed upon the church of God!

Accept this, then, as our apology for entering upon an exposition of the *unfulfilled* prophecy now before us. Let me assure you, that we of this day, as including all the nations of the earth, the church of God, and as individuals, have an interest in it. We may fail to convince you of this. With God alone "is the residue of the spirit." The angel who "talked" with St. John on the subject relating to this EIGHTH HEAD, declared, "*here is*

---

[1] Luke xix. 42.   [2] *Ibid.* xxiv. 25.

the mind which hath wisdom:" *i. e.*, to understand it. That wisdom cometh only from above. In regard to ourself, all we ask is, " hear, before you strike."

To proceed. We claim to have demonstrated, that Napoleon I. was the *last* of the seven heads of the Roman beast, as emperor of the Franco-Roman empire, which head, having been slain by the sword of military violence after " continuing a short space," *reappeared* in the person of his nephew, Louis Napoleon III., as the same seventh head *revived.* But the angel speaks of an eighth head,—not, mark, of the Roman beast, for he has only *seven*—but as being " of *the seven,*" in the sense of origin or source, as in the Greek, ἐκ τῶν ἑπτά ἐστι, *i. e., out of* or *from*, the seven.

The meaning, therefore, can only be, that the revived seventh and eighth headships, centre in and belong to *the same person.* In no sense can the eighth head (as Mr. Faber and others affirm), be said to be " *one* of the seven." By no arithmetical process can you make seven count eight. Nor is the prophecy to be understood to teach that the *functions* of the revived seventh and eighth headships are *so united into one,* as that they are exercised *simultaneously.*

We shall now proceed to show, agreeably to the tenor of the prophecies respecting this eighth head when taken as a whole, that the circumstance of this revived seventh head being connected with the *same person* who is accounted an eighth, arises from the fact of the *mutation* which it is destined to undergo. In analogy to the mutations of the beast with seven heads and ten horns, which first appears with seven crowns upon its *heads ;* then with the crowns transferred to its *ten horns,* while upon its heads is inscribed the name of blasphemy; and then *without crowns,* as the scarlet-colored beast with its body full of names of blasphemy, etc;—which symbols denoted the successive changes of the *same beast* from its Pagan, through the various stages of its Papal antichristian forms, while each were entirely separate and distinct from the other:—so here. It is the revived seventh head relinquishing its *merely secular* power, for that of an *absolute politico-religious* headship.

It follows, therefore,—unless what we have said of Louis Napoleon III. as the revived seventh head of the Franco-Roman empire can be disproved—that when he shall have fully run his course and accomplished his "destiny" as the *secular* sovereign of that empire, he will appear upon the prophetical platform as

AN EIGHTH HEAD, OR THE LEADER OF THE LAST GREAT DEMOCRATIC POLITICO-RELIGIOUS CONFEDERACY OF THE ANTICHRISTIAN NATIONS, AGAINST THE ABRAHAMIC JEWISH RACE AND THE GENTILE CHRISTIAN CHURCH.

In other words, we mean to say, that under this *new* and *distinct* form of the symbolic eighth headship, Napoleon III. is designated in this prophecy as none other than St. Paul's "MAN OF SIN AND SON OF PERDITION"— for the "angel" declares of this "eighth" head, that he "*goeth into perdition*"—even he "who opposeth and exalteth himself above all that is called God, or that is worshipped; so that he as God, sitteth in the temple of God, showing himself that he is God. . . Even him, whose coming is after the working of Satan with all power and signs and lying wonders, and with all deceivableness of unrighteousness in them that perish; because they received not the love of the truth, that they might be saved. And for this cause," adds the apostle, "God shall send them strong delusion, that they should believe a lie; that they all might be damned who believe not the truth, but have pleasure in unrighteousness."[1] **In a** word, the Holy Spirit, in this prophecy and that of the apoca**lypse,** points us to him, in, through, and by whom, as the "eighth" head, "**the** dragon, **which** is the Devil and Satan," will openly and visibly manifest himself as THE LAST ANTICHRIST, or the DEVIL INCARNATED—alias HUMANITY DEIFIED!

Nor should we overlook in this connection those portentous words of the Lord Jesus:—*I* am come *in my Father's name,* and ye RECEIVE ME NOT: if *another* **shall** come *in his own name, him ye will receive.*"[2] It will be well here to call to mind the Napoleonic *prestige* of the "nephew," as derived from that of the "uncle;" and also the full-length portrait already given of his incomparably peculiar intellectual and moral characteristics;[3] than which, no attributes can be conceived as centring in any *one man,* better fitted to realize all that is implied in Christ's prophecy as above, concerning "him who is **to come in his own name.**"

One other prophecy we must here advert to, **before** passing on. It relates to the *final doom* of this Antichrist and his democratico-infidel confederacy, and THE AGENT by whom it will be effected. When "that wicked shall be revealed," says St. Paul, "THE LORD shall consume him by the spirit of His mouth, and destroy him by the brightness of His (παρουσια, *i. e., personal*) coming.[4]" We here remark by the way, that the word παρουσια, **wherever** used in the New Testament, and to whomsoever applied, always means a *personal,* and not a figura-

[1] 2 Thess. ii. 3, 4, and verses 9-12.
[2] John v. 43.
[3] See pages 83-86.
[4] 2 Thess. ii. 8.

tive coming. The παρουσια or coming of St. Paul's "man of sin and son of perdition" or the last Antichrist, will be a *personal* coming. And the same word, παρουσια, being applied to the "coming" of the Lord Jesus Christ, that coming also must be *personal*.

If, then, these prophetico-historic statements concerning this wonderful man, Louis Napoleon III., can be sustained by the legitimate laws of interpretation, they will not only furnish us with renewed cause of praise and adoration for the disclosures of that infinite wisdom which, "knowing the end from the beginning," hath prophetically designated *the very person* with whom is to close the work of persecution of the church and people of God, Jewish and Christian, *commenced* by his ancestral prototype, the Babylonish head of gold, more than 2,500 years ago, and which has been *continued* by the "little horn" of Papacy and its Roman ally; but will prepare all those of them who shall be exposed to it, to meet, undaunted, that season of unparalleled tribulation and suffering which, as we shall see in the proper place, will mark his career as the EIGHTH HEAD.

We are aware how the mind instinctively recoils at the thought, that *the man should now be living*, in whom all that St. Paul and others of the prophets have spoken of shall be verified as the last incarnated Antichrist. Hence the denial, by some writers, of a *future personal Antichrist*. This denial is made to rest upon the alleged *identity*, first, of the "little horn" of Daniel's fourth beast, chap. vii. 8, with, second, the "little horn" which sprang out of one of the four notable horns of Daniel's he-goat, or "the king of fierce countenance," chap. viii. 8–19; and both of these, third, with "the king who did according to his will," as described in chap. xi. 31, and verses 36–45: which symbols being one and all thus indiscriminately merged into the *same* power, and that power declared to be the PAPACY, they have interpreted the hierophantic imagery employed by the Holy Spirit to portray their *separate* characters and exploits, as denoting the same things with those of the eighth apocalyptic head.

Now, it is by thus confounding things which differ, that the subjects of God's prophetic word have been involved in the greatest confusion and perplexity, and has caused many a sincere inquirer after truth to turn from its pursuit in disgust. It requires but a cursory glance at the passages referred to, however, in order to see that they *differ* in their origin, in the places and times of their appearance, in their exploits, and in their final doom. The "little horn" of chap. vii. comes up among the "ten horns" of Daniel's nondescript beast, and hence is of *Roman* origin. Its characteristics, having eyes as the eyes of a man, and a mouth speaking great things against the Most High, denote the Papacy and the Popedom of Rome, which came to maturity in A. D. 533. And it is finally destroyed by its own vassals, the ten horns of the Roman beast. The "little horn" of chap. viii., the "king of fierce countenance," on the other hand, is of *Arabian* origin, having sprung from that province as one of the four divisions into which Alexander's Greek empire was divided, and does not make his appearance upon the stage until about eighty years *after* that of the little Roman horn. His characteristics clearly mark him out as the SARACENIC or TURCO-MOHAMMEDAN power. And it finally falls after a mysterious manner, being "broken without hand;" or, as the Apocalypse represents it, chap. xvi. 12, as the "*drying up*" of the mystical Euphrates." And as to the last, "the king who does according to his will," he is neither Roman nor Arabian.

Having subjugated all the Latin nations to his despotic sway, he is ALL HEAD. His characteristic is, that "he shall exalt himself, and magnify himself above every god, and shall speak marvellous things against the God of gods," etc. This neither the Pope nor Mohammed have ever done. And when this "wilful king" is destroyed, it will be by the *personal* agency of the Lord Jesus Christ. Besides, as to the *respective fields* of their exploits. That of the "little horn" of chap. vii. was limited to the *western Roman* empire, where he was to persecute "the saints of the Most High who were to be given into his hands." That of the "little horn" of chap. viii. was raised up as a scourge for the punishment of the apostate *Eastern* or *Greek* branch of the empire. While that of the "wilful king," alias, the last Antichrist, will be extended over *all countries* throughout Christendom. Having, therefore, thus briefly exposed the fallacy of the above theory, which carries with it the proof that the coming of the last Antichrist is *still future*, we shall proceed to lay open what "the mind of the spirit" has revealed concerning this tremendous power. We shall begin with,

THE PROPHETICO-HISTORIC RISE, CAREER, AND DOOM OF THE APOCALYPTIC EIGHTH HEAD, OR THE LAST ANTICHRIST.

I. THE CHRONOLOGICAL PERIOD ASSIGNED FOR HIS APPEARANCE.

We must here premise, that the career of the "little horn" of the Papacy, as a spiritual and ecclesiastico-secular power, and the Roman body politic, as a civil power, were to run *a parallel course,* from the time of the appearance of the former upon the prophetical stage. Accordingly, **the** period allotted to the action of each *was the same.* The saints were to be given into the hands of the "little horn" of the Papacy, "*until a time, times, and the dividing of time,*"[1] which, as a prophetical number, when deciphered, amounts to 1,260 years of lunar time; while "power was to be given unto the seven-headed and ten-horned beast" as inclusive of his several mutations, of "*forty and two months,*"[2] each month of 30 days, making 1,260 days, "each day" reckoned "for a year."[3] To this period, however, there is an addition of *two shorter dates.* It is to be explained thus: Although the "*dominion,*" that is, the ecclesiastico-secular power of the "little horn" was to "be taken away," yet the "*lives*" of the ten horns or kings were to be "prolonged for a *season* and a *time.*"[4] Hence, to the 1,260 years' career of the Papacy is added 30 years, thus extending it first to 1,290; and to the 1,290 years is added 45, thus extending it to 1,335 years; which last number spans the *whole period* allotted to them.

But the point is, to determine *the time* of the appearance of the "little horn" upon the stage of action. Chronologists differ in regard to it, the variations lying between A. D. 533 and 606. We adopt the former date, viz. 533, as the *actual* commencement of the "little horn's" career, that being the year when, by the edict of the Emperor Justinian as a successor of the Roman Augustus in the line of the *sixth* head or polity, John II., the then patriarch of Rome, was constituted SUPREME PONTIFF or vicar of Jesus Christ on earth throughout Christendom.

Inasmuch, however, as the 1,260 years, being a *cardi-*

---

[1] Dan. vii. 25. [2] Rev. xiii. 5. [3] Ezek. iv. 6.
[4] Dan. vii. 12.

nal prophetic number, is that on which hinges the time fixed for the " coming " of the last Antichrist, or eighth head, we deem it indispensable that we settle the question of the *exact year* when it commenced. We submit the following authentic historical data, as demonstrative that that year was A. D. 533.

The principal source of information on this subject, is derived from the annals of Baronius, the chief Romish ecclesiastical historian. " JUSTINIAN being about to commence the Vandal war, an enterprise of great difficulty, was anxious previously to settle the *religious disputes* of his capital," occasioned by the increasing prevalence of the Nestorian heresy, to which the emperor was particularly hostile. Hence, " whether through anxiety to purchase the suffrage of the Roman bishop, the patriarch of the west, whose opinion influenced a large portion of Christendom; or to give irresistible weight to the verdict which was to be pronounced in his own favor, he decided the *precedency* which had been contested by the bishops of Constantinople from the foundation of the city; and, in the fullest and most unequivocal form, declared the Bishop of Rome THE CHIEF of the whole ecclesiastical body of the empire. His letter was couched in these terms:

" Justinian, pious, fortunate, renowned, triumphant, emperor, consul, etc., to John, the most holy Archbishop of our city of Rome, and Patriarch.

" Rendering honor to the apostolic chair, and to your Holiness, as has been always and is our wish, and honoring your Blessedness as a father; we have hastened to bring to the knowledge of your Holiness all matters relating to the churches. . . *Therefore, we have made no delay in subjecting and uniting to your Holiness all the priests of the whole East.*

" For this reason we have thought fit to bring to your notice the present matters of disturbance, etc. . . For we cannot suffer that anything which relates to the state of the church, however manifest and unquestionable, should be moved, without the knowledge of your Holiness, who are THE HEAD OF ALL THE HOLY CHURCHES: for in all things, as we have already declared, we are anxious to *increase the honor and authority of your apostolic chair,*" etc.

" To this letter the Bishop of Rome returned an answer, ' giving the papal sanction to the judgment already pronounced by the emperor on the heresy.'" The letter of the emperor also 'further mentions, that the archbishop [of Constantinople] also had written to the Pope, '*he being desirous in all things to follow the apostolic authority of his Blessedness.*'

In the Pope's letter, " He observes that, among the virtues of Justinian, ' one shines as a star, his reverence for the apostolic chair, *to which he had subjected and united all the churches*, it being truly the head of all ; as was testified by the rules of the fathers, the laws of princes, and the declarations of the emperor's piety.' " Besides—

"The authenticity of the *title* [of the Pope of Rome as universal bishop], receives unanswerable proof from the edicts in the ' Novellæ ' of the Justinian code.

" The preamble of the 9th states that ' as *the elder Rome* was the founder of the laws, so was it not to be questioned that *in her* was the supremacy of the pontificate.'

" The 131st, on the ecclesiastical titles and privileges, chap. 2d, states : ' We therefore decree, that the most holy Pope of the *elder Rome is the first* of all the holy priesthood ; and that the blessed Archbishop of Constantinople, *the new Rome*, shall hold the *second rank after* the holy apostolic chair of the elder Rome.' "

But now, as to *the dates* of these transactions.

" The emperor's letter must have been sent *before* the 25th of March, 533. For, in his letter of that date to Epiphanius, he speaks of its having been already despatched, and repeats his decision, that ' all affairs touching the church shall be referred to the Pope, *head of all bishops,* and the true and effective corrector of heresies.'

" In the same month of the following year, 534, the Pope returned an answer repeating the language of the emperor, applauding his homage to the see, and adopting the title of the imperial mandate."

This edict of Justinian in A. D. 533 is further confirmed by the following facts: Belisarius, the general of Justinian, sailed with the fleet and armies from Constantinople in the summer of A. D. 533; landed in Africa in September, and reduced Carthage on the 15th of that month; completed the conquest of Africa in the course of the following autumn and summer, and returned to Constantinople in the autumn of the year 534.[1] But it was during the years 533 and 534, that the memorable correspondence between Justinian and Pope John of Rome was conducted, the conquest of Africa by Belisarius having paved the way for it, it having been conducted by those who connected the establishment of orthodoxy with that of the Pope of Rome as *the centre of unity, the determiner of controversy, and the head of all the churches.* In proof of this, according to the tables of Contius, Lugdini, 1618, the letters which passed between Justinian and the Pope were dated partly in the third and partly in the fourth consulship of the emperor; in which last, Paulinus was his colleague, and which correspond respectively to the years 533 and 534 of the Christian era. On this subject Gibbon says, "One awful hour reversed the fortunes of the contending parties;" for, when "intelligence of the success of Belisarius in Africa reached the emperor, December 16, 533, impatient to abolish the temporal and spiritual tyranny of the Vandals, he proceeded without delay to the *full establishment of the Catholic church.*" "The temple was now resigned to the Catholics, who loudly proclaimed the creed of Athanasius and Justinian." The new power, styled the "eternal oracles," comprehending both the "*civil* and *ecclesiastical* constitution of the Roman empire," "were proclaimed on solemn festivals at the doors of the churches."

---

[1] Gibbon's Decline and Fall. Vol. iii. chap. xii. pp. 167-193.

Thus, "the supremacy of the Pope of Rome had by those mandates and edicts received the fullest sanction that could be given by the authority of the master of the Roman world. But the yoke sat uneasily on the Bishop of Constantinople; and on the death of Justinian, the supremacy was utterly denied. . . Toward the close of the sixth century, John of Constantinople, surnamed for his pious austerities the Faster, summoned a council, and resumed the ancient title of the see, 'Universal Bishop.' The Roman bishop, Gregory the Great, indignant at the usurpation," . . . "furiously denounced John, calling him an 'usurper, aiming at supremacy over the whole church,' and declaring, with unconscious truth, that whoever claimed such a supremacy, was Antichrist.

"The accession of Phocas at length decided the question. He had ascended the throne of the East by the murder of the Emperor Mauritius. The insecurity of his title rendered him anxious to obtain the sanction of the *Patriarch of the West*. The conditions were easily settled. The usurper received the benediction of the *Bishop of Rome*; and the Bishop in A. D. 606, vindicated his title from his rival, the Patriarch of Constantinople, that had been almost a century before conferred on the Papal tiara by Justinian. He was thenceforth 'head of all the churches' without a competitor,—'Universal Bishop' of Christendom. That Phocas suppressed the claim of the Bishop of Constantinople is beyond a doubt. But the highest authorities among the civilians and annalists of Rome spurn the idea that the profligate usurper Phocas was the founder of the supremacy of Rome; they ascend to *Justinian* as the only legitimate source, and rightly date the title from the memorable year A. D. 533."

Well, having settled this important point, by adding to A. D. 533 the 1,260 years, it brings us down to A. D. 1793, when, according to the word of the Lord, that "judgment was to sit, which should take away the *dominion*," or the secular power, of the "little horn," to "consume and to destroy it *unto the end*."[1] And so, the work commenced, as we have shown, with the French Revolution in A. D. 1793.

---

[1] Dan. vii. 26.

It was not, however, to fall instantaneously, but by a succession of blows at the hand of retributive justice. "Its *life*," or spiritual power, "was to be prolonged for a season and a time." It requires no argument to prove, that for the thirty years from 1793 (the excess of the 1,290 over the 1,260 years), the Papacy as a spiritual power, inclusive of a partial restoration of its secular prerogatives (consequent of the return of Pius VII. in A. D. 1814 from his Napoleonic exile in Savonia in Lombardy to Fontainebleau in France, and thence back to Rome), continued to flourish with greater or lesser vigor down to A. D. 1823. Also, that from thence, for the next 42 out of the remaining 45 years, down to A. D. 1868 (the excess of the 1,335 over the 1,290 years), the "*lives*" of the same vassal ten horns or kings of the ecclesiastico-secular power of the Papacy assumed renewed vigor; until, having become intolerant throughout the Italian dominions, the predicted "judgment" of Almighty God had begun *again* to take effect, so that the "little horn" has been stript of the last lingering shreds of its political or temporal power, Rome and Venice only remaining to be freed.

Still, the "*lives*" of the "ten horns" or "kings" survive. The famous "ENCYCLICAL LETTER of Pope Pius IX."[1] has galvanized its *spiritual* power into renewed energy. Yes. ROMANISM IS DESTINED TO BECOME ONCE MORE DOMINANT THROUGHOUT CHRISTENDOM! But, thank God, that dominancy will be short-lived! It cannot reach beyond the preordained limit assigned it in A. D. 1868, when *the whole period* of the 1,335 years allotted to the career of the "little horn" will have run out. For, the "ten horns" or "kings" of the principal-

---

[1] See Appendix.

ities of western Europe, "which have received no kingdom as yet; but receive power as kings one hour with the beast,"—for they, including Victor Emanuel, hold their power only under the *sufferance* of the present revived seventh secular head of the Franco-Roman empire—these "ten kings," we repeat, at the expiration of that prophetical period, being of "*one mind*, shall give their power and strength unto the beast. . . For God hath put it in their hearts to fulfil his will, and to agree, *and give their kingdom unto the beast until* the words of God shall be fulfilled."[1]

This consummation, therefore, only awaits the *withdrawal* of the French troops from Rome, at the signal given by Napoleon III. This will constitute the finishing stroke of his secular policy. That he will do this, take the following scrap from the *N. Y. Herald* of December 21st, 1860:

"The Bishop of Versailles sought an interview with the Emperor, to try and make him feel the woes of the church, and to remind him of the end of his uncle. The Emperor listened to him patiently, with his cigar in his mouth, and at last said: 'Monseigneur, your distress does you credit, but the temporal power—*i. e.*, of Pope Pius IX.—is no longer compatible with our civilization, and we must put an end to it, as I put out my cigar.'"

On the other hand, we read, in regard to the *spiritual* power of the Papacy, that the "ten horns upon the [secular Roman] beast *shall hate the whore, and shall make her desolate and naked, and shall eat her flesh, and burn her with fire.*"[2] Terrifically portentous symbols! They denote her total and irremediable destruction! Aye, and that *at the very hands* of those "ten vassal kings," who, for the long period of 1,335 years, have been subordi-

[1] Rev. xvii. 13, 17.   [2] Rev. xvii. 16.

nated to her despotic sway! And this ruin, mark, as the righteous retribution of Heaven upon her for having made herself " drunken with the blood of the saints, and with the blood of the martyrs of Jesus," [1] *she brings upon herself.* Yes, we repeat: that very " encyclical letter of Pope Pius IX." will do the work! For, incensed at length at the insolence, the intolerance, the utter falsity, and the unexampled impositions so long practised upon the nations of Christendom by the infinite superstitions, delusions, and corruptions of the PAPACY, in their wrath, they will as with " *one mind* " arise, and exterminate the last vestige of it from the earth!

And, in conclusion: this work accomplished, and the " let " or hindrance to the παρουσια, or *personal* " coming," of " the man of sin and son of perdition," alias the last Antichrist, as predicted by St Paul, being thus " taken out of the way ; " *then* will be ushered upon the platform of the prophetical earth, the *inauguration,* at the hands of the ten uncrowned kings, of the previously revived seventh head of the Franco-Roman empire, into his seat of power as the EIGHTH HEAD, by the united transfer of " their power and strength " UNTO HIM!

[1] Rev. xvii. 6.

CHAPTER VI. [CONTINUED.]

SECTION II.

LOUIS NAPOLEON III., AS THE EIGHTH HEAD OF THE UNIVERSAL LATIN EMPIRE.

I. The steps which are to immediately precede the *Introduction* of Louis Napoleon III. upon the stage of action as the eighth apocalyptic head.

II. His *Inauguration*, as such, into his seat of power, at the hands of the ten Roman "horns" or "kings," REV. xvii. 13, 17.

WE have said that the prophecy relating to the EIGHTH apocalyptic head is still *future*. But the subject of it *has not yet completed* his career, as the revived seventh *secular* head of the Franco-Roman empire. Everything, however, in the national, political, and moral condition of the world and of the church, as we shall see, clearly indicate that his *inauguration* into his seat of power as the eighth head, *is nigh at hand*. We have demonstrated that the prophetico-chronological period of 1,335 years, allotted in the Divine purpose to *the whole* contemporaneous career of the Papal ecclesiastico-secular and the Roman civil powers, commencing in A. D. 533, terminate together in A. D. 1868.

It will here be in place to premise, that, in view of the present state of things, as in the past, the "LITTLE HORN" of Papacy holds a dominancy over the *ten crowned horns* of the Roman beast, analogous to that of the DRAGON over the *seven crowned heads* of the same beast. The harlot-rider still retains her seat upon the back of the "scarlet-colored beast," *alias*, "the beast with two horns like a lamb, and who speaks as a dragon." This she does in the confident, but, as the sequel has shown, the unfounded hope of permanent restoration to *political* power. So also, she still retains her grasp as a *spiritual* power upon the "ten horns" or "kings." But, there being left to her of her *secular* dominions nothing but Rome and Venice, the position of these ten horns, at the time present, is, that while they are *reputed* "as kings, they have received *no* kingdom as yet." It suffices them for the time being, that they shall have wrested the ten-crowned kingdoms from the "little horn" by the process of Italian nationalization under the crown of Victor Emanuel. Hence their present attitude as having, in themselves, "*no kingdom.*" The terms of the prophecy, however, show that this arrangement is *temporary* only. Another move upon the platform awaits them, which no human diplomacy can avert. And, when the Popedom shall have been finally stripped of its remaining territorial possessions,—Rome and Venice,—the seven-headed, scarlet-colored beast will appear with his "ten horns" *uncrowned;* for, God will have put it in their hearts to fulfil His will, and to agree, and "give their kingdom unto the beast"—*alias*, Müller's "tame eagle" and "Corsican wolf"—Napoleon III, as the "EIGHTH" head.

In what we have further to offer on this subject, we speak, as we all along have done, not as a prophet, but as an *interpreter of* prophecy. The above prophetic imagery, taken in connection with Italian affairs and those of other nationalities, present a prospective state of things *vastly different* from that apprehended by the popular mind. Instead of that *speedy conversion* of Italy and other nationalities by the *ordinary* instrumentalities of the day under this dispensation about which so many fondly dream, consequent of their throwing off from their necks the long-continued galling yoke of papal despotism, we are led to look for results *directly the reverse*. This statement, at least to most minds, may seem at first view both bold and unfounded. But, let us see.

Our business now is, to prove what we have affirmed and now repeat, regarding NAPOLEON III., as he who is destined soon to appear upon the great prophetical platform of these " last times," as the great *God-denying or apostatico-democratic head of the last Antichristian confederacy, alias,* THE LAST ANTICHRIST. We submit the following considerations to your candid and prayerful thoughts.

I. The steps which are to immediately precede his introduction upon the prophetical stage of action.

II. The agents, at whose hands he is to be inaugurated into his seat of power.

III. The prophetico-historic marks, which designate who, and what he is.

IV. The prophetic exploits of this last Antichrist and his confederated hosts, and

V. Their final doom.

I. We are to present to your view, first, *the steps which are to immediately precede Napoleon III.'s introduction upon the prophetical stage of action.* We here observe that, *prior* to the transfer to him by the "ten kings" of "their kingdom," "power, and strength," or, during his progressive steps to the acme of his ambition as the eighth apocalyptic head, it will be signalized by *the working of miracles,* in authentication of his mission as such. That Louis Napoleon III. is warily but resolutely advancing in the path that he marked out for himself while yet an exile in the United States, and when, in A. D. 1835, he gave to the world the "*Idées Napoleoniennes,*" and which he has elaborated in his recently published "History of Julius Cæsar," has been confirmed by each successive step of his progress from A. D. 1848 to the present time. Let us then suppose that, despite of his stripping the Popedom of its *temporal* power, he contemplates the seizure of the triple crown of Pope Pius IX., as his uncle did the iron crown of Charlemagne in A. D. 1804. This would not necessarily involve the *unseating* of his harlot-rider from his back. She is still permitted to retain her seat there as the *spiritual* head of the Papacy, and will so remain, until the seven heads of the "scarlet-colored beast" shall be merged into one as an EIGHTH head. But, that the above is not mere supposition, " he has permitted or caused a pamphlet to be issued, in which it is proposed that *he himself* should be a sort of POPE, and unite the *political* and *religious* sovereignties in his own person—a thing which may possibly be consummated at no distant day."

"The title of the above pamphlet is, '*The Emperor Pope.*' It has been principally sold among official persons. It argues that Victoria is Queen and Pope; that the Protestant sovereigns of the Germanic confederation exercise both political and religious power; that in Sweden, Denmark, and Norway the kings are Popes; that Alexander II., Emperor of Russia, is Czar and Pontiff; that Otho is king and Pope at Athens; that the Sultan of Turkey is emperor and Pope; and that the Emperor of France should not be behind them," etc. Pretty fair logic, this! "It is also given on 'good authority' that Louis Napoleon has actually submitted the question to some of the French bishops, on the subject of a *French Patriarchate*, at least with practically independent powers." (See Catholic Herald, December 15, 1860.)

"It is also worthy of notice in this connection, that soon after the last Encyclical of the Pope was promulged, so fiercely condemning all the ideas of progress, and the authority of peoples, which enter so largely into Napoleonism, there appeared a pamphlet, written by M. Caylu, called '*César Pontife*,' in which the following passage occurs: '*Let Cæsar then be Pontiff;* not, however, in the sense commonly attributed to the word, but as the director, or rather the protector, of the national church regenerated, recognized, and approved by a council. Such, according to us, is the only answer to the encyclical. The question of orthodoxy or of schism is not in our competency; and besides, may not people break with the temporal power of the Pope-king without becoming Protestants? Has not the encyclical of Pius IX. shut up the source of diplomatic compromise? We accept the challenge, and we answer in words as terrible to the temporal Papacy as those which the hand of the angel traced on the palace walls of the King of Babylon,—CÆSAR PONTIFF! To great evils we must apply great remedies. If there be any other solution, serious and possible, we should be glad to hear of it, and to accept it beforehand. If there be none, then the state must look to it without delay; for the civil authority and liberty of conscience are imperilled.'"

Now, it is not difficult to conceive with what facility the present reigning pontiff may succumb to such an eventuality. Believing, as he does, that the *perpetuity* of holy mother church depends solely on the *continued unity* of the mitre and the sword, and finding that the latter has been wrenched from *his* grasp, he may not only yield his assent to, but may exert a direct agency in effecting a combination of, the ecclesiastical and political power in the person of his rival. And, this being consummated, a change in the functions of the present head of the Papacy naturally follows, from that of the *Pope* to that of the "*false prophet*" spoken of, Rev. xix. 20. There we are told, that this "false prophet *wrought miracles* before"—WHOM? The answer is, "*the beast from the earth*," who, having "two horns like a lamb and who spake like a dragon," even he who "exerciseth all the power of the first beast before him," *i. e.*, the seventh secular head, or Napoleon I.; "and causeth the earth and they which dwell therein, *to worship the first beast* whose deadly wound was healed;"[1] and also commands "them that dwell on the earth, that they should *make an image*

---

[1] Rev. xiii. 11, 12.

to the beast which had the wound *and did live ;*"[1] *i. e.,* the revived seventh secular head, or Napoleon III.

Now, such a purely national *combination* of the spiritual and temporal power of the Emperor of the French, would add incalculably to the strength and glory of THE EMPIRE. This the sagacious emperor knows full well. That he should, therefore, constitute himself *the head* of the church in his own empire, is not unreasonable. And, that he may have formed the purpose to do so, and *will* do so *if* necessary to carry out his schemes, is evident from the two articles already alluded to. Indeed, the war may be said already to have commenced between the episcopate and clergy of France, and the sovereign. In this war, the emperor will of course expect to encounter opposition from the Catholic party, the French bar, and the Legitimist and Orleanist body, at the *first step* of an open rupture with Pius IX. and the hierarchy of France. But the Catholic party is so weak, and the temporal dominion of the Pope so much opposed to the Italian sympathies of the French people, that this opposition will be easily overcome. In fact, the emperor's *schemes of reform* in extending the functions of the Senate and legislative body, by which the French people secure a voice in the government of the empire, followed, as they already have been with the entire liberation of the press, and the removal of all restrictions upon the right of popular discussion, will more than check-mate all these movements of his enemies, by securing the approbation of the Legislature, press, and populace of France, *and even of England*, to the projects of aggrandizement which he contemplates.

"It is also rumored in the religious circles, that very

---

[1] Rev. xiii. 14.

strange and important measures and changes are maturing, of such gravity and importance, that a French religious journal declares it impossible to give them publicity through the press. It is said that the choice of a new Pontiff has already been made or resolved upon; but that Pius IX. will not tender his resignation until he has obtained a secret pledge from all the members of the Sacred Council that their votes will be given to *an illustrious layman*, who at one sitting would be made a priest, a bishop, and a cardinal. This much is certain: amongst all these remarkable hypotheses (and religious journals confess it, among others the *Union de l' Ouest*), that some great events are expected to occur in Rome very soon.

"Pius IX. frequently lets escape him references to the approaching eventuality, and in coming out of his oratory, his most intimate prelates, from day to day, gather indications which make clear the situation, and show that the Holy Father no longer attempts to deceive himself as to the future. These are the last death-rattles of the temporal power."

With this additional halo of glory encircling the brow of his imperial majesty, therefore, taken in connection with the excitable and impulsive character of the French nation, we have only to take into account their *idolatrous* veneration of his Napoleonic *prestige*, to be satisfied of the certainty of his *transition*, by their united voice, from his revived seventh to his eighth headship. Or, if any doubt this, we would ask them to look, first, at their "*worship* of the first beast whose deadly wound was healed," as verified in the unexampled pageantry attendant upon the transfer of the remains of Napoleon I. from St. Helena to France, and the universal homage paid at his shrine by *all nations;* and then turn, second, to the *miraculous wonders* which will be wrought to deceive them and all other nations, in attestation of the mission of the revived seventh as an eighth head. The *result* will be,

II. *His inauguration, as such, into his seat of power, at their hands.* We must here ask indulgence for a little scope on this subject.

First, then, we are to bear in mind that Italy is but *one* of the "ten horns" or "kings" of the territorial Roman earth. Now, we are all cognizant of the fact, that Italy owes her deliverance from the dominancy of Austria to the timely interposition in her behalf of the present ruler of France; also, of the acknowledgment, on her part, of his incomparable diplomacy and transcendent power; and that, at *his* significant nod, they proclaimed Victor Emanuel as king of Italy. But the prophecy declares of *all* the "ten horns" or "kings," that "God hath put it in their hearts to fulfil His will, *and to agree and give their kingdom unto the beast,* until the words of God shall be fulfilled." The other *nine* "kings" therefore are, 1. Lombardy; 2. Ravenna; 3. Naples; 4. Tuscany; 5. France; 6. Austria; 7. Spain; 8. Portugal, and 9. Great Britain. Now *all* these European powers, however reluctantly on the part of some of them, have united in *recognizing* the independence of the Italian States. Nor this only. Despite the decree of the so-called Holy Alliance in A. D. 1815, that no member of the Napoleonic family should ever again occupy the throne of France, they have all *paid their homage* to Napoleon III., as the *emperor* of France.

The question therefore is, How are we to account for this? One would suppose that the only solution of this astounding *politico-moral* phenomenon was to be found in the fact that these crowned potentates of earth were all

> "————— mad, insane most grievously,
> And most insane *because* they know it not."
>
> POLLOCK.

The fact, this, precisely: for it perfectly accords with the symbolic imagery of the book of Daniel,—the *maniacy* of the Babylonian monarch, Nebuchadnezzar,[1] and the four rampant beasts,[2]—denotive of corresponding *politico-moral* characteristics on the part of those RULERS of the Gentile nations who, for so long a period (2,520 years[3]), were to "destroy the earth;"[4] but who, when the time came, should *themselves* be "destroyed."[5] Hence the Pauline prophecy respecting them, that, as the confederates of that "wicked one" who is to be "revealed,"[6] even the eighth head, "God shall send them strong delusion, that they should believe a lie."[7] The apostle also speaks of the *form* of development of this "strong delusion." The "*coming*" of this "wicked one," he says, "is after the working of Satan, with all power, and signs, and lying wonders, and with all deceivableness of unrighteousness in them that perish; *because* they received not the love of the truth, that they might be saved."[8] And oh, when we reflect *how long* the admonitory voice of a compassionate God has sounded in the ears of these Gentile rulers of Christendom,—"Kiss the Son, lest He be angry, and ye perish in the way, when His wrath is kindled but a little;"[9] and their *equally long neglect* to "take heed" to it; can we impeach the rectitude of the divine "Governor among the nations," if at

---

[1] Dan. iv. 1–18; and vers. 28–25.
[2] Dan. vii. 1–8, etc.
[3] See pages 39–41.
[4] Rev. xi. 18.
[5] Ib., see also Dan. ii. 34, 35; vii. 11, 12; and verse 26.
[6] 2 Thess. ii. 3, 8.
[7] Ib. verse 11.
[8] Ib. verses 9, 10.
[9] Ps. ii. 12.

the last He sends upon them these retributive "strong delusions?" Every pious mind is ready to respond, as with a thousand tongues, No! And to exclaim, "Just and true are thy ways, Thou King of saints!" And, therefore, what the Pauline prophecy as above gives only in outline, St. John, under and during the pouring out of the sixth vial of the Almighty's wrath upon the symbolic "river Euphrates," or the TURCO-MOHAMMEDAN POWER,[1]—which vial is *now* being poured out,—St. John, we repeat, fills up in the following prophecy, symbolic of the *manner in* which and the *purpose for* which, these "strong delusions" will be inflicted. To this subject we now invite your special regard.

The prophecy is as follows:

"And I saw *three unclean spirits like frogs* come out of the mouth of the dragon, and out of the beast, and out of the mouth of the false prophet.

"For they are *the spirits of devils, working miracles*, which go forth unto the kings of the earth and of the whole world, to gather them to the battle of the great day of God Almighty—and he gathered them together into a place called in the Hebrew tongue ARMAGEDDON." (Rev. xvi. 13, 14, 16.)

It will be necessary here to explain, *en passant*, first, that the phrase, "*the whole world*," in this prophecy, is to be understood as applying more specially to the prophetical platform of the ROMAN EARTH, that having been the great theatre of action of the "ten horns" or "kings" of the beast, although other nations will be made to feel the *influence* of the miracle-working wonders of the "three frog spirits." This phraseology, "the whole world," is applied to the Roman empire, Luke ii. 1, 3, 5:

---

[1] Rev. xvi. 12. See also appendix.

but there were other nations which lay *outside* of it, and hence were not included in the Roman taxation. Besides, it is the "ten horns" or "kings" *only*, that "give their kingdom, power, and strength to the beast." The second remark is, that there will be an *interval* between the gathering of the nations and their kings by the agency of "the three frog spirits," and the GREAT "BATTLE" which is to transpire in "the field called Armageddon."

We proceed, now, to the other parts of the prophecy. And,

1. As to the *source* or *origin* of this tripod of "frog spirits." The first issued "out of the mouth of the *dragon*," which the Holy Spirit interprets to symbolize "that old serpent called the Devil and Satan,"[1] or "the god of this world," who, as "the prince of the power of the air, worketh in the children of disobedience." The second, "out of the mouth of the *beast*," denotive of the body politic of the Roman empire, symbolized by the nondescript monster of Daniel having ten horns, and the same with the apocalyptic beast with seven heads and ten horns under his several transmutations. And the third, "out of the mouth of the *false prophet*," who is an offshoot of the eleventh or Papal "little horn" of Daniel's fourth beast.

These three diabolical powers, therefore, constitute a *trinity in unity*, in antagonism with the TRIUNE PERSONALITY of the infinite and eternal Godhead, the Father, the Son, and the Holy Ghost. For, as the Father gave his Son Jesus "all power in heaven and earth;"[2] and also after the ascension of Jesus gave to the church "another comforter, even the Spirit of Truth:"[3] so the dragon gave to his two offshoots, the beast and the false prophet,

[1] Rev. xii. 9 : xx. 1, 2.   [2] Matt. xxviii. 18.   [3] John xiv. 16, 11.

"his power, and seat, and great authority."[1] Yes, "all the kingdoms of the world and the glory of them," during man's lapsed state, being "*delivered*" over to the *satanic usurper* of Messiah's rights, he "giveth to whomsoever he will."[2] Then further.

2. As *consequent* of the combined miraculous powers put forth by this trio of "frog spirits" as emanating from the triune powers of all evil, their influences extend over the *elements* of nature, the *political* economy or diplomacy of nations, and the *ecclesiastical* affairs of religious systems. And, what is to be specially noted in this connection, is the fact that these combined influences, whether they relate to the one or the other, are all put forth under a *religious* guise. Hence St. Paul:—"If *Satan* transforms himself into an angel of light" in order to deceive "the kings of the earth and of the whole world," "it is no marvel," he adds, "if *his ministers* also be transformed into the ministers of righteousness:"[3] aye, "wolves in sheep's clothing."[4] We have, however, the Holy Spirit's interpretation of their character. They are declared to be "*the spirits of devils.*"

But, as there are "THREE" of these "unclean frog spirits," each having its own distinct official functions, and filling its appropriate sphere in the accomplishment of the diabolical work assigned to it, the question is,

3. *What are we to understand by them?* We reply, that the *first*, which issues forth "out of the mouth of the dragon,"—who, as "the father of lies," *commenced* his satanic work in Eden with *a lie*, and is therefore called "a liar from the beginning," now *ends* his work through this leading "frog spirit," by infusing into the minds of

---

[1] Rev. xiii. 2.
[3] 2 Cor. xi. 13, 14.
[2] Luke iv. 5, 6.
[4] Matt. vii. 15.

"the kings of the earth and of the whole world" *a spirit of lying, chicanery, and fraud*—including all sorts and degrees of peculation, forgery, counterfeiting, etc.—*together with perfidy and treason*, both in church and state. That the *second* "frog spirit," that comes "out of the mouth of the beast,"—who derives "his seat, and power, and authority from the dragon"—infuses into the minds of the masses, *the principles of an unbridled and licentious anarchy*, which despises and tramples alike upon all constitutional systems, divine and human. And that the *third*, or the "frog spirit" which proceeds "out of the mouth of the false prophet," inspires the same masses with *the corrupting creed of an idolatrous and God-denying atheism.* But in addition to this:—

4. The *mission* of these "three frog spirits," or "spirits of devils," coincides exactly with the *period or season* alluded to by "the loud voice from heaven" which St. John "heard, saying, 'Woe to the inhabiters of the earth and of the sea! for the Devil is come down unto you, having great wrath, because he knoweth that he hath but a short time.'"[1]

Now, this "loud voice from heaven" falls in with the effusion of the sixth apocalyptic vial, which dries up the mystical river "Euphrates," symbolic of the gradual exhaustion of the Moslem Turco-Ottoman or Mohammedan power.[2] For, it is *immediately after* the final extinction of that power, that St. John saw the "three unclean frog spirits" go forth to "the kings of the earth and of the whole world."[3] And, that we of this day are living under the pouring out of *the last dregs* of this vial, we would ask, who that is at all observant of the existing

---

[1] Rev. xii. 12. [2] See Appendix.
[3] Compare Rev. xvi. verses 12 and 13, 14.

national, political, and religious state of the TURKISH EMPIRE, that "sick old man," as the Czar of Russia, Nicholas I., facetiously styled him, is not looking for its *speedy erasure* from the list of European nations? And, although we may trace the *incipient* workings of those political and moral elements, which have prepared the way for the appearance upon the prophetical stage of these " frog spirits," from the period of the earliest outbreak of the French Revolution in A. D. 1768—brought on by the effusion of the first one of the seven vials or last plagues; yet, each succeeding vial of judgments upon the Papal and Mohammedan Antichrists having become *more intensified* in their effects down to this hour, the guilty nations of earth and the apostate portions of the church, both Papal and Protestant, are being hurried on, as with lightning speed, to their *exposure* to the more powerfully combined workings of this tripod of " the spirits of devils," LYING, ANARCHY, and ATHEISM.

5. And, mark you! the *culminating point* of these diabolical influences will be, the formation of that LAST DEMOCRATICO-INFIDEL or antichristian confederacy of which we have spoken. Yes, the nations of earth, in view of the *acknowledged instability* of the time-worn and moss-covered thrones and dynasties of the Old World, whether autocratic, despotic, or monarchical, and of that of the New World as well; and being aware also, not only, but incensed at the *evident inadequacy* alike of both the ancient and modern systems of religion, whether Judaic, nominally Protestant, Papal, or Mohammedan, to meet the wants of mankind; and finally, being further cognizant of the fact of the existence in every government under heaven of the *permeating leaven* of a rabid spirit of Jacobinism; we repeat, in the light of this condition of the world, national, political, and religious, and

impelled by the judicially irresistible influences of the *strong delusions* " which shall be sent upon them as the just punishment of their rejecting " the love of the truth that they might be saved," while that salvation was so freely proffered to them: the universal cry of " LIBERTY, LIBERTY!" " EQUALITY, EQUALITY!" " UNITY, UNITY!" will sweep before it all existing political systems and religious institutions of *mere human* device!

But, *you doubt this.* Nor are we surprised at it, being at war, as it is, with all your long-cherished opinions and prejudices. Shocked at the very thought of such an eventuality, you are ready to denounce it as a chimera. But let me remind you of one fact: Man is a *religious* being. Of another fact: That man, rather than have *no* religion, is ready to take up with one that is *false;* aye, and vastly more so than to adopt that which is *true.* On this point we are sure of your verdict in our favor, when we remind you of the *vast preponderance* in point of numbers, between the devotees of the *false* religious systems of the Pagans, Papists, Mohammedans, and others, compared with that of nominal Protestants, which we hold to be the *true.* Why, at this very moment, the proportion in favor of the former over the latter is as 1,145,000,000 to 80,000,000; and, out of these 80,000,000 Protestants, not more than 15,000,000 are enrolled as communicants of all the churches in Christendom! Let me then once more recall to your mind the fact, that in the mission of this tripod of " the spirits of devils," they do not go forth " to the kings of the earth and of the whole world" as mere politicians: but, as bearing the proportions of *an immense consolidated spiritual power*, antagonistic to all existing systems of religion! And so, as, immediately preliminary to its organization and introduction upon the stage, the " ten horns" or "kings" of the Roman earth will have struck down and totally annihilated the existing Papal superstition, the way will be prepared for the speedy gathering together of its antichristian hosts.

Then, too, we are to recollect that these "three unclean frog spirits" or "spirits of devils," are clothed with *miraculous* powers. Now, mankind, we know, are not invulnerable to persuasion, when backed with miraculous demonstrations. Why, since the appearance of that great apostle of the *miracle-working spiritualists* of our day, Uriah Clark, from his humble home in Hydesville, New York, in A. D. 1848—*the very year* that Louis Napoleon was elected President of the French Assembly, and who *himself* is a spiritualist—they claim that in the United States there are at least 2,000,000 of decisive and 5,000,000 of nominal believers; and that on the eastern continent (Christian) they may be reckoned to number at least from 1,000,000 to 2,000,000; while they swell the number throughout the globe to hundreds of millions! Supposing, then, that "the kings" of the Latin earth were the united eye-witnesses of *one* of the miracles of the "three frog spirits," that of the False Prophet, for example, who is to come "with *all* power and signs, and lying wonders," etc. What, think you, would be the *effect* of this? Let prophecy answer. It forewarns us that these "kings" and their subjects will "*worship the dragon* which gave power unto the beast," not only; but that they will also "*worship the beast*," *i. e.*, the EIGHTH HEAD, "saying, Who is like unto the beast? Who is able to make war with him?" But then it is declared that *all* these "spirits of devils" shall work "miracles," that they may "*deceive* them that dwell on the earth." We again ask, therefore: What, suppose you, will be the effect of this *combined* miraculous display of power among the masses? The Holy Spirit forewarns us, that when they shall transpire, such will be their captivating influence, that they "shall deceive, if it be possible, the very elect."[1]

And, as most of those *now living* may witness these demonstrations of miraculous power, we would affectionately address to all a note of warning. Inasmuch, then, as nothing but the truth of God in the mind, and the grace of God in the heart, will be able to *fortify* any soul against being led captive by these "strong delusions," we would only say, "Let him that thinketh he standeth take heed lest he fall."

All others—and this is our closing remark on the subject in hand—all others, embracing "the kings of the earth and of the whole world," having *fallen a prey* to the miracle-working wonders of these diabolical agencies, "the spirits of devils," will concentrate their forces, and will *organize* themselves into that last stupendous antichristian confederacy of the nations, either actually or as allies, at whose hands the apocalyptic eighth head, NAPOLEON III., will be inaugurated into his seat of power.

[1] Matt. xxiv. 24.

CHAPTER VI.

[CONTINUED.]

SECTION III.

THE PROPHETICO-HISTORIC "MARK, NAME, OR NUMBER" (666), REV. XIII. 16-18, WHICH DESIGNATES THE EIGHTH APOCALYPTIC HEAD, SHOWING THAT THEY POINT TO LOUIS NAPOLEON III.

> I. This mark, name, or number, as applied to his *ancestry*.—The name and character of Papal Rome, as found in the Hebrew, Greek, and Latin languages.—To his *own name*.—Louis (Ludovicus).—Napoleon.—Louis Napoleon Bonaparte.

We have now pointed out, I., the successive steps which are to immediately precede the introduction of the eighth apocalyptic head upon the prophetical stage of action; and II., the agents at whose hands he is to be inaugurated into his seat of power.

But, in order to remove all doubt from the mind as to the application of the preceding prophetical exegesis to Napoleon III. as the eighth apocalyptic head, we now proceed to consider, III., *The prophetico-historic mark, name, or number, which designates him as such*. With the single remark, that we are now to look upon Napoleon III. as having retired from the stage of action in his capacity of the revived seventh head of the secular Franco-Roman empire; and that we are to contemplate him exclusively in his character and exploits as the EIGHTH HEAD OR LEADER OF THE LAST ANTICHRISTIAN CONFEDERACY OF THE NATIONS; St. John says of him, Rev. xiii. 16-18:

> "And he causeth all, both small and great, rich and poor, free and bond, to receive a mark in their right hand, or in their foreheads:
> "And that no man might buy or sell, save he that had the mark, or the name of the beast, or the number of his name."

And then the apostle adds:

"Here is wisdom. Let him that hath understanding count the number of the beast: for it is the number of a man; and his number is six hundred three-score and six."

It is here to be observed, in the first place, that the above prophecy, taken in connection with the context, furnishes additional evidence, that the revived seventh and eighth headships centre in and are exercised by THE SAME PERSON. It is the more important to recognize this distinction, in order to discriminate between the power that *confers* the mark or name or number of the beast, and HE by whom that number is *interpreted*.

Now, the power who *confers* this "mark, name, or number" upon the eighth head, is THE "BEAST," which St. John saw "coming up out of the earth, having *two horns like a lamb*, but who *spake as a dragon*," and who, as such, "exerciseth all the power of the *first beast* (Napoleon I.) which was before him," and who "causeth the earth and them which dwell therein to worship the first beast, whose deadly wound was healed." This act of *worship* is imposed upon and is now being performed *by all nations* in the church in Notre Dame, Paris, by paying their homage over the ashes of the first Napoleon.

The apostle then goes on to point out *the means* employed by the "beast" in conferring this "mark," etc. " He doeth *great wonders*, so that he maketh *fire* to come down from heaven on the earth in the sight of men, and *deceiveth* them that dwell on the earth *by the means* of those miracles which he had power to do in the sight of the beast; saying to them that dwell on the earth, that they should *make an image* to the beast, which had the wound by a sword, *and did live:*" not, mark, as the revived seventh, but as the EIGHTH HEAD. For "*the image*" here spoken of was not set up under the former headship. It is just here where the *transition* in the prophecy takes place from the revived seventh to the eighth headship. And so, in *confirmation* of his authority as the revived seventh head to impose said "mark" etc. upon the eighth, it is said that "he had power to *give life* unto the image of the beast, that the image of the beast should both speak, and cause that as many as *would not worship* the image of the beast *should be killed*."

Without presuming to be wise above what is written, we pretend not to positively decide in what this "image" will consist. It is pertinent, however, to observe, that it will form the counterpart of its ancient archetype, the "*golden image*," set up by the Babylonian monarch, Nebuchadnezzar, in the plains of Dura, in the province of Babylon, and which all "people, nations, and languages were commanded to fall down and worship," under pain of being "cast into the midst of a burning, fiery furnace," in case of disobedience.[1] It is in place to remark, however, that the Napoleonic "image" has *no* "mark, or name, or number, assigned to it. That is reserved for "THE BEAST" alone. Hence we read, that the seventh revived head "causeth all," by his decree, "both small and great, rich and poor, free and bond, to receive *a mark* in their right hand, or in their foreheads: and that *no man might buy or sell*, save he that *had* the mark, or name of the beast, or the number of his name." In a word, it is clear that the two headships, united as they were in the same person, *coöperate* each with the other in the transfer of the functions of the former to the

---

[1] Dan. iii. 1-7.

latter, the *first* using its influence in the support of the tyranny of the *last*.

But one important thing was omitted in this transaction. That was, to *decipher* "*the number* of the beast." That omission, in mercy to us, was reserved to be disclosed by the HOLY SPIRIT. Hence the additional statement:—"Here is wisdom. Let him that hath understanding *count the number of the beast;* for it is the number of A MAN: and his number is SIX HUNDRED THREE-SCORE AND SIX."

Now, the veriest tyro knows, that it was customary with the Hebrews, Greeks, and Romans, to use the *letters* of their alphabets to keep accounts by, instead of *figures*, which are of much later invention. This ancient custom, in part, prevails to this day, as may be seen in books, medals, monuments, and public buildings, *e. g.*, MDCCXCIII. is put for 1793, which, in Hebrew characters, are deciphered thus, אזטג (3971), (aleph, zayan, teth, gimmel), *i. e.* 1793; and in Greek, thus: αζθγ (1793), (alpha, zeta, theta, gamma), *i. e.* 1793.

Accordingly, in the above passage, the *mystical* number, 666, is represented by the Greek numerals χ′ (600), ξ (60), ς (6), (chi, xi, sigma), *i. e.* 666. Our Saviour also, in the same book, calls Himself " α " (alpha) and " ω " (omega), *i. e.*, " the *first* and the *last*," these two letters being the first and the last in the Greek alphabet. Nor is it a little astonishing, that the above number 666, without a single unit over or under, as we shall show, should be found in the composition of the *name* of " this beast," as the EIGHTH " HEAD " spoken of in the above passage when written and counted as *numerals* in the three languages, *Hebrew*, *Greek*, and *Latin*, that composed the inscription placed by Pilate over the head of our blessed Lord on the cross.

7*

In order, however, to give completeness to the revelations concerning this eighth head, it is reasonable to expect that some light would be furnished on the subject of his *zoological origin*. Nor will it lessen our amazement, should it turn out that the " mark, or name, or number " of his ancestry, and that of his own, when counted as numerals, should be found to produce the exact number of 666. Let us, then, apply it,

I. TO HIS ANCESTRY—*The name and character of Papal Rome, as found in the Hebrew, Greek, and Latin languages.* When applied to the PAPAL Beast as *a man*, a Roman of the *Latin* nation, this number will be found exactly to make out the "*mark*" of his name in the above three languages, thus: רמעכוש, *Romanus*, λατεινος, *Latinus*. But when considered as numerals, or figures (of which both words entirely consist), they may then be called the *number* of his name, the Hebrew words, רמעכוש, a *Roman*, from Romulus, the founder of Rome, and רומיית, *Romiith*, the city of Rome, and with which corresponds the Greek word, λατεινος, Latinus, thus

Romanus—a Roman.		Romiith.		Latinus.	
ר Raish,	200.	ר Raish,	200.	λ Lambda,	30.
מ Mem,	40.	ו Wav,	6.	α Alpha,	1.
ע Tzadi,	70.	מ Mem,	40.	τ' Tau,	300.
נ Noon,	50.	י Yod,	10.	ε Epsilon,	5.
ו Wav,	6.	י Yod,	10.	ι Iota,	10.
ש Sheen,	300.	ת Pay,	400.	ν Nu,	50.
	———		———	o Omicron,	70.
	666.		666.	ς Sigma,	200.
					———
					666.

From this we pass to observe, as a singular circumstance in reference to the *character* of the Papal " little horn," that the title or frontlet,—*Vicarius filii Dei*—(Vicar of the Son of God), which the Popes of Rome have assumed to themselves, and caused to be inscribed over the door of the Vatican, exactly makes up the number of 666, when deciphered according to the numerical signification of its constituent letters, thus:

Vicar	of the Son	of God.
V I C A R I V S	F I L I I	D E I
5, 1,100, 1, 5	1,50,1,1,	500, 1. Total, 666.

One other fact. It is a matter of historic verity, that in A. D. 666, Pope Vitalian first ordained that public worship should be exclusively performed in the *Latin* tongue, from which time they *latinized* everything— masses, prayers, hymns, litanies, canons, bulls, the acts of councils—etc., etc.; nor are the Scriptures read—and that by priests alone—in any other language under popery than the Latin. Hence this language has been communicated unto the people as the mark and character of the whole empire!

Now for the fact just alluded to. Another designation is applied to this power, on the principle of the interchangeable use of the terms king and kingdom, as denoting the same thing, viz., that of "The Latin Kingdom." Dr. Adam Clarke, in his commentary on Rom. xiii. 1, in connection with verses 6, 7, having shown by quotations from the acts of Romish councils, Papal bulls, etc., that they apply to the hierarchy of Rome the above name, says: "if this application of this name to that power be correct, the Greek words signifying 'the Latin kingdom,' must have this number." He then adds, that the most concise method of expressing this name among the Greeks was as follows: Η λατινη βασιλεια, which is thus numbered:—

	The	Latin					Kingdom.					
Η	λ	α	τ	ι	ν	η	β	α	σ	ι	λ	ε	ι	α
8,	30,	1,	300,	10,	50,	8,	2,	1,	200,	10,	30,	5,	10,	1.	Total 666.

"No other kingdom on earth," says this learned divine, "can be found to contain 666. This is the ἡ σοφια, the wisdom or demonstration. A *beast* is the symbol of a *kingdom;* and Η λατινη βασιλεια, being shown to contain, exclusively, the *number* 666, is the demonstration."

But, in regard to the facts here presented, it is to be specially noted, that however these various titles, orders, etc., may be applicable to the purposes above specified; yet, that they can only be used as designating the Papal "little horn" of Daniel as *an Antichrist;* and hence, that they cannot be restricted to a *succession* of Popes is evident from the circumstance that a complete fulfilment of *all* the conditions of this prophetic "mark, or name, or number of the beast," relates to a *single individual*—some ONE MAN. Hence the Holy Spirit declares emphatically, that this number 666 *is the number of* A MAN," *i. e.*, of one who shall be, pre-eminently, THE ANTICHRIST, or that "Wicked One" (ανομος, *anomos*), "THE MAN OF SIN AND SON OF PERDITION," of St. Paul.

And now, having demonstrated that Louis Napoleon III. is the revived seventh head of the Roman beast, in which capacity he now exercises the *secular* power of the Franco-Roman emperorship; and also, that, as the eighth head, being zoologically "*of* the seven," he undergoes a *mutation*—which takes place when the "ten horns" or "kings" of the Roman earth, being "of one mind, agree to give their power and strength or kingdom to him"— at which time he assumes the functions of a *religious* or *spiritual* head: let us see whether HIS NAME, in *Hebrew*,

Greek, and *Latin*, furnishes this significant number of 666. Take the name thus :—

Louis. (LVDOVICVS.)

The two names, *Louis Napoleon*, are those by which the present ruling Emperor of France is universally known. The laws of symbolic prophecy, however, require that they be translated into languages in which the *letters* are used as numerals. Take then, first, the *Latin*. This, as we have seen, is the language of the Roman empire and of the Papal church, of which the French emperor is reputed as "the eldest son," and who, in the prayers offered up for him in the church of Notre Dame, is styled *Ludovicus*, the French of which is *Louis*. Take this name,

L V D O V I C V S.
50, 5, 500, 5, 1, 100, 5.   Total 666.

But, to this it is objected, that though the name of Ludovicus, the Latin for Louis, does, according to the Latin valuation of its letters, make up the number 666, if the *o* and the *s* are left out of the account, yet it is demanded, " by what principle of interpretation or fairness are they left out ? Spell the name *without* the *o* and the *s*, and you do not have Ludovicus. Spell the name *with* the two letters, and you have two letters which cannot enter into its numeral value, and, therefore, Ludovicus = 666, as the name and number of the 'beast' is fancy, and nothing more."

To this objection we reply, "that there are only *seven* letters that have any numerical value in the Latin alphabet, viz.: $M = 1000$, $D = 500$, $C = 100$, $L = 50$, $X = 10$, V or $U = 5$, and $I = 1$, and all the rest are counted as *ciphers*, and of course the addition of ever so many ciphers to a given number can never increase its value. There is, in truth, no point whatever in such an objection. The fact has never been disputed by prophetical writers, that Ludovicus does not really contain 666. Seebachius was the first that fixed upon Ludovicus as the name of the Beast, on account of France being considered the *principal* of the kingdoms of the beast, but many others have adopted the name." [1]

And so, if we take the other name,

NAPOLEON,

by putting it into the *Greek* form, *dative* case, in the word Ναπολεοντι, as if inscribed upon a monument, we arrive at the same result, thus:

$$\begin{array}{ccccccccc} N & α & π & o & λ & ε & o & ν & τ & ι \\ 50, & 1, & 80, & 70, & 30, & 5, & 70, & 50, & 300, & 10. \end{array}$$ Total, 666.

But it is demanded: "By what system of interpretation or fairness is the name *Louis* Napoleon deliberately *misspelt*, when using the Greek letters, in order to make that name square with this theory of the beast's number? *Louis* is spelt Λοις, whereas it ought to be made to spell Λουις. In like manner *Napoleon* is turned into Ναπολεον, whereas it ought to be turned into Ναπολεων," etc.

The answer to this is, that, in reference to the name *Louis*, " the proper sound of the first syllable is Lo-o, or *Loo*. Now, *ou*, expresses *oo* or *o*, in French; but it has no legitimate sound in English." Webster says, " Missouri, in Fr. Missouri, all very proper for Frenchmen: for Englishmen the letters used lead to a false pronunciation. It

[1] See Proph. Times, June, 1864, p. 95.

is to be regretted that our language is doomed to be the heterogeneous medley of English and foreign languages."[1] And again: "It is much to be regretted that British authors and travellers admit into their writings foreign words, without conforming them in *orthography* to regular English analogies... I would not refuse to admit foreign words, but I would compel them to submit to the formalities of naturalization."[2]

"By these principles, which pervade Webster's entire Introduction, the *u* in Louis would never have been permitted in English." "From the sentence 'Louis Bonapart emperor governor,' we have dropped a *u* from every word but the first; and it has no business in that. We want the sound of *o* in move, or *oo* in boot, and *ou* does not in English legitimately express that sound; nor does *oo* express the sound definitely, but *o* does; and therefore I am advocating no chimera or fancy, but a strictly scientific and exact fact. *Louis* is, in English, false orthography. *Lois* is specifically correct. Move and prove, are in French, mouvoir and eprouvoir. The *e* in Napoleon in English sound, is *short*. Now this, as has been shown, gives the exact number of the *name* Λοις Ναπολεον."

Again: "In Liddell and Scott's Lexicon, under the head of the letter *o*, it is shown that Λοις is a usual interchangeable form for Λουις, the diphthong *ou* being frequently written as the single letter *o*, where it is stated that 'in early times the vowel *o* was not called ομικρον but ου.' Bock remarks that in Attic inscriptions before Euclides (Ol, 94, 2), the diphthong *ou* is found only in ου, ουκ, ουτος with their derivatives, and in some proper names: elsewhere always *o*. That *o* in many words must

---

[1] Dic. p. 9.   [2] Ib. p. 77.

have sounded very like the diphthong ου, appears from divers Œlic forms, such as βολα for βουλα, βολομα for βουλομα, οραυος for ουρανος. We have in the Attic, μουνος, νουσος, κουσος, ουνομα for μονος, νοσος, κοσος, ονομα, and ουδος, ουρος for οδος, ορος. Hence it appears that ου is sometimes written as ο and *vice versa.*

"Furthermore. With regard to Ναπολεον, it is stated in the same Lexicon that ο (*omicron*) was a usual Œlic for ω (*omega*), so that Ναπολεον might thus, according to one of the Greek dialects, be spelt Ναπολεον without doing inadmissible violence to its proper Hellenistic orthography. But an additional reason for writing the word in Greek with a *short*, rather than a *long* penultimate ω, is found in the fact that we do not pronounce or spell Napoleon in English as Napoleoon, and therefore, in translating it into Greek, it does not seem reasonable to spell its last syllable with a long or double ω, as ων (*oon*), but rather with a short ο as ον (*on*).

"Thus the Greek Lexicon furnishes us with satisfactory warrant for translating the words *Louis Napoleon* into Λοις Ναπολεον . . . and hence, by the institution of this critical and exegetical scrutiny into the alleged untrustworthiness of the above-mentioned hermeneutical interpretation of the apocalyptic number of the pre-figurative wild beast, the above-named objection is demonstrated to be substantially fallacious and untenable.

"It is here worthy of remark, that there is a third method in which Louis Napoleon's name contains 666 in Greek. If his name, *Buonaparte*, be turned into *Greek*, it becomes καλομερος or καλονμερος; and, indeed, the Duchess of Abrantes describes Napoleon's lineal descent from the Greek family of *Calomeros*. Now the initials, L. N., for Λοις Ναπολεον, placed before Καλονμερος, contribute to make together the number of 666, thus:

Λ   N   κ α λ   ο   ν   μ   ε   ρ   ο   s.
30, 50, 20, 1, 30, 70, 50, 40, 5, 100, 70, 200,   666.

And, in conclusion, "it should be remembered, that the principal form in which Louis Napoleon's name is considered to contain the fatal number of 666 in Greek, is in the *dative* case in the word Ναπολεοντι; and no one is able to discover the slightest flaw in this method. Now, whether Napoleon be written in Greek in the nominative as Ναπολεον, or, as before proposed, Ναπολεων, it will, at least, be unhesitatingly admitted that Ναπολεοντι is the dative form of the word; and the reason why Antichrist's name ought to contain 666 in the *dative* rather than in the nominative case, is thus explained by the Rev. Robert Polwhele in his pamphlet, "The Sealed People, or those who *escape* the Great Tribulation:"

"The name to be deciphered in the number 666, is the name of THE BEAST, to be borne by those who *worship his image*. Not being the name of those who are to bear it upon their foreheads or hands, it is not in the nominative case; but it is a mark or sign of *dedication*, and therefore in the *dative* case, just as might be inscribed on temples or altars, implying that the temple or altar was dedicated or devoted to such a deity. The perception of this truth, that the *name* is one to be borne by the worshippers as a sign or mark of dedication, is that exercise of the understanding which is to be inferred from the expression with which the enigma is introduced (Rev. xiii. 18), and which is necessary in order to solve it. And the word Ναπολεοντι, the *name* of Napoleon, by its dative inflection, suggestive of *dedication* or subserviency to him by the *worshippers* who bore his name, is the solution of this wonderful enigma."

The English author of "Napoleonism Unveiled" similarly observes, in reference to the view that the Apocalypse was written in the *Greek* language, and that, consequently, the name of the beast, and his number, must also be in Greek, that,

"The dynastic name of the Emperor Napoleon in its *dative* case,

Ναπολεοντι (the inflection used in the Greek and other languages whenever dedication or subserviency is implied), forms the number of the beast *in the very language* in which the Apocalypse was written. Taking all things into consideration, so extraordinary a fulfilment has never before taken place. The mysterious origin of the name, and its significant meaning, the political power and influence with which it is invested, the desire of the Emperor to perpetuate its use by his successors, and lastly, its forming the *mystical* number 666, all contribute to impress upon the mind strong convictions of its being *the very number* of THE BEAST of which St. John prophesied in Patmos."

Finally, on this subject. We cannot omit a reference to an additional fact, namely: that the whole name of this eighth head

LOUIS NAPOLEON BONAPART,

when put in *Hebrew*, furnishes precisely the same result, as the preceding in Latin and Greek, thus:

ל	Lamed.	30.	
א	Aleph.	1.	
ו	Wav.	6.	LOUIS
י	Yod.	10.	
ס	Samech.	60.	
נ	Noon.	50.	
פ	Phay.	80.	
ל	Lamed.	30.	
א	Aleph.	1.	NAPOLEON
ו	Wav.	6.	
נ	Noon.	50.	
ב	Baith.	2.	
נ	Noon.	50.	
פ	Phay.	80.	
ר	Raish.	200.	BONAPART.
ט	Teth.	9.	
א	Aleph.	1.	

Total, 666.

The writer from whom this article is quoted very justly remarks: "If there has ever been another case of so many and such remarkable coincidences in harmony with the scriptural designations of THE LAST ANTICHRIST, it has never come to our knowledge." To this we would add that, taken in connection with the foregoing proofs that Louis Napoleon III. is the predestined eighth head pointed out in Rev. xvii. 11, and it amounts to a moral demonstration, that it was to *him alone* whom our blessed Lord referred in His address to the Jews of His day when He said: "*If another come* IN HIS OWN NAME, *him ye will receive.*" In a word, this last Antichrist will be constituted of an embodiment of the "*many Antichrists*" predicted by St. John (1 John ii. 18), in all their Pagano-Papal, Mohammedan, and democratico-infidel characteristics!

In the light of these facts, therefore, we shall claim it as having been demonstrated by a lexicographical, mathematical, and moral certainty, that Louis Napoleon III. is the predestined EIGHTH HEAD or leader of the last great democratico-atheistic confederacy that is soon to be ushered upon the stage of action. Now, the prophecy declares,

1. That in regard to this antichristian confederacy, or UNIVERSAL LATIN EMPIRE, it will embrace "all, both small and great, rich and poor, free and bond," who "*receive* the mark, or name, or number of the beast in their right hands, or in their foreheads." In other words, that it will include all those nationalities throughout Christendom, political and ecclesiastical, which, by enlisting under his banner, or dedicating themselves to his service, *shall swear allegiance to him.* On this subject permit us here to repeat what we have often observed, that the *secular* press, compared with the religious, and

including the pulpit, are by far the more reliable, though undesigned, expounders of God's prophetic word in regard to the "SIGNS OF THE TIMES" we live in. We would refer you, in illustration of this remark, to an editorial article in the *New York Herald* of August 23d, 1865, occasioned by the trial, in Buffalo, of one Charles J. Colchester, who, claiming to be a *spiritual medium* (that is, one who holds communication with the spirit world, and who performs the miracle-working wonders of raps and table-tippings, etc.), and having been required to take out a license as a juggler, has peremptorily refused to do so, on the ground of his religious rights as a *spiritualist :* and has been prosecuted by the Commissioner of the United States Government. This writer, after speaking of the importance of this "very curious trial," and expatiating on the pending issues *pro* and *con*, says:

"The signs of the times convince us that something extraordinary is going to happen in the religious world. Perhaps *a new religion* is to be inaugurated with miracles and wonders and the opening of the heavens. The upheavals of all the old forms and creeds which usually announce *the beginning* of a new dispensation, are not wanting in this dispensation. In England we find Bishop Colenso and his party denying the truth of the Pentateuch, and the pious authors of 'Essays and Reviews' ridiculing the thirty-nine Articles of the Church of England. In France, Renan argues against the divinity of Jesus. In Germany Strauss is the apostle of poetical infidelity. At Rome, the Pope denounces all other religions as false, and praises his own to perfection, while Protestants, in their turn, stigmatize the Pope as an impostor. In New England, the parsons all differ, each one seeming to consider himself a little Christ. The 'North American Review' calls Theodore Parker a modern Jesus. The Mormons have started a new church, and are obtaining thousands of proselytes. The Universalists, who are convinced that nobody will be damned, fraternize cordially with the Beecherites, who believe that everybody will be damned except themselves. *The greatest laxity of opinion is almost everywhere allowed.* Throughout Christendom, it is tacitly conceded that the Bible *must not be believed literally*, which is the next thing to *not believing it at all.*" And then the writer adds: "In the midst of all this confusion of creeds and breaking up of sects, come the phenomena of *spiritualism!* Who can say that there is not going to be *a new revelation*, and that it will not begin at the court-house in Buffalo?" etc., etc.

Now, despite the flippancy which characterizes some portions of this article, we must insist upon its general truthfulness, as a picture of the *existing* moral and religious condition of things throughout Christendom—*ridiculing* the fundamental truths of our common Christianity, whether as set forth in "the thirty-nine articles of the Church of England" or other formularies; *denying* the Divinity of the Lord Jesus Christ; the *tendency* of the unregenerate mind to self-deification; the *latitudinarianism* and *fraternizing* of religious sects whose teachings are as divergent as the nether poles; the *denial* that the Scriptures are to be interpreted LITERALLY, and which, as this writer says, "is the next thing to not believing them at all;" the *conflict* which is now being waged between Popery and Protestantism; and, though last, not least, the *wide-spread* influences of Mormonism and spiritualism: these, and a "legion" of other moral antagonisms to "the faith at first delivered to the saints" as "THE SIGNS OF THE TIMES," are but a verification of the Pauline prophecy, that "the time would come when men *would not endure* sound doctrine," but that, "after their own lusts they would heap to themselves teachers, having itching ears;" and that they would "*turn away* their ears from the truth, and be *turned unto fables.*"[1]

Such, then, being the present aspect of things throughout the Christian world, what, suppose you, will they be when, *superadded* to all these unchristianizing and de-

---

[1] 2 Tim. iv. 3, 4.

moralizing and disorganizing influences, the apocalyptic "three unclean frog spirits" or "spirits of devils" shall be let loose upon "the kings of the earth and of the whole world?" Can we reach any other conclusion than that, being prepared for their mission by the preëxisting state of things, "GOD," as He has said, "will put it in their hearts to agree, *and give their kingdom to the* BEAST?" And this act, on their part, will involve the *surrender* of themselves to his power, by receiving his "mark, or name, or number of his name in their right hands and in their foreheads," and by their *idolatrous worshipping* of his image. But, in the next place, the prophecy forewarns us,

2. "*That no man may buy or sell*, SAVE HE that hath the mark, or the name of the Beast, or the number of his name." Yes, a being deprived of the ordinary sources of subsistence, confiscation of property, etc., will be *the penalty* to all such!

This, then, will be that UNPARALLELED TRIBULATION that shall come on all the nations of the earth predicted by our Lord, "Such as never was since the beginning of the creation which God created unto that time, nor ever shall be."[1] Nor this only. It will be that apocalyptic "hour of temptation" to the nominal church of God, which will "*try* them that dwell upon the earth;"[2] or the same with that *ordeal* predicted by St. Paul in the words, "Every man's work shall be made manifest: for the day shall declare it, because it shall be revealed by fire: and *the fire* shall try every man's work of what sort it is. If any man's work *abide*, . . . he shall receive a reward. If any man's works shall be *burned*, he shall suffer loss: but he himself shall be saved, *yet so as by fire*."[3]

---

[1] Matt. xxiv. 21. Mark xiii. 19.   [2] Rev. iii. 10.   [3] 1 Cor. iii. 11-13.

CHAPTER VI.

[CONTINUED.]

SECTION IV.

THE PROPHETICO-HISTORIC EXPLOITS OF THE APOCALYPTIC EIGHTH HEAD AND HIS ANTICHRISTIAN CONFEDERACY.

I. *The first act* of the eighth head—Restoration of the Jews to their own land—Palestine—Its successive changes—Seven maps in illustration.

II. *His second act.*—Desecration of the temple, etc.

HAVING now shown, I., the custom of the ancient Hebrews, Greeks, and Romans, in keeping their accounts by the use of the *letters* of their alphabets instead of figures; and also that Christ himself and the apostle St. John adopted the same custom in the apocalypse; and having, II., demonstrated the *mystical* " mark, or name, or number" 666, as occurring in Rev. xiii. 16–18, points us to the apocalyptic EIGHTH HEAD of Rev. xvii. 11, and that this number, in the Hebrew, Greek, and Latin numeral figures, is found *in the name* of the present emperor of the Franco-Roman empire in all those languages, irrefragably proving thereby that he is the veritable predestined " Man of sin and son of perdition " predicted by St. Paul: we proceed in accordance with our plan, to furnish an exposition,

IV. *Of the prophetico-historic exploits* of this eighth apocalyptic head and his antichristian confederacy. We are now about to enter into and explore a field of scriptural exegesis, which may appear *new* to most of our readers. Let us not forget, however, that the great facts and truths of divine revelation are parabolically compared to " *a treasure hid in the field,*" which " treasure," in all its richness and fulness, is not to be found except at the cost of "*selling all* that a man hath," in order to "*buy* that field." Nor can we gain possession of it separate from the severest toil and perseverance. Some miners in a golden region, with pick-axe and spade in hand, having obtained *a few ingots* of the precious metal, but tiring in the way, may imagine that they have exhausted the field of their explorations, and abandon the work; while others, having entered the same region, undismayed by apparent obstacles, and digging far down below the surface, at length, to their great joy, strike the *principal vein* of the coveted ore, and their persevering toil is crowned with an abundant reward.

We are aware that this illustration, when applied to the subject in hand, may be thought invidious, and that it savors of self-adulation. *We* are not, however, responsible for either inference. We leave the facts to speak for themselves. Of this we are sure, that *all boasting* is excluded, for, to use the language of St. Paul, "Who maketh us to differ from another? And what have we that we have not received? And *if* we have received it why should we glory, as if we had not received it?"[1] This we know, that there are in the inexhaustible "treasury" of God's deeply "hidden mysteries of His will,"[2] "things" that are "*new*" as well as "*old;*"[3] not indeed that there are or can be any "things" *superadded* to those already given;[4] but, that those who seek "wisdom" as they "seek silver, and search for her as for hid treasures," shall "*understand* the fear of the Lord, and *find* the knowledge of God;"[5] and so, like unto a "scribe which is instructed unto the kingdom of heaven, shall bring forth out of his treasure things *new* and *old*."[6]

[1] 1 Cor. iv. 7. [2] 2 Eph. 1–9. [3] Matt. xiii. 52.
[4] See Rev. xxii. 18, 19. [5] Prov. ii. 1–5. [6] Matt. xiii. 52.

How far *we* may have succeeded in exhuming from this "treasure hid in the field," any of the "*new*," but ignored and long neglected "things" which God hath revealed for our "instruction in righteousness,"[1] we shall leave for the reader's candor to decide, in regard to those facts and truths which we are now about to submit to their reflections. They relate to, IVth,

THE PROPHETICO-HISTORIC EXPLOITS OF THE APOCALYPTIC EIGHTH HEAD AND HIS ANTICHRISTIAN CONFEDERACY.

Having already explained those prophecies which point out, first, the *agents*—the "ten horns" or "kings" of the Roman earth—who by their united act "give their power and strength and kingdom" to this eighth head; and second, his *inauguration* at their hands into "his seat, and power, and great authority;" and third, the "*gathering together* of the kings of the earth and of the world," by the wonder-working miraculous influences of the "three unclean frog spirits" or "spirits of devils," and their consolidation into the last antichristian confederacy, etc.; we now observe,

I. That the first act of this eighth head will be, *the restoration of God's covenant people, the Jews, to their own land.*

No subject occupies a more prominent place in the prophecies of the Old and New Testaments, than those which relate to the *future restoration* of Judah and Israel, or the ten tribes, to the land called CANAAN or PALESTINE, promised to their fathers. Before proceeding to an exhibit of this *first act* of the eighth head in their restoration, therefore, the importance of an historical acquaint-

[1] 2 Tim. iii. 16.

ance with the *changes* to which the Holy Land has been subjected, from its first occupancy to its final possession by the covenant seed of Abraham, will justify the space appropriated to a consideration of—

THE PREDICTED ENLARGEMENT AND NEW DIVISION OF THE PROMISED LAND AMONG THE TWELVE TRIBES OF ISRAEL, WHEN RESTORED.

This would seem very naturally to occur to a reflecting mind not only as possible and probable, but as necessarily arising from those changes to be produced by the *mundane convulsions* of various portions of the earth spoken of in Scripture. For example: The rending of Mount Olivet on the east of Jerusalem by an earthquake, removing one half of it toward the north, and the other half toward the south, with a very great valley between,[1] cannot fail to produce a total alteration in the topographical aspect of Palestine from what it now is. Indeed, the *design* of the covenant God of Israel in subjecting the land of promise to these and the like great physical revolutions, is, to verify to them the possession of it, in accordance with the geographical boundaries assigned to it in the stipulations of the compact originally made with their fathers, Abraham, and Isaac, and Jacob, but the *full extent* of which they have never yet enjoyed. Let us, then, take a view,

I. *Of the successive geographical developments of this remarkable country, from its earliest history down to the present time.*

1. Prior to Abraham's call to leave Ur of the Chaldees in Mesopotamia to repair to Canaan,[2] that country

---

[1] Zech. xiv. 4, 5.   [2] See Gen. chap. xii.

was occupied by the following HEATHEN NATIONS, viz., the Kenites, and the Kennizites, and the Kadmonites; the Hittites, the Perizzites, and the Rephaims; the Amorites, and the Canaanites, and the Girgashites, and the Jebusites."[1] Their respective localities are all laid down in the Scriptures of the Old and New Testaments, thus: —The *Kenites* were located westward of the Dead Sea, and extended their southern boundary into the confines of Arabia Petræa.[2] The *Kadmonites*, or eastern people (supposed to be the same with the Hivites[3]), occupied the northeast, south of Mount Lebanon, in Mispeh or Gilead. The *Hittites*, descendants of Heth, the second son of Canaan, dwelt in the south, near Hebron.[4] The *Perizzites* occupied the central parts of Canaan, scattered, more or less, among the other tribes.[5] The *Rephaims*, a race of giants, dwelt on the west of the Dead Sea, extending to the Mediterranean.[6] The *Amorites* were located both on the east and west of Jordan, and possessed the two powerful kingdoms of Sihon and Og, with others.[7] The *Canaanites* embraced some of the tribes of that name, which dwelt in the midland between the Mediterranean and the Dead Sea, and extended also toward the coast of Jordan eastward. The *Girgashites* (supposed to be the ancestors of the Girgasenes of the New Testament, Matt. viii. 28; Mark v. 1; Luke viii.

[1] Gen. xv. 19-21.
[2] Compare Exod. iii. 1, with Judg. i. 16; Numb. xxiv. 21; and 1 Sam. xv. 16.
[3] Numb. xiii. 20-22; Josh. ix. 1; xi. 3; Judg. iii. 3.
[4] Judg. i. 26; 2 Sam. xi. 6; 1 Kings vii. 6; xi. 1.
[5] Gen. xiii. 7; Josh. xvii. 15; Judg. i. 4; iii. 5; 1 Kings ix. 20, 21; 2 Chron. viii. 7; Ezra ix. 1.
[6] Josh. xv. 8; xviii. 5, 16-20; 2 Sam. v. 18, 22; xxiii. 13: 1 Chr. xi. 15; xvi. 9; Isa. xvii. 5. See also Gen. xiv. 5; xv. 20.
[7] Numb. xxi.-xxxii.; Deut. i. 44; Josh. xii.—xv.—xix.; Judg. vi. 10; 2 Kings xxi. 11; Amos ii. 9.

26) occupied the country directly north and east of the sea of Tiberias.¹ The *Kennizites* appear to have been located southeast of the Kenites.² And the *Jebusites* dwelt between the Mediterranean and the northern part of the Dead Sea, in the mountainous regions adjacent.³

(The opposite map will illustrate their respective localities.)

But, as we have said on a former occasion, these heathen tribes were reputed by Him " whose is the earth and the fulness thereof"⁴ as *intruders* into a territory which, in His divine purpose, had been selected as THE THEATRE for the display of his mighty wonders, through that people whom He should " choose to be his peculiar treasure above all the nations of the earth."⁵ Hence the call of Abram, in A. M. 2083, to leave his native country and kindred in Ur of the Chaldees, and repair to Canaan.⁶ Obedient to the Divine mandate, Abram " came forth " and " dwelt " for a while in " Haran." Thence he passed through the land by the way of Sichem, and came to " the plain of Moreh (and the Canaanite was then in the land). And the Lord appeared unto Abram, and said, *unto thy seed will I give this land.*"⁷ " Lift up thine eyes, and look from the place where thou art, northward, and southward, and eastward, and westward. For *all the land which thou seest*, to *thee* will I give it, and to *thy seed* for ever."⁸ But, upon the changing of his name from Abram to ABRAHAM, this covenant of God was *renewed* to him, and subsequently to Isaac and Ja-

---

¹ Josh. xxi. 11. See also Gen. x. 16.
² Josh. xv. 17 ; Judg. i. 13 ; iii. 9-11 ; 1 Chron. iv. 13 ; xxvii. 15.
³ Numb. xiii. 29 ; Judg. i. 21 ; 2 Sam. v-xxiv. 16 ; Zech. ix. 7.
⁴ Ps. xxiv. 1.   ⁵ Exod. xix. 5.   ⁶ Gen. xii. 1.
⁷ Gen. xi. 31, 32 ; xii. 6, 7.   ⁸ *Ibid.* xiii. 14, 15.

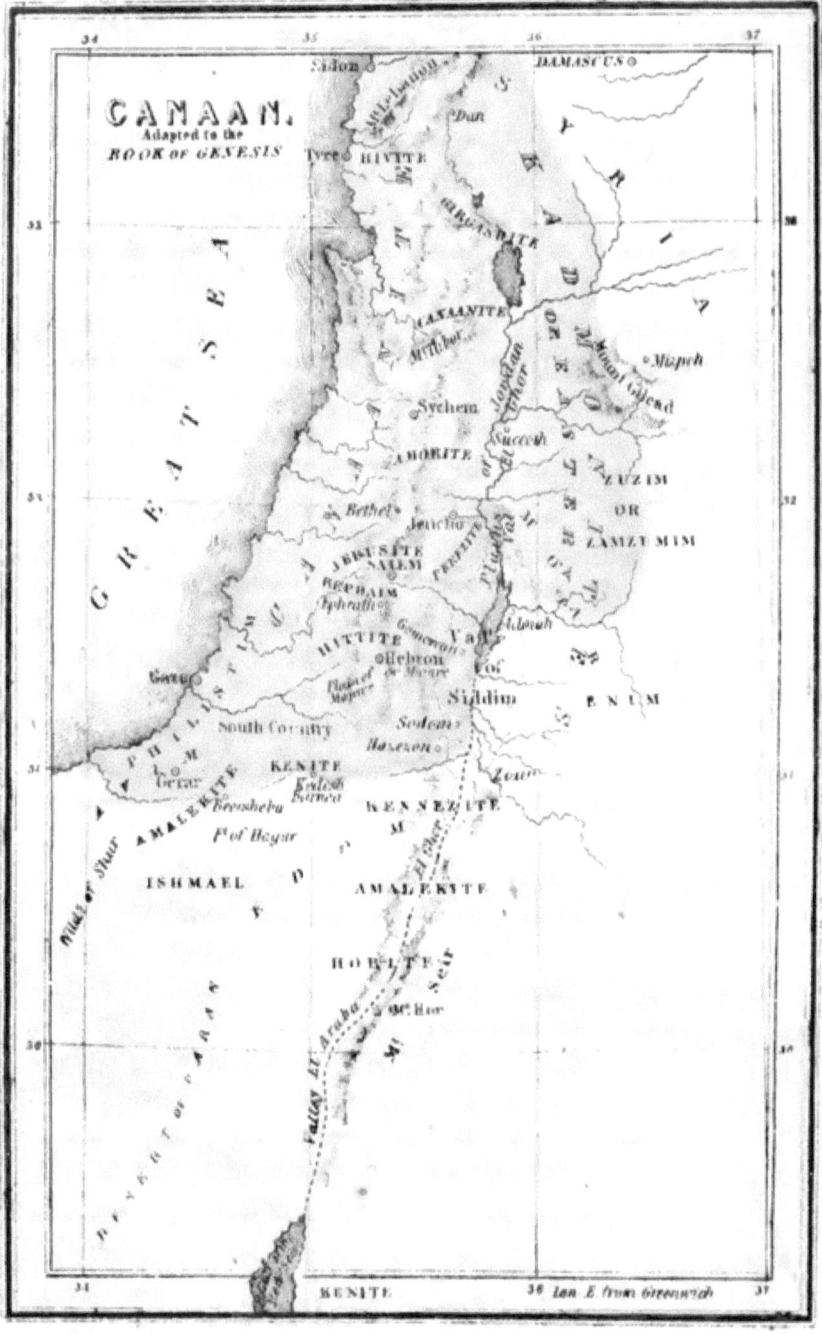

cob.¹ A period, however, of 470 years (including the 430 years of sojourn and bondage of his seed as "strangers" in Egypt, and the 40 years of wanderings in the wilderness after the exode), was to elapse,² *before* they were to enter into the possession of the promised land. The time having at length arrived, under their leader, Joshua, the successor of Moses, the Israelites crossed the Jordan, and entered into CANAAN. From this point, therefore, we are to take a view of the geographical extent of the Holy Land,

2. *From the time of Joshua*, in A. M. 2583, *to the end of the Judges*, in A. M. 3057. It is to be borne in mind, that the entire extent of the land of Canaan, as preoccupied by the heathen tribes above named, was bounded on the north by Mount Lebanon; on the west by the Mediterranean; on the east by the Desert of Arabia, and the land of the Ammonites, Moabites, and Midianites; and on the south by the land of Edom, and the wilderness of Paran, etc. It was about 200 miles in length from north to south, and about 80 miles from east to west; and lay between the 32d and 34th degrees of north latitude, and the 36th and 37th degrees of east longitude, from London.

Of this land, however, *in its full extent*, as we shall see, the Israelites were not to be put into immediate possession. As already stated, the Most High, having, for the purpose of His own glory, given the land in covenant to Abraham and his seed, issued the command, "And ye shall *dispossess* the inhabitants of the land, and dwell therein; *for I have given you the land to possess it.*"³ But he adds, concerning the nations to be ejected and destroyed, "I will not drive them out before thee in *one*

---

¹ Gen. xvii. 5-8; xxvi. 2, 3; xxviii. 13, 14.
² *Ibid.* xv. 7-16; Numb. xiv. 26-35.   ³ Numb. xxxiii. 53.

year, lest the land become desolate, and the beasts of the field multiply against thee. But *by little and little*, I will drive them out from before thee, until thou be increased and inherit the land."[1]

And now, Joshua, having received the Divine command "to *divide for an inheritance*" the whole land "from the wilderness, and this Lebanon, even unto the Great River, the river Euphrates, all the land of the Hittites, and unto the Great Sea,"[2] or Mediterranean; yet, although in his first expedition against its heathen intruders, he subdued all the southern part of the promised land, and in his second the northern, together with all his other extensive conquests, "there remained yet *very much land* to be possessed."[3] Five years were devoted to the division of the land by Joshua.[4]

(The opposite map, compared with No. I., will show the *exact correspondence* between the extent of the land *before* and *after* its division.)

After *the death* of Joshua, it was the great sin of Israel, that when they were able, they "*did not* utterly drive out" their enemies from the land, as they had been commanded. For this sin they were severely rebuked and chastised during the time of the Judges.[5] These conquests were reserved for *further completion* by David and Solomon.[6] Particularly under the reign of the latter king, there was a nearer approximation toward the securing of the *utmost* geographical boundaries stipulated in the original covenant compact. This may be gathered,

3. From a view of the geographical extent of Canaan

---

[1] Exod. xxiii. 29, 30.   [2] Josh. i. 4, 6.
[3] Josh. xii.–xiii. 1: 2–6; xi. 18.
[4] Compare Numb. xiv. 30, 33, 34; with Josh. xi. 18; and xiv. 10.
[5] Judg. i. 21–26; ii. 1–3.   [6] 2 Sam. viii. 3–14; 2 Chron. ix. 26.

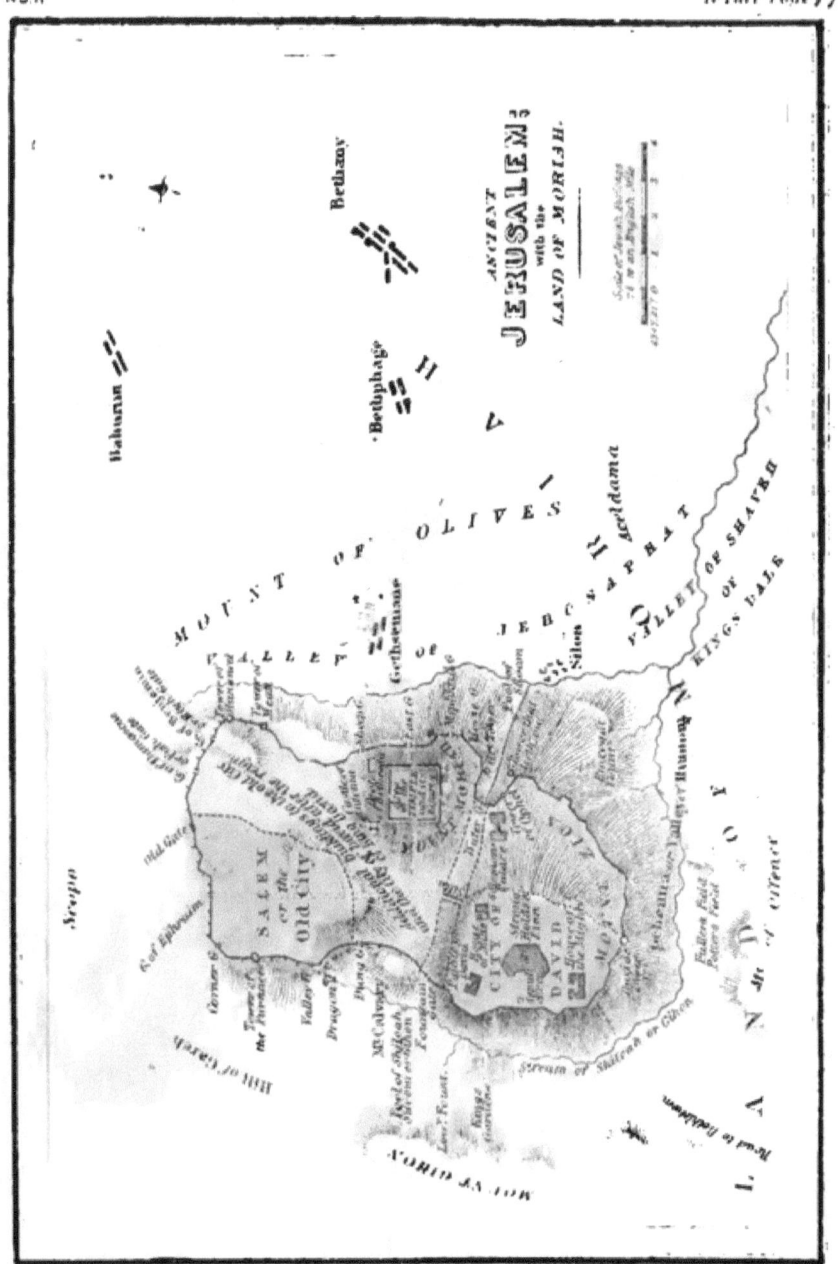

during the period of the Kings. Thus we read: "And Solomon reigned over all the kingdoms from the river (Euphrates) unto the land of the Philistines, and unto the border of Egypt . . . for he had dominion over all the region this side the river (Euphrates) from Tiphsah (or Thapsacus, situated thereon), even to Azzah, or Gaza, with her towns and villages, unto the river of Egypt (or the Nile) southward, and the Great Sea (the Mediterranean) westward,' even over all the kings on this side of the river,"[2] (Euphrates).

It is to be observed, however, that though the nations occupying the *adjacent countries* to the then possessions of Israel were *tributary* to David and Solomon; yet this was not their possessing the land according to the *original* grant, as promised by their covenant God. Nor did they invalidate the divine grant, in that they occupied *a part only* of the specified territory, and the subjection merely of others. Otherwise it could not be proved that the Lord had promised them any part of the land for *actual* possession. But Heaven stands pledged to Abraham, that unto his seed shall *the whole prescribed territory* be given.

(The accompanying maps will illustrate the geographical boundaries of the Holy Land, in three different aspects, viz., the first, *under the kings;* the second, *during the captivities;* and the third, as they were *in the time of Christ.* It will be seen at a glance, that they underwent no material change from that of their first arrangement, when occupied by the Canaanites.)

This event, however, is *still future.* It awaits,

4. *The enlargement* of the Holy Land, in accordance

[1] Josh. xv. 47.
[2] 1 Kings iv. 21-24. See also Horne's Introduction, etc. Vol. III. pp. 4-6.

with the *whole extent* of the boundaries prescribed by the original stipulations of the covenant. These extensive boundaries may be gathered from the following statements: First. When Abram dwelt in the plains of Mamre, "In that same day, the Lord made a covenant with him, saying, Unto thy seed have I given this land, *from the river of Egypt (the Nile), unto the Great River, the river Euphrates.*"[1] The "river of Egypt," or the Nile, as the boundary mark of the promised land in this passage, necessarily includes Idumea and the land of Goshen, north of the eastern branch of that river; while the allotment embraces also a considerable part of Syria, comprehending the whole territory from the Euphrates on the northeast, and the whole of Idumea to the Nile on the southwest. Again,

Second. After the giving of the law at Mount Sinai, saith the Lord, "*I will set from the Red Sea even unto the sea of the Philistines* and *from the desert unto the river*," etc.[2] As, by other specifications, we find that part of Stony Arabia included, which is embraced between the gulphs and the Red Sea, it is evident that the expression, "from the Red Sea even to the sea of the Philistines," points to the Elanitic Gulph on the southeast, and all west from it to the Mediterranean, or "sea of the Philistines." And so also the phrase, "from the desert to the river," gives us the desert of Egypt and Arabia,[3] through which the Israelites were just passing, as their southern boundary, from which, "the whole land unto the river," (Euphrates), is embraced in this important grant. This promise was again *renewed*, when Moses and the Israelites were in Horeb.[4] Now, Mount Horeb lay between

---
[1] Gen. xv. 13-31. [2] Exod. xxiii. 31.
[3] Gen. xvi. 7; Exod. xv. 22.
[4] Deut. i. 6-9. See also chap. xi. 22-24; Josh. i. 2-4.

the gulphs and the Red Sea, 140 miles *south* of what subsequently became the boundaries of the land as possessed by them; yet, in the wide range thus set before them, they are still called to go into all the places *even* "*in the south of Horeb*," which is situated only about 50 miles north of the most southern extremity of the peninsula. But,

Third. These boundaries, as laid down in Numb. xxxiv., taken in connection with others with which it corresponds in the parallel passage from Joshua, chap. xv., will tend to show in a clearer light the limits of the land in its full extent. It is here said, that the "*south quarter* shall be from the wilderness of Zin [southward, or leading toward the south, Josh. xv. 1,] and "along by the coast of Edom [or Idumea], which was the uttermost part of the south coast." And again. "And your south border shall be the outmost coast of the salt sea, eastward," or from the southeast corner of the Dead Sea. "And your border shall turn from the south to the ascent of Akrabbim," or the mountains of Accaba (Arabic, ascent), which run toward the head of the Elanitic or eastern gulf of the Red Sea. "And as for the *western border*, ye shall have the Great Sea," (or the Mediterranean), for a border."[1] "And this shall be your *north border:* from the Great Sea you shall point out Hor-ha-hor,"[2] (not "Mount Hor," as rendered in our English Bible, confounding it with that on the southern border, but) "the double mountain," or Mount Lebanon, which formed the northern frontier of Palestine, dividing it from Syria, and running eastward from the neighborhood of Sidon to Damascus. "And ye shall point out

---

[1] Numb. xxiv. 6.
[2] Compare also Numb. xxiv. 7; Josh. xiii. 5; Ezek. xlviii. 1.

your *east border* from Hazar-Enan to Shephan, and the coast shall go down to Riblah, on the east side of Ain: and the border shall descend, and shall reach unto the side of the sea of Chinneroth eastward. And the border shall go down to Jordan, and the goings out of it shall be at the salt sea: THIS SHALL BE YOUR LAND, WITH THE COASTS THEREOF ROUND ABOUT."

Such was the admirable geographical chart of the *original* land of promise, dictated by the covenant God of Abraham, Isaac, and Jacob, and described with so much precision by Moses, as an eye-witness of it. With a map before us, an ideal line drawn from the Mediterranean on the *west*, to Thapsachus on the Euphrates in the *east* (latitude 35 degrees 20 minutes north), will give the *northern* boundary; and on the south of Idumea, extend the view from Eziongeber along the shores of the Red Sea, including the various curvatures forming its gulphs, till the line reaches Suez (the Etham of Scripture, Exod. xii. 20; Numb. xxxiii. 6), and stretching over to Cairo, in lat. 30 deg. north, and long. 31 deg. 14 min. east (the Rameses of Scripture, Exod. xii. 37; Numb. xxxiii. 3), traverses the northern bank of the eastern branch of the Nile to the Mediterranean, which gives the *southern* boundary. The Mediterranean *north* from the river Nile, and *west* to the 37th degree north latitude, will give the *western* boundary. While the *eastern* boundary extends far beyond the east of Hazar-Enan, Shephan, Ain, the river Jordan, and the sea of Cinneroth and the Salt or Dead Sea. We now pass on,

II. *To the new division*, which awaits the above enlarged extent of the Holy Land among the twelve tribes. That the two houses of Israel and Judah, when restored to their own land and reunited into one nation, shall enter upon the possession of it *to the full extent* of the original promise, is most explicitly declared by Ezekiel, chap. xlvii. 13, 14. "Thus saith the Lord God; this shall be the border whereby ye shall inherit the land, according to *the twelve tribes* of Israel (Joseph shall have two parts). And ye shall inherit it, one with another; concerning which I lifted up mine hand to give it unto your fathers: *And this land shall fall to you for inheritance.*" The prophet then proceeds, verses 15–21, to give the *exact boundaries* of the land, which will be found to correspond with those given in the preceding articles. And then follows its *division* among the twelve tribes, in the closing chapter of his book. This division will be *totally different* from that made by Joshua. That division, as the most casual inspection of the map of Palestine adapted to his time will show,[1] was regulated by no regard to regularity or order. It was made evidently with a respect to what territory was from time to time *acquired*, and which could therefore be made available for occupancy by the different tribes. Indeed, its exceeding irregularity cannot but impress any mind with the conviction, *that it was not designed* to be permanent. And this is confirmed by the fact, that the new division is marked by the most distinct specifications in regard to the relative situations of the whole, *all running parallel* to each other in a straight line from east to west. These specifications are recorded in Ezek. chap. xlviii. verses 2–7, and 23–27. They will proceed in the following order: Beginning at the *north border*, they will mark out the portions of Dan, of Asher, of Naphthali, of Manasseh, of Ephraim, of Reuben, and of Judah. The prophet then describes another portion of the land called "the holy oblation," verses 8–22. Then follow the allotments

---

[1] See the map, page 174.

of the remaining tribes—of Benjamin, of Simeon, of Issachar, of Zebulun, and of Gad. The *regularity* of these new divisions of the land among the twelve tribes is so obvious, that further remark is unnecessary. We must, however, ask your indulgence for a further notice of that part of this new arrangement called,

"THE HOLY OBLATION." This is reserved as "*an offering unto the Lord.*" Its length is given at 25,000 reeds,[1] and its breadth 10,000, being the first half of that portion in the centre of which will be erected "the sanctuary," or *new temple*, according to the model of Ezekiel. The area of this sanctuary will cover a square of five hundred cubits, with an additional fifty cubits round about for the suburbs thereof.[2] (The opposite view will give an idea of the ground plan and internal arrangements of the various apartments in this new temple, and of their uses.) To this *first half* of "the holy oblation," is added another portion of the same dimensions, *i. e.*, 25,000 reeds in length by 10,000 in breadth.[3] Thus, "All the oblation shall be 25,000 by 25,000 (reeds) : ye shall offer the holy oblation four square, with the possession of *the city*."[4] Then further: "The holy portion of the land" adjoining "the border of Judah,"[5] besides that it embraces "an holy place for the sanctuary," it "shall be *for the priests*" also, "the ministers of the sanctuary, which shall come near to minister unto the Lord, and it shall be a place for *their houses*."[6] The other portion of the same size which joins "the border of the priests," "shall also *the Levites*, the ministers of the house," who formerly had no inheritance, "have for themselves, for a

---

[1] The reed being 6 cubits long (Ezek. xl. 5), or nearly 11 feet English.
[2] Ezek. xlv. 1-3 ; and xlviii. 8.   [3] Ib. verse 13.
[4] Ib. verse 20.   [5] Ib. xlviii. 8.
[6] Ezek. xlv. 4.

A VIEW OF THE GROUND WORK OF THE SANCTUARY

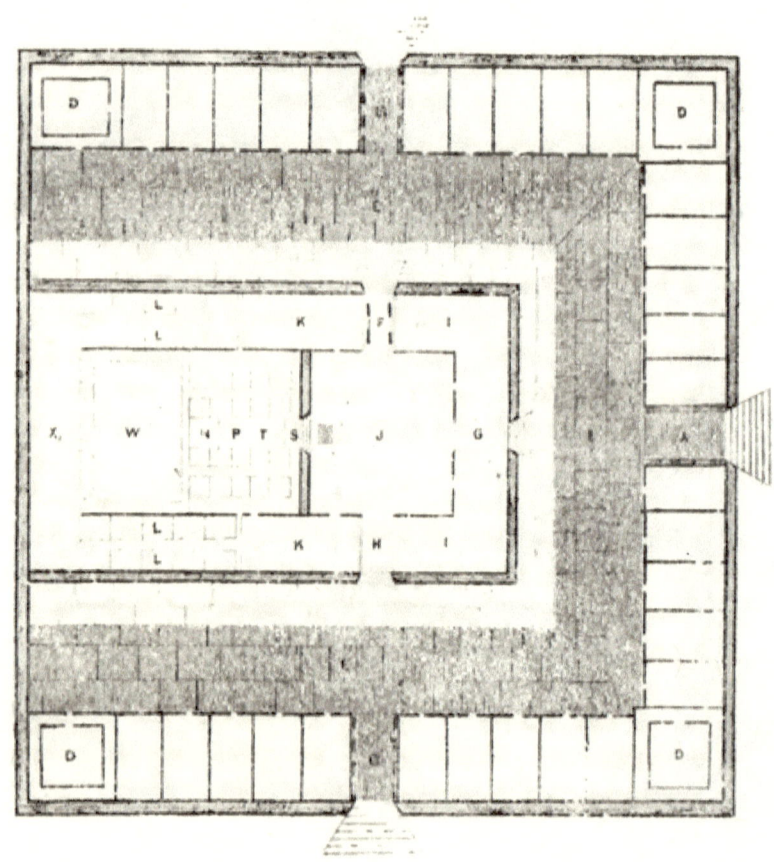

Which shall hereafter be built for Divine Worship by the twelve Tribes of Israel; with notes explanatory of the same.

EXPLANATORY NOTES.

A. East Gate of the Outer Court and Porch, with its Chambers.................... Ezek. ch. XL. 6—9.
B. North Gate .... " " 20—23.
C. South Gate .... " " 24—27.
D. Courts.. " XLVI. 21—24.
E. Paved Outer Courts, 100 cubits broad, with 30 Chambers round about......... " XL. 17—19.
F. North Porch of the inner court and tables. " " 35—43.
G. East Gate of the inner court and porch.... " " 32—34.
H. South Gate .... " " 28—31.
I. Singers' Chambers................................ " " 44
J. The Inner Court, with the Altar .... " XLIII. 13—27.
K. Priests' Chamber .... " XL. 45—46.
L. Holy Chambers and Walk between......... " XLII. 1—14.
M. Kitchen for the Priests .... " XLVI. 19—20.
N. Most Holy Place .... " XLI. 3—4.
P. Table before the Lord .... " " 22
S. Porch of the Temple .... " XL. 48—49.
T. The Temple or Holy Place................... " XLI. 1—2.
U. Side Chambers of the Temple, and Walk between. .... " " 5—11.
V. Wall, 90 cubits long and 5 thick, around the building.. " " 12
W. The building before the separate place, 70 cubits broad, 90 long....................... " " "
X. The Separate Place.

possession of *twenty chambers*."[1] Still, this leaves 5,000 reeds in width, over against the 25,000 from east to west, to complete the square of the oblation. It is supplied thus:—" And the 5,000 that are left in the breadth, etc., shall be *a profane place* for the city, for dwelling and for suburbs, and the city shall be in the midst thereof."[2] . . "And they that serve the city, shall serve it out of the tribes of Israel."[3]

These three compartments, therefore, into which "the holy oblation" is divided, consisting of *two* of 10,000 reeds each in breadth, and *one* of 5,000, all being of equal length, render it in whole a square of 50 miles.

And finally, the prophet, speaking of "*the residue in length*," *i. e.* the land which lay "over against the oblation of the holy portion," says, it "shall be 10,000 eastward, and 10,000 westward. . . And the increase thereof shall be *for food* to them that serve the city."[4]

(The accompanying map will illustrate the *original covenant boundaries* of the Holy Land, as already described, and also *the new division* of it among the twelve tribes of Israel, together with *the holy oblation*, etc., which occupies the central portion of it between the allotments of Judah on the north and of Benjamin on the south.)

Now, as we have said, the land of promise, as formerly possessed by Israel, was *very limited*, compared with that given to them in the *original* covenant compact. This will appear from one of the marks by which the new boundary on one side, viz., the east, is to be ascertained. The former boundary extended only to the *west side* of the river Jordan: "From the land of Israel to Jordan."[5] Whereas, when they shall enter into the

---

[1] Ezek. xlv. 5.   [2] Ib. xlviii. 15.   [3] Ib. verse 19.
[4] Ib. verse 18.   [5] Ib. xlvii. 18.

whole possession, the limits will extend *far east* of that river.

This, then, is the land to which Israel will be restored at the hand of the EIGHTH HEAD.

But it is here to be specially noted, that this restoration of the Jews will take place while they are still in their *nationally unconverted state, and under circumstances of great suffering.* Thus the prophet Ezekiel: "And the word of the Lord came unto me, saying, Son of man, the house of Israel" (or Judah, for so they are styled in several places) "is to me become dross: . . . and *because* ye are all become dross, I will gather you into the midst of Jerusalem . . . as into the midst of a furnace, *to blow fire upon it and to melt it*: So will I gather you in mine anger and in my fury . . . and I will leave you there, and will melt you. . . And ye shall know that I the Lord have poured out my fury upon you." [1]

We repeat: it is under these circumstances that the Jewish nation will be restored to the land promised to their fathers.

But, at whose *instigation* will the Jews be brought back to Palestine? Recalling to mind what we have said of their restoration in a nationally unconverted state, etc., we now return to consider, I. *The first act* of the apocalyptic eighth head in regard to them. LOUIS NAPOLEON III., having placed himself at the head of his antichristian hosts, the prophet Daniel tells us that he will enter into a "*league*"[2] with them, *to restore them to their own land*. This "league," however, he tells us, will be made with them as those who "*do wickedly against the covenant*,"[3]

---

[1] Ezek. xxii. 17-22. See also chap. xx. 33-38.
[2] Dan. xi. 23.   [3] Ib. verse 33.

etc., inasmuch as it will involve their continued rejection of Jesus as "the minister of the circumcision for the truth of God, to *confirm* the promises made unto their fathers."[1] And so, this eighth head, whom Daniel styles "*a vile person*," taking advantage of their eagerness to enter into a league with him for their restoration, "shall *corrupt them by flatteries*."[2] That is, he will guarantee to them a restoration to Palestine, *upon condition of their promised allegiance to him*, when he shall have "entered peaceably even upon the fattest places of the provinces," where he "shall do that which his fathers have not done, nor his father's fathers."[3] Nor this only. For, "*after* the league made with him, he shall *work deceitfully*,"[4] etc.

But, we must turn over to the prophet Hosea, for a more detailed account of this transaction. Having charged "*the priests and house of Israel*" that they "had dealt treacherously against the Lord," he says: "Now shall A MOUTH devour them, with their portion." Then he exclaims: "Blow ye the cornet in Gibeah, and the trumpet in Ramah: cry aloud at Beth-aven, after thee, O Benjamin. The princes of Judah were like them that remove the bound: therefore will I *pour out my wrath* upon them like water. . . I will be unto Ephraim as a moth, and to the house of Judah as rottenness,"[5] etc.

Now, these terrible denunciations are directed against Ephraim and Judah, at the time *immediately* prior to their restoration, the *manner* of effecting which, the prophet proceeds to describe in the following words: "When Ephraim saw his sickness, and Judah saw his wound, then went Ephraim to *the Assyrian*, and sent to *King Jareb: yet could he not heal you, nor cure you of your wound*,"[6] etc.

[1] Rom. xv. 8.   [2] Dan. xi. 33.   [3] Ib. verse 24.
[4] Ib. verse 23.   [5] Hosea v. 8–14.

The import of the above prophecy is simply this: that Ephraim, or those remaining fragments of the ten tribes who *returned* to Jerusalem in the time of Jeroboam I., and Judah, sensibly feeling their degraded condition, will devise a plan to *extricate* themselves. To this end, they apply to the King of "Assyria,"—the *antitypal* apocalyptic eighth head, vel LOUIS NAPOLEON III.,[1] as adumbrated by those cruel oppressors of Israel and Judah, the Assyrio-Babylonian King, Nebuchadnezzar, and his predecessors. This is confirmed by the historic fact, that the Assyrian monarchs exercised the prerogative to mediate in the settlements of all difficulties in reference to inferior and dependent powers, and to dictate the conditions with the authority of despots. This antitypal "Assyrian" grants their request, and this results in a *joint* "*league*," by which the Jews become INCORPORATED WITH HIS CONFEDERACY. But, although their covenant God leaves them to their own device to consummate their plans, yet He declares that this eighth head will *utterly fail* to restore them to national peace and prosperity, not only, but that HE from whom they have once more *turned away*, will execute the most terrible vengeance both upon them and their Assyrian ally.

We pass to another point in this connection. The prophet Isaiah calls upon "all the inhabitants of the world, and dwellers on the earth," thus: "See ye, when he lifteth up an ensign on the mountains; and when he bloweth

---

[1] We have recently received information from two well authenticated sources, that a deputation from the associated Jewish Society throughout Europe have been sent to the Emperor of the French, desiring him to issue a decree *for the restoration of the Jews to their own land;* but that his reply to them was, that though he would grant their request, yet that *the time* for it had not fully come, etc. In that he was right. The above edict must await his *transfer*, by the "ten kings," from his revived seventh to his eighth headship, which cannot be till after the close of A. D. 1868.

the trumpet, hear ye,"[1] etc. Now, *who is it*, that answers as the antecedent to the relative pronoun "HE," in this passage? The answer is, that it is none other than the apocalyptic EIGHTH HEAD, who, having made the "*league*" which guarantees to the Jews their restoration to Palestine, now lifts up his "*ensign*,"—that is, the "mark, name, or number of his name,"—and "*blows the trumpet*"—which is the edict issuing from THE "MOUTH" of him who "speaks as a dragon,"—to his antichristian confederated hosts and their allies; for the predicted time will then have come, when "*the present* shall be brought unto the Lord of hosts, of a people scattered and peeled, and from a people terrible from their beginning hitherto; a nation meted out and trodden under foot, whose land the rivers" —the typical Assyrians above alluded to—" have spoiled" in ages past, "to the place of the name of the Lord of Hosts, THE MOUNT ZION."[1]

And now, talk about the *political* and *moral* upheavings, and commotions, and revolutions which, like the underground earthquake commotions of terra firma, are convulsing all the time-worn dynasties of the old world, with their hoary-locked *ecclesiastical* institutions; why, they will dwindle into absolute insignificance, compared with the *effects* produced by the "lifting up of this ensign" to the nations by, and the issuing of this edict from the mouth of, this eighth head.

But, do the prophecies throw any light upon the AGENCIES *that are to be employed* in this ingathering of the unconverted Jews to Palestine? Let us see. We turn to the prophecy of Isaiah, chap. xviii. 1-3:—"Ho!" —mark here, not "*Wo to*," as in our English translation, but—"Ho! THE LAND OF OVERSHADOWING WINGS, which

---

[1] Isa. xviii. 7.

is beyond the rivers of Ethiopia: (or Cush): that sendeth ambassadors by the sea, even in vessels of bulrushes upon the waters, saying, Go, ye swift messengers, TO A PEOPLE," i. e., THE JEWS, "TERRIBLE FROM THE BEGINNING HITHERTO; a nation meted out and trodden down, whose land the *rivers* have spoiled. All ye inhabitants of the world, and dwellers on the earth, see ye, *when he lifteth up an ensign on the mountains; and when he bloweth a trumpet*, hear ye," [1] etc.

Now, the question here is, *to what nation or people*, occupying " the land of overshadowing wings," does this prophecy point us? Expositors have written much on this subject, only to "darken counsel by words without knowledge." Evidently, the metaphorical phraseology, "sendeth embassadors by the sea, even in vessels of bulrushes upon the waters," points to some GREAT MARITIME POWER. But, there are a number of such powers. How are we to determine *which one* is intended by this prophecy? This much we know. "That the ancient prophets designated different countries by metaphors, or by their national emblems or ensigns." For example. They spake of Babylon under the symbol of the *winged lion;* Medo-Persia of a *bear;* Greece of a *four-headed and four-winged leopard;* and Rome of a *non-descript beast*. Then also, Cyrus is symbolized by a *ram;* Alexander the Great, by a *he-goat;* and Rome, or the Roman army, by an *eagle*, etc. So, too, in modern times, we see the same thing. Turkey has her *crescent;* England has her *lion and unicorn;* Scotland her *thistle;* Ireland her *shamrock;* and, the United States of America, her *eagle*.

But, here are *two* nations, as we see, the Roman and the American, each having the *eagle* as their respective ensigns. Does the above prophecy give any clue by

[1] Isa. xviii. 2, 7.

which to determine which one is meant? It does, and that most emphatically. On the one hand, the ROMAN EAGLE is always represented as "perched up on high with *folded wings,* betokening its selfishness and self-complaisancy, with its piercing eye gazing on all around, and watching an opportunity to pounce upon and devour the hapless bird that might chance to come within its reach." Whereas, on the other hand, the AMERICAN EAGLE, with its outstretched or "*overshadowing wings,*" grasps with one foot the olive-branch, and with the other, the weapons of defence; the former betokening the emblem of *peace and welcome* to the agitated and oppressed nationalities of the old world; and the latter of *protection* to all who seek for repose under her expanded embrace.

This fact, therefore, taken in connection with the *locality* of this "land of overshadowing wings," viz., that it lies "beyond the rivers of Ethiopia," or Cush, and we must insist that it can refer to none other than to the UNITED STATES OF AMERICA! For, doubtless, by the "*rivers*" in this prophecy, we are to understand the Nile and other Ethiopian rivers which lay to the *west;* and as the prophecy points to "the land of overshadowing wings," and *not* to that of the lion and unicorn, or those of the thistle or shamrock, as laying "*beyond* these rivers," it can refer to none other than to the *northern* and *southern* continent of America!

Little, probably, did our forefathers think, when they adopted as their national insignia the eagle with outstretched wings, that they were giving birth to A MIGHTY MARITIME NATION spoken of by prophecy at least 2,500 years *before* the "Declaration of Independence of these United States!" For however England, at the present time, may bear away the palm in comparison with the maritime power of France, yet we ask,—and this fact will furnish additional evidence of the truth of the application of the above prophecy to these United States,—to *whom* are both England and France indebted for *all* that is really valuable in their floating craft, but to the preeminent genius of *the sons* of " the land of overshadowing wings, which sendeth ambassadors by the sea, even in vessels of bulrushes upon the waters ? " Besides, it is conceded on all hands, if we mistake not, that the United States, both in a commercial and naval point of view, commands the sea by a floating craft which, in number, quality, power, and swiftness, *outrivals* that of any other nation. And, though neither a prophet, nor the son of a prophet, we nevertheless express a strong conviction, as predicated of " the signs of the times," that this " land of overshadowing wings " is designed, in the purpose of God, to retain the preëminency she now holds over all other nations, in the field of new and more astounding modes of travel than the world has ever yet known.

In regard, then, to the agents that will be employed in the great maritime work of restoring the Jews to Palestine. Yielding all that may be justly claimed by France and England in this matter—and, in that *initiatory* process, as we have seen, France will take the lead—and hence, not intending to deny them a participation among " the ships of Tarshish " in conveying the Jews back to their long-alienated land ; yet we must nevertheless insist, that it is *principally* to this " land of overshadowing wings," to whom the command will be issued, " *Go ye swift messengers*, to a nation scattered and peeled ; to a nation terrible from their beginning hitherto ; a nation meted out and trodden down, whose land the rivers " (i. e., the Babylonian, Medo-Persian, Grecian, and Roman invaders of Palestine) " have spoiled,"—during the long period of the " seven times " or 2,520 years of their exile, as a "*present to be brought to the Lord of hosts in the mount Zion.*"[1]

Well. You are perhaps ready to ask, "Is this 'land of overshadowing wings'—this 'land of the star-spangled banner'—this 'land of the brave and home of the free,' to be *merged into* and *form a part of*, the last great democratico-atheistic confederacy of nations under this eighth head?" To this we reply, No.[2] Unlike Great Britain—including England, Scotland, and Ireland, all embraced under one crown,—

THE UNITED STATES OF AMERICA IS NOT ONE OF THE "TEN HORNS" OF THE TERRITORIAL ROMAN EARTH,

Whose "ten kings give their power, and strength, and kingdom to the beast."

We repeat: unlike Great Britain. This, of course, implies that Great Britain *is* one of the "ten horns" of the territorial Roman earth. We have heretofore assumed this as an historical fact. We are aware, however, that since the time of the Reformation, and especially under the crown of Edward VI. and of the martyrs, Cranmer, Latimer, and Ridley, it is alleged that Great Britain, having thrown off the Papal yoke, has been and still remains thoroughly Protestant. The question therefore turns upon the single point, whether Great Britain was originally a Protestant nation, but for a time subjected to the obedience of Rome; or whether, from the first, she was purely Romanized, and as such took her place among the "ten horns of the beast," and that, maugre her professed Protestantism, she still holds her position among them as such?

[1] Isa. xviii. 2, and verse 7.   [2] See pages 22–23 of this work.

Against this latter hypothesis, our minds, from long cherished associations with her character as a Protestant nation, are ready to recoil. We must, however, in this matter, as in others of a like nature, yield to the force of evidence. In this view, we beg to submit the historical facts following:

In the first place, we concede the fact of the early introduction of Christianity into the British isles. Tertullian of the second century says: that "all nations have believed . . . and those places of the *British isles*, which were unapproachable to the Romans, are altogether subject to Christ."[1] Bede also, speaking of the tenth persecution under the bloody Diocletian in the early part of IVth century, says: "At length it reached *Britain* also, and many persons, with the constancy of martyrs, died in the confession of their faith."[2] And so, Gildas, the earliest British historian whose works are preserved, says that "the sun of righteousness shone upon *this frozen isle* a little before the reign of Boadicea by the Roman legions, A. D. 61."[3] Gildas wrote about A. D. 560.

But, from the testimony of Churton, regarding the period between A. D. 303 and 314, it is more than doubtful if any Christian churches could be found in *England* at this time. He says: "In the time of Diocletian, it pleased the Almighty to permit the cause of the truth, for the space of ten years (A. D. 303 to 314), to undergo the severest trial which the world has ever known. Gildas, the earliest British historian, tells us that *at this time* the Christian churches throughout the world were leveled with the ground; all the copies of the Scriptures which could anywhere be found were burned in the public streets, and the priests and bishops of the Lord's house

---

[1] Adv. Jud. C. 7. [2] Bede, B. 1, c. 6.
[3] Gildas de Excid. Gent. Britannia, p. 9. Ed. Joss. Evan's Prim. Ages.

were slaughtered, together with their charge; so that in some provinces *not even a trace* of Christianity could be found.[1] Then, pursuing the track of history up to A. D. 426, although the Romans sent an army to assist the natives of *Britain* against the inroads of the Picts and Scots; and even admitting the exemption of that province from the fate of the others as just alluded to; yet, the *Saxons*, A. D. 449, possessed themselves of the eastern parts of the island, and, pushing on in savage war, drove great numbers of the Britons westward, *even into Wales*, where their posterity and language are preserved to the present day. Mr. Churton, in reference to these calamitous times, says: "It is impossible to find anything more disastrous than the *state of Britain* at this time. A famine had followed the ravages of the Picts and Scots; then arose a bloody war among the native chiefs and the Roman Britons; those who had lived with the Romans in their cities, [*i. e.* the *native* Britons], and learnt their language, were cut off *almost to a man*." . . . "From this time," he continues, " *Christianity began to disappear* from the most important and fruitful provinces of Britain. As the Saxons founded, one after another, their petty kingdoms, they *destroyed the Churches*, and *the priests fled before them*."[2]

Then again: even admitting the presence of a large number of *British bishops* at the council of Arles in A. D. 315, still it by no means follows, as is alleged, that they were *prelatical* bishops in an uninterrupted line of succession from (St. Paul or?) St. John, and that from them were derived the *English* succession of bishops. For, besides the incongruity of these statements, with the above historical facts from Churton, between A. D. 303 and

[1] Churton's Early Eng. Chh. p. 20.
[2] Churton's Early Eng. Chh. p. 32.

449; during the long interval that elapsed of 150 years, while some of the refugees from the persecutions under Diocletian found their way to *France*, and settled in that part " called Brittany (or Arles)—from which it received its name,"—Britain was now occupied by two peoples totally distinct in language, in religion, and in laws, viz., the *old Britons*, who, with their flocks, had fled to Wales, and the *Saxon* invaders of their once peaceful homes, all the latter of whom were enveloped in *heathen darkness*, and were engaged in the most rancorous hatred and " deadly wars " up to A. D. 596, *when Pope Gregory the Great sent* AUGUSTINE, *with other Romish monks, to convert the* SAXONS *to Christianity*. The source of his mission, its objects, the sphere of its operations, its character, and its results, each require a passing remark, in connection with the subject in hand.

And first : of *Gregory the Great*. In reference to the period of which we now speak, the once mighty empire of Rome was a mere wreck, forlorn and powerless. And yet, marvelous as it may seem, *at this very time*, the mind of Gregory conceived the gigantic project of making *Rome* the centre of an *universal spiritual kingdom*. It was the offspring of that ambition which often survives the wreck of fortune. The political state of the world, and the aspirations of ecclesiastics after " the preëminence," were maturing the way for the extension and establishment of the office of " universal bishop." This title, as conferred upon the Bishop of Rome, John II., by Justinian in A. D. 533, being subsequently ignored by the *eastern* church, it was now actually assumed by Gregory's cotemporary and rival, John, the patriarch of Constantinople, whose " strange and daring arrogance " Pope Gregory denounced as indicating " that the times of Antichrist were at hand."[1] And yet the Roman breviary tells us that Gregory "crushed the arrogance of John!"[2] Gibbon says of him, that "his virtues, and even his faults, a singular mixture of simplicity and cunning, of pride and humility, of sense and superstition, were happily suited to his station and the temper of the times. In his rival, the patriarch of Constantinople, he contemned the antichristian title of UNIVERSAL BISHOP, which the successor of St. Peter was too haughty to concede, and too feeble to assume."[3]

The *idea* of the conversion of the Saxons was conceived by Gregory before his election to the popedom. Bede[4] informs us, that being one day at Rome in the market-place, among other articles of merchandise exposed to sale were "some boys, their bodies white, their countenances beautiful, and their hair very fine." Having asked what was their country and their religion, he was told that they were "Pagans, from the island of *Britain*." . . . "He therefore asked again, what was the name of the nation?" And it was answered that they were called Angles. "Right," said he, "for they have an *angelic* face, and it becomes such to be co-heirs with the angels in heaven." "What is the name," proceeded he, "of the provinces from which they are brought?" It was replied, that the natives of that province were called Deira. "Truly are they *De irâ*," said he, "withdrawn from wrath and called to the mercy of Christ. How is

[1] Bede's Epist. Lib. IV., 78.
[2] Die XII. Martii. In festo Sanctii Gregorii.
[3] Gibbon's Decline and Fall.
[4] Called "the venerable Bede;" he was a monk, and, though a native historian of the eighth century, yet he paid unreserved obedience to the Pope of Rome; and so highly are his works esteemed by the Romish church, that they are referred to as evidence in the Catechism of the Council of Trent, and quoted for edification in the Roman breviary.

the king of that province called?" They told him his name was Ælla; and he, alluding to the name, said, "*allelujah*, the praise of God the Creator must be sung in those parts."[1]

Under these circumstances it was, that Gregory I., the alleged 64th Pope, in the apostolical line of succession from Peter, A. D. 596, "sent AUGUSTINE, with other monks, to preach to the English," or *Saxons*, the Pope having appointed that Augustine should "be consecrated *bishop*, in case they were received by the English."[2] The whole company, at first intimidated by fear of the fierce and barbarous character of the Saxons, and from their ignorance of their language returned home.[3] But "Augustine, being strengthened by the confirmation of the blessed Father Gregory, returned to the work of the word of God, with the servants of Christ," *i. e.*, the monks, about forty in number, "and arrived in *Britain*." They landed on "the large island of Thanet on the east of Kent," of which "ETHELBERT was at that time the most powerful king." Through "interpreters of the nation of the Franks," furnished "by the order of the blessed Pope Gregory,"[4] they were admitted to hold audience with the king, who, though at first influenced by a superstitious fear of an exposure to "magical arts," yet, "bearing a silver cross for a banner, and the image of our Lord and Savior painted on a board,"[5] "Augustine," says Bede, "by God's assistance, *supported with miracles*," (though not possessed of "the signs of an apostle," the miraculous gift of tongues), "reduced king Ethelbert and his nation from the worship of idols to the faith of Christ."[6] Bede then informs us, that the king "permitted them to reside

---

[1] Bede, Book II., c. 1. [2] Ib. Book I., c. 23.
[3] Ib. Book I., c. 23.   [4] Ib. c. 24.
[6] Ib.   [6] Ib. Book II., c. 3.

in CANTERBURY, which was the metropolis of all his dominions."[1] And from thence, Bede tells us, "Augustine sent Laurentius the priest, and Peter the monk, to Rome, to acquaint Pope Gregory that the nation of the English" (the Saxons) "had received the faith of Christ, and that he (*i. e.*, Augustine) was himself made their *bishop.*"

Thus, then, as it appears, AUGUSTINE was the *first Anglo-Saxon bishop* of Canterbury in York, of which he subsequently became the first *archbishop.* But the question is—was Augustine a *popish* or an *anti*-popish prelate? If the former, then it follows that the Anglo-Saxon church of GREAT BRITAIN, under the mission of Augustine, became one of the "*ten horns*" of the ecclesiastico-political papal beast. If the latter, then—as is alleged by those who *deny* the popish origin of Augustine's mission—it follows that Great Britain has "ever been legally and ecclesiastically *independent* of," the church of Rome.[2]

In support of this latter statement, it is affirmed that Augustine was consecrated by the Archbishops of *Arles* and of *Lyons* in Gall, (France,) and that "the Gallican churches derived their episcopate" according to "the ancients themselves," from St. John; and hence, that Augustine, being "the first Saxon bishop, as well as the first Archbishop of Canterbury," therefore, "the *English* bishops received their succession, *not*, as is often affirmed, from Rome, but from *Arles*,"[3] etc. But, were these Gallican Archbishops of Arles and Lyons *Protestants?* So far from it, even admitting that they derived their consecrations through the line of the bishops of Ephesus, as alleged to have been founded by St. John; yet, following the ecclesiastical records up to A. D. 533, by the edict of

---

[1] Bede, Book II., c. 3.   [2] Chapin's Primitive Church, p. 359.
[3] Chapin's Prim. Church, p. 392.

Justinian, as we have shown,[1] John II, the *Patriarch of Rome*, was constituted the UNIVERSAL HEAD OF ALL THE CHURCHES THROUGHOUT CHRISTENDOM, and hence, these *Gallican* bishops became subordinated to *his* authority. PAPAL FRANCE, is one of the " *ten horns* " of the " *Beast*." Gall and Lyons are *in* France, and are also PAPAL.

Then further: in addition to this fact, as we have seen, Augustine *derived his mission* for the conversion of the Anglo-Saxons from Gregory, Bishop of Rome. Accordingly, " in A. D. 598, he (Augustine) wrote to Gregory, *Bishop of Rome*, for advice touching certain points of inquiry. One of the questions was, in what manner he ought to deal with the bishops of Gall and Britain? . . . In answer, Gregory tells him, that he had *nothing to do* with the bishops of Gall, who were subject to the Bishop of *Arles* as their metropolitan; but, that he ought to have authority over the *British* bishops,"[2] etc. It is hence affirmed from this statement, that *there were* canonical and lawful bishops in Britain *before* Augustine went there;" and consequently that, " according to the existing canons of the church—the sixth canon of the council of Nice, A. D. 325," which enacts, "that the ancient customs and rights of the church should not be changed,"—" he (Augustine) owed allegiance to the metropolitan of *Britain*,"[3] etc. And in proof, it is alleged that there were *seven British bishops* who met Augustine in the conference held on the banks of the Severn. But if this be so, it follows inevitably, that Augustine, through whom, as the connecting link between the *Anglo-Saxon* succession and that of *Ephesus* through the lines of Lyons and Arles, and who is declared to be " the *first* Saxon bishop" and " the *first* Archbishop

---

[1] See pages 125-129 of this work. [2] Chapin's Prim. Church, p. 33.
[3] Ib. 360.

of Canterbury," (agreeably to the above canon,) was a SCHISMATICAL USURPER of the *preëxisting* "customs and rights" of the British church! What then becomes of the alleged *unbroken succession* of the English Protestant church!

But, no. For, on the one hand, while we are assured that "the earliest history of the *British church* has been involved in much obscurity, by the destruction of the records of that church;" and that "much doubt and uncertainty have been thrown over it, by the manner in which it has been treated by later monkish historians, to whom we are indebted for very much of the history of those times;"[1] yet, *authentic* history shows how much at variance with fact is the pretense of Augustine's *schismatical infringement* of "the customs and rights of the so-called preëxisting metropolitanship of the old British church. That *no such order* existed in that part of the dominion of Ethelbert, where Augustine was established as the Archbishop of Canterbury, is evident from the fact already alluded to, namely, that "the old British churches, existing *anterior* to the Anglo-Saxon invasion, had been *utterly swept* from North Britain." Mr. Churton says: "The *last British bishops*, Theonas of London, and Thadioc of York, retreated with the remnants of their flocks into *Wales*."[2] And, in regard to "the *number* of bishops in England" in the time of Augustine, the venerable Bede makes mention of *one*—"the Bishop of Luidhard, whom the pagan king, Ethelbert of Kent, had agreed (as the condition exacted by her parents) should accompany his wife, Bertha, a Christian lady of the royal family of the *Franks*, to preserve her faith,"[3] etc. Beyond this *one* bishop, therefore—and who with his royal *protege*

[1] Chapin's Prim. Church, p. 362.   [2] The Early Eng. Ch., p. 33.
[3] Bede, Book XXV., c. 25.

were of the *Romish* church—*there was none other in England* " at this time." And, as to those who met Augustine on the banks of the Severn, they were the *expatriated bishops of the old British churches*, existing *anterior* to the Anglo-Saxon invasion, and who, as already stated, fled for refuge, some to *Brittany* in France, and some to *Wales*. Bede informs us, that "the bishops, or doctors," whom Augustine, with the assistance of the converted king Ethelbert, drew together to confer with him at a place which is to this day called "Augustine's Ac" (Oak), were "of the *next province* of the Britains," etc., *i. e.*, *Wales*. The *object* of Augustine and the king in this conference with them was, to convert them over to the *Romish faith*. The *first* effort however having signally failed, a *second* conference was appointed, which brought together *seven* of the above expatriated bishops, and many of their most learned men from the monastery of Bancornaburg, or Bangor, over which the abbot Binooth, who bore a prominent part in the debate with Augustine, is said to have presided at that time.[1]

In regard, therefore, to *this particular period* of the history of these old expatriated British bishops who fled to Wales, it is by a confounding the two, or an identifying of the *English* succession with the *old British* churches, that it is sought to sustain the presence of "at least *one* archbishop, and *seven* bishops in England, when Augustine landed there." In support of this hypothesis, it is further urged that the alleged "arch-episcopate of *Caerleon*," to which these bishops belonged, was identical with what is claimed to have been "the *Anglo-Saxon* portion of it" in Kent, England, "when Augus-

[1] Bede. See also Chapin's Prim. Chh., p. 361.

tine landed there." But we ask: what "*portion*" of the old "British church" could that have been, when Mr. Churton tells us, that "the *last British bishops*, Theonás of London and Thadioc of York, retreated with the remnants of their flock, into *Wales?*" and that, as another writer states, *six years before* the conference between Augustine and Dinooth, they having fixed their seats at "Kaerleon ar Wye—*Caerleon upon Wiske*."[1]

But, even granting that there *was* a "portion" of the old British church in Kent "when Augustine landed there." It is nevertheless an historical fact, that, though at first they "practically denied at the very outset, the supremacy of the Pope, as it is now claimed;" yet we are assured that "the *Anglo-Saxon* portion of it" was "converted by missionaries *from Rome*."[2] And who, pray, were these missionaries, but AUGUSTINE and his forty monks? Aye, and their Romish conversion *followed* that denial of the Papal supremacy which they at first made; for what sort of conversion can that be, against which the mind rises up in revolt "*from the very outset?*" It is clear, therefore, that this "portion" of the BRITISH CHURCH, whether large or small, became ROMAN.

The *manner* in which this was brought about may be gathered from the following: This triumph of the "missionaries from Rome" was occasioned on the one hand by Wilfred's refusal, on the appointment to his bishopric of York, to receive consecration at the hands of the *Scottish bishops* of Lindisfarn or Durham, and Litchfield, and his repairing to *Paris*, where he obtained it from Agilbert, the archbishop; and on the other, from the *re-ordination* of Chad, at the instigation of Theodore, he having

[1] Chapin's Prim. Chh., p. 861, note.   [2] Ib. p. 371.

been previously ordained bishop of York, on which occasion *two Welsh bishops* were present and assisted."[1] These bishops were of that class of the old British bishops of *Wales*, whom, on the banks of the Severn, Augustine failed at the *first conference* to subdue to the obedience of the Roman see, which did not transpire till about A. D. 668, as above stated.

And finally, as to the *agency* employed by Rome in the accomplishment of this work, it was on this wise. In reply to their *second* refusal to comply with Augustine's demands, "that they would do none of those things, nor receive him as their archbishop," Bede reports him " in a violent manner to have foretold, that in case they would not join in unity with their brethren, they should be *warred upon* by their enemies; and if they would not preach the way of life to the English nation, they should *at their hands undergo the vengeance of death*. All which, through the dispensation of the divine judgment, *fell out exactly as he had predicted*."[2]

Yea, verily. For, " under Theodore and Wilfred, the *Welch* Christians were not even allowed to receive the Sacrament with the *English*, unless they *conformed*." Bede relates, that at one time " there were slain of them who came to pray (Presbyters) about 1,200 men, and only 50 escaped by flight."[3]

Thus, says Mr. Churton, speaking of Theodore, " he found the church (*English*) divided, he left it united; he found it a missionary church, scarcely fixed in more than two principal provinces; he left it—what it ever will be while the country remains in happiness and freedom—

---

[1] Churton's Early Eng. Chh. pp. 75-86.   [2] Bede, Book II. c. 2.
[3] Bede, Ib.

THE ESTABLISHED CHURCH OF ENGLAND."[1] From the above facts, therefore, it appears,

1. That AUGUSTINE, by whom, under the auspices of Pope Gregory, the *Saxons* were converted to the *Roman faith*, was by him appointed the *first Saxon bishop*, and the *first archbishop of* CANTERBURY, his consecration having been received at the hands of the *papal* archbishops of Lyons and Arles.

2. That Augustine *was not* a USURPER of the preexisting " customs and rights " of the *British* church.

3. That GREAT BRITAIN, having been " *at the very outset*," reduced to the obedience of the *Roman* church, was thereby constituted *one of the* " *ten horns* " of the Papal " beast." And,

4. As it is admitted on all hands, that " the Church of England as by law established," derived her alleged *unbroken* succession of bishops in a direct line from the Canterberian archiepiscopate of AUGUSTINE; it follows that, maugre her professed Protestantism, she has *never lost her position* as one of the " ten horns " of the Roman beast.

Like his predecessors from Leo X. in the time of Henry VIII., Pio Nono, the present reigning pontiff, so far from having *relinquished* his claim to her as such, has seized upon and holds her, as one of the brightest gems which adorns his triple crown. The church of Rome has ever looked upon her simply as guilty of *schism;* and " schism " consists of a rupture " IN the body,"[2] not of severance *from* it. And, though *excommunicated* by the Papal bull of Leo X., yet excommunication implies possible submission and *restoration*. This restoration the Church of Rome claims to have already

---

[1] Churton's Early Eng. Chh. pp. 75, 76. [2] 1 Cor. xii. 25.

virtually achieved. For this, "the Church of England as by law established,"—though partaking largely of the *Protestant* element of the Reformation, yet—having retained in her Ritualism so much of the leaven of the *Romish* missal, she is indebted to herself. The Romeward tendencies thence resulting is seen in the developments of the virus of *Tractarianism*, which, like a sinew of "iron and brass," binds her to her *original* sphere, as one of the "ten horns" of papal Rome.

And, in regard to the *political* and *moral* character of the British nation, one of her own writers, in speaking of her, says:

"We repeat, once more, that this country is, at this moment, *the most guilty of the whole world.* That our Indian wars have been massacres more bloody than the massacre of St. Bartholomew; that our opium-poisoning in China is, with one exception, the greatest crime ever committed by the human race; that we persist in these enormities from year to year, until our hearts are hardened beyond remedy; that we, alone, maintain the Mahommedan empire of Turkey, and we alone, have set up the crescent and trampled on the cross; that these dreadful sins must have a dreadful end, and that the least we can expect is, *the humiliation* of the British empire, as a commutation of sentence, in place of the *humiliation* of the British name; and that we shall never be a prosperous, happy, or Christian nation, until we are stript of every atom of our ill-gotten spoil. Until then, the day of the Lord will be against *us*, as against all iniquity."

. . "A haughty spirit is before a fall;" but "before *honor* is *humility*." [1]

The following satire from the same pen is placed in

---

[1] Purdon on "The Last Vials," March 1st, 1862, pp. 11, 12.

juxtaposition with the *political* and *moral* characteristics and acts of Napoleon III.

"But what *we* at least ought most to admire, is the moral and religious excellence of this man. We are, as every one knows, the best of nations—the most moral, upright, and pious. We have never yet committed a fault, except in that unfortunate invasion of Affganistan. That was the Uriah case of the modern David. And is not the Emperor Napoleon following our example? Shall not *he* make false pretenses as well as we? Shall not *he* rob other nations as we have robbed the East? Shall not *he* provoke men to quarrels, and then kill them by thousands because they have been provoked? Shall we enjoy the luxury of slaughtering 80,000 Hindoos in one year, from love to the Gospel, and not indulge *him* with a little carnage from love to something else? This would be most unreasonable indeed. Shall *we* poison the souls and bodies of 400,000 Chinese every year, with opium, and not allow the *Emperor* to destroy a tenth part as many by any other process he pleases? It is true that *he* is not so bad as WE! He does not destroy *one tenth* as many lives—but still he does his best, and we must make allowance for the timidity of young beginners. It is not every man who has had so long an apprenticeship in robbery, poisoning, and hypocrisy, as the British nation has enjoyed. But our good example will not be thrown away, and in the mean time let us not discourage our weak but willing *imitator*."[1]

No. It will be found ere long, that the "example" of the British nation "*will not be thrown away.*" Let the reader but fix his eye on those "coming events which cast their shadows before;" especially in connection

---

[1] Purdon on "The Last Vials," March 1st, 1862, pp. 14, 15.

with the events of the year 1866 and 1867. He will find *within* that interval, that the British nation will *acknowledge* herself to be one of the "ten horns" of the Roman beast; and he will find, *immediately after* the close of A. D. 1868, her *recognition*, willingly or unwillingly, of the HEADSHIP of Louis Napoleon III. over "THE UNIVERSAL LATIN EMPIRE."

On the other hand, in regard to this "land of overshadowing wings," *alias*, THE UNITED STATES OF AMERICA. Founded upon the principle of a universal toleration of all religions, we are "*a church without a bishop and a state without a king.*" The principles of our Protestantism flowed down to us through *another channel* than that of Rome. Far back in the annals of the past, the *source* whence has flowed, in unbroken continuity, the stream of primitive Christianity in contrast with its Romish perversions, must be sought for in those ancient dwellers among the Cottian mountains of the Alps, called the VAUDOIS, or WALDENSES, the faithful remnants of whom are to this day to be found in the valleys of Piedmont, whom neither the fire nor sword of Papal persecutions have ever succeeded either to subdue or exterminate. The same uncorrupt stream was transmitted from them through the ALBIGENSIAN and BOHEMIAN Protestants against the corruptions of Rome, until at length it diffused its healing waters over large portions of *continental Europe*, while it extended its hallowed influences to *England* also, whence the rise of the WICKLIFFITES or LOLLARDS. But there is a marked difference to be observed in those characteristics which distinguish the continental from the Anglican Reformations. The former consisted in a *throwing off* and a *total separation from* the long protracted dominancy and prevalent corruptions of the Church of Rome. Hence, however they may be reputed as *separatists*, they cannot in consistency be denominated *schismatics*. Hence, too, those English *non-conformists*, when driven by persecution from their fatherland to seek for shelter on AMERICAN soil landed on Plymouth Rock, planted those seeds of *civil and religious liberty* which, according to the " voice of prophecy," was to give birth to this " LAND OF OVERSHADOWING WINGS." It is these antagonistic principles to the despotic and monarchical systems of the Old World, both in church and state—so indelibly stereotyped in the " Constitution of these United States,"—that renders her at once the object of the hate and the dread of the crowned heads of Europe, and particularly those of France, Austria, and England. Save the *Jewish* nation, there is none other under the wide heavens, which, within the same short period, has been signalized by such national strides; and, with the above exception, none other that is destined to so glorious a future.

Nevertheless, it becomes us, in deep humility, to confess before God that *we are a sinful nation, laden with iniquity.* Blest of the Most High as no other Gentile nation has been blest, we have " despised the riches of God's goodness, and forbearance, and long-suffering ; not knowing that *the goodness of God* leadeth to repentance."[1] May we not, therefore, reasonably fear that we shall be called again to "*pass under the rod*" of Divine chastisement ? And, so, coming down to our own times, and resuming the subject of previous remark ; from the widely-diffused *influences* of the miracle-working wonders of the " three unclean frog spirits," or " spirits of devils," who go forth to " *deceive* " not only the " ten kings " of the Roman earth, but also of " the whole world," other

[1] Rom. ii. 4.

nationalities, *not* of the "ten horns," will become *allies* to this eighth head, and of which OURS, unless we repent, will be one. On the other hand, the unconverted Jewish nation, when first restored, though *not* one of the "ten horns," will not only be *absorbed into*, and form *a part of*, that great antichristian confederacy, but they will HAIL THIS EIGHTH HEAD AS THEIR MESSIAH!

But you doubt—you hesitate. The very suggestion even of such eventualities is so astounding—and especially to those who look into the Bible as they look into an old counting-room waste-book or ledger—that you are ready to pronounce it improbable, not only, but impossible. Let me then say that, as it respects *our own* country, while blest with equal light, and with far greater advantages for good than any one or indeed all nations beside, yet it is undeniable that, partaking with them of that moral depravity common to fallen creaturehood, we are at the same time subject to the influence of that *same leaven of antichristianism in all its forms*, national, political, civil, social, and religious, though not of so *rancorous* characteristics, as that of the nations of the Old World. Who, then, will venture to affirm the impossibility, in view of these facts, that this "land of overshadowing wings" *will not form an alliance* with this apocalyptic eighth head, for the purposes above specified?

And as to the other statement, that the *Jews*, when restored in their unconverted state, will hail this eighth head as their Messiah, what will this be, we ask, but a *literal* verification on their part, of that notable prophecy of our Lord respecting them as a nation,—"*I* am come in my *Father's name*, and ye RECEIVE ME NOT: if another shall come *in his own name*,"—*i. e.*, with the "mark, or name, or number of the beast," already explained, "HIM YE WILL RECEIVE." We appeal then, from what *you* know of the antecedents and existing characteristics, political and moral, of that world-renowned "pacificator" and draconic-mouthed dictator of all the crowned heads of Europe, the present reigning emperor of France ; who can say that, when, having passed from his *revived seventh* to his EIGHTH headship, and exhibiting before them " all the power and signs and lying wonders," with all the "deceivableness of unrighteousness" of the LAST ANTICHRIST, the Jews *will not* " receive him " AS THEIR MESSIAH ? True, when Jesus was upon earth, and claimed to be the veritable " KING OF ISRAEL," that was to " Sit upon the throne of His Father David," the Jewish nation demanded of Him, " Show us a *sign* from heaven that we may believe." And " SIGNS " the most marvellous, stupendous, and unprecedented, such as healing the sick, giving limbs to the maimed, eyes to the blind, ears to the deaf, tongues to the dumb, the casting out of devils, stilling the boisterous waves of the sea, yea, and raising the very dead to life, were *continually* wrought before them. And yet, " HIM they received not ! " Wherefore ? Ah, the manger at Bethlehem as His birth-place ; His being the reputed son of an humble carpenter ; and being so poor that He had not where to lay His head, with them *eclipsed* all these evidences of His Messiahship, and they rejected and crucified Him as an impostor ! But, how changed the scene, when this EIGHTH HEAD shall have stept upon the stage ! With a *prestige* which inheres in no other one man ; attended with those gorgeous and captivating trappings unparalleled in the history of earthly potentates ; and, as Daniel says, " shall have power over the treasures of silver and gold." [1] etc. ; and withal, " shall do great wonders, so that he *maketh fire come down*

---

[1] Dan. xi. 43.

from heaven on the earth in the sight of men, in attestation of his mission; ah, who, we repeat, will affirm that, under such circumstances between the two claimants, the TRUE and the FALSE, the Jews *will not* hail Napoleon III. as their MESSIAH?

Well. Let us now suppose the Jews to have been restored, and to have placed themselves *under the rule* of their false Messiah. What then? We must here premise by the way, that, besides that the JEWS can boast of numbering among their race many of the most renowned scholars in every country whither they are scattered, and who exert a powerful influence in the diplomatic, professional, literary, commercial, and other departments of state; they are also the *wealthiest* of any other nation in the world. Indeed, it is doubtful whether at this time there is a single cabinet of all the crowned heads of Europe, which is not in one way or other, held in surveillance by those mammoth bankers, the Jewish millionaire Rothschilds of France. Hence, having once reached their destination, from their undying love to their covenant soil, each will emulate the other in *wiping out* the last vestiges of those footprints of the destroyers from among the Gentiles who have so long laid it waste. "For I will cause to return *the captivity of the land* as at the first, saith the Lord. Thus saith the Lord of hosts: again in this place, which is desolate, without man and without beast, and in all the cities thereof, *shall be an habitation* of shepherds causing the flocks to lie down,"[1] etc. Nor this only. For, "Behold, the days come, saith the Lord, that THE CITY," *i. e.* JERUSALEM, "shall be built to the Lord, from the tower of Hananeel unto the gate of the corner,"[2] etc. And, this rebuilding of "the Holy City,"

---

[1] 1 Jer. xxxiii. 11-13. [2] Ib. xxxi. 13.

will include THE RE-ERECTION OF THE TEMPLE after the model prescribed by the prophet Ezekiel, (see Ezek. xli—xlii.), which in its dimensions, costliness, and magnificence, will incomparably surpass those of either Solomon, Zerubbabel, or Herod.

And so, the restored commonwealth of " the house of Judah " will speedily rise to national and political distinction in the earth. But mark : this will all transpire while the Jews are yet *in* " *league* " with their false Messiah. Accordingly, the prophet Ezekiel, referring to this very period, says : " And the word of the Lord came unto me, saying, Son of man, say unto her, 'Thou art the land that *is not cleansed,* nor rained upon in the day of indignation. There is *a conspiracy of her prophets* in the midst thereof, like a roaring lion ravening for prey. . . . *Her priests* have violated my laws, and have profaned my holy things: . . . *Her princes* in the midst thereof are like wolves ravening for the prey, to shed blood, and to destroy souls, to get dishonest gain. And *her prophets* have daubed them with untempered mortar, seeing vanity, and divining lies unto them, saying, Thus saith the Lord God : and the Lord hath not spoken. *The people* of the land have used oppression, and exercised robbery, and have vexed the poor and the needy ; yea, they have oppressed the stranger wrongfully."[1] And no marvel this, when we consider that they have placed themselves under the iron rule, and are influenced by the *example* of him who, having come to them " in his own name," has come " *after the working of Satan,* with all power and signs and lying wonders."

But, the Jews will not yet have reached the *climax* of their national sins. This is to be gathered from the

---

[1] 1 Ezek. xxii. 23-30.

following: "And thou shalt say to the rebellious, even to the house of Israel, (or Judah), Thus saith the Lord God, O ye house of Israel, let it suffice you of all your abominations; in that ye have brought into my *sanctuary*,"—*i. e.* into their newly erected temple—"*strangers, uncircumcised in heart,* and *uncircumcised in flesh,* to be in my sanctuary, to pollute it, even my house, when ye offer my bread, the fat and the blood, and they have *broken my covenant,* because of all *your* abominations."[1] By this we are to understand, that upon the rebuilding of the temple in Jerusalem, the ORDINANCE OF SACRIFICES, etc., shall be restored for the people, and the priests and Levites, as aforetime, shall stand to *minister* before them.[2] Now God commanded that these offices should be filled by "the sons of *Zadok*, of the tribe of *Levi*."[3] But, instead of this, and as a consequence of their compliance with the conditions stipulated in their "league" with their false Messiah, it opens up the way for,

II. His *second act* in this tragical drama. For, we read that, as the last Antichrist, "who shall oppose and exalt himself above all that is called God, or that is worshipped," he as God, shall seat himself *in the temple of God,* showing himself that he *is God.*"[4] And therefore, as such, he will proceed to select his priests, etc., *not* from the legitimate and divinely appointed "sons of Zadok," but from his Gentile confederates, "*strangers*," like himself, "*uncircumcised* both in heart and in the flesh!"

And now see: *on account* of these and the like "abominations" of the restored Jews, their covenant God brings upon the nation, Jeremiah's and Daniel's predicted time of "Jacob's trouble,"[5] or that season of UN-

---

[1] 1 Ezek. xliv. 6, 7. [2] Ib., verses 10–16.
[3] Ib., verse 15. [4] 2 Thess. ii. 3, 4.
[5] 1 Jer. xxxi. 7; Dan. xii. 1,

PARALLELED "TRIBULATION" spoken of by our Lord, "Such as was not since the beginning of the creation which God created to that time, nor ever shall be."[1] Yes, they will *once more* be brought " to pass under the rod "[2] of God's chastising hand. For, " He will gather them in the midst of Jerusalem ; " . . . and " He will blow upon them in the fury of his wrath, and they shall be melted in the midst thereof, as silver in the midst of a furnace," etc.

Now, this fearful visitation of the Lord's wrath upon the Jews as figuratively portrayed in the above prophecy, as we shall show, will be *literally* verified to them at the hand of that very false Messiah, who had " corrupted them by flatteries " to enter into a " league " with him. It will be on this wise. We read, Dan. xi. 23, that " *after* the league made with them, " he shall work *deceitfully*." Aye, still practising the same deeply mysterious, cunning, deceitful, and treacherous policy *then*, as that which has thus far marked his diplomatic career as the revived seventh *secular* head of the Franco-Roman empire ; the Jews, having at length discovered by their bitter experience the " *deceitfulness* " of him with whom they had entered into a "league" for their protection, and horrified at the *desecration* of their temple by his blaspheming footsteps, together with that of their God-appointed priesthood and rites; with one voice they will exclaim, " *My leanness, my leanness, woe is me!* the treacherous dealers have dealt treacherously : yea, the treacherous dealers have dealt very treacherously." And, under the deep conviction withal that Louis Napoleon III., as the eighth apocalyptic head is THE ANTICHRIST, they will rise

---

[1] Matt. xxiv. 21; Mark xiii. 19; Luke xxi. 25, 26.
[2] Ezek. xx. 36, 37.

up as one man IN OPEN REVOLT against him and his atheistic Gentile confederates!

We are now approaching *the end* of these prophetico-historic expositions. The above-named revolt of the Jewish Nation against Napoleon III., although at first not cognizant of the purpose of God in regard to it, will be found to initiate those *last acts* in this connection, with which these prophetical revelations close.

The subject will conclude with our next chapter.

CHAPTER VI.

[CONCLUDED.]

SECTION V.

CONTINUATION OF THE PROPHETICO-HISTORIC EXPLOITS OF THE APOCALYPTIC EIGHTH HEAD AND HIS ANTICHRISTIAN CONFEDERACY.

> III. His *third act.*—Invasion of the Holy Land, and its capital, Jerusalem.—IV. His *final doom,* with that of his Magogian confederacy.—Conclusion.

THE close of the preceding section left the Jewish nation in *open revolt* against the blasphemy and treachery of their false Messiah. This revolt introduces upon the prophetical platform the next act of this despot,

III. *His invasion of the Holy Land and its capital, Jerusalem.* Daniel's "wilful king," *alias,* the last Antichrist, having "planted the tabernacle of his palaces between the seas in the glorious holy mountain,"[1] being in-

---

[1] Dan. xi. 36-45.

cited by emotions of jealousy at the rising greatness and prosperity of the Jewish commonwealth, and of indignation at their revolt against his authority, resolves to marshal his confederated hosts,—the *Gog* and *Magog* army of Ezekiel,[1]—with a view to invade the Holy Land, bury its capital in ruins, and to totally annihilate the Jewish race. This will be his " going forth unto the kings of the earth and of the whole world, *to gather them to the battle of the great day of God Almighty*," mentioned Rev. xvi. 14 ; and it is the same with the Lord's " gathering all nations against Jerusalem to battle," of which the prophet Zechariah speaks, chap. xiv. 1, 2. This mighty confederacy of the antichristian nations will be constituted, principally, as we have said, of the kingdoms or principalities of the " ten horns " or " kings " of the *Latin earth*,[2] but will also embrace as its *allies*, those nations enumerated by the prophet Ezekiel, chap. xxxviii. 1–7 :—" Gog of the land of Magog, the prince of Rosh, Mesech, and Tubal ; and Persia, Ethiopia or Cush, Libya or Phut, Gomer and Togarmah," etc.

We must here observe, by the way, that the reader will do well to compare Ezek. chapters xxxiv. 17–21 ; xxxviii. 1–17 ; and xxxix. 1–24, on this subject. We also remark, that the learned Mr. Faber, in his work on the Jews[3] (pp. 234–247), argues at great length that the above invasion of Jerusalem refers exclusively to the " compassing of the camp of the saints about, and the beloved city," by the " Gog and Magog " army *at the close* of the millennial era, recorded Rev. xx. 8, 9. But

---

[1] Ezek. xxxviii. 2, 3, 16, 18, xxxix. 11.
[2] Rev. xvii. 12, 13, 17 ; xix. 19.
[3] " A General and Connected View of the Prophecies relative to the Conversion, Restoration, and Future Glory of the Houses of Judah and Israel," etc. Boston. Published by Andrews & Cummings, 1809.

what is decisive in proof, that the Gog and Magog hosts of Ezekiel are *entirely separate* and *distinct* from those of the Apocalypse, is the fact, that in Ezek. xxxviii. 16, the gathering of Gog and Magog against the Jews in the latter days, and their signal overthrow by the interposition of "the Lord" in their behalf as described in Zech. xiv. 3, 4, and Rev. xix. 11–21, that it is to the end that "the heathen may know God;" that is, that they shall, by being witnesses of these things, be *turned from dumb idols to serve the living God*," an event which is undeniably *pre* and not *post*-millennial.

Then, in addition to this, Ezekiel's description of the magnitude of this army, the number of their weapons, and the process prescribed for burying their carcasses, and burning the weapons used by it (Ezek. xxxix. 9–13), can never be applied to the *apocalyptic* Gog and Magog hosts.

Again. Mr. Faber is entirely in error when he represents, as in page 245, that "the antichristian confederacy is a *Roman* one," whereas "the Magogean confederacy *is not*." This error arises from the failure on the part of Mr. Faber to recognize the fact of the continuation of the old national landmarks *during* the millennial era, and also *after* its close. Thus Zechariah, referring to that era, says: "And it shall come to pass, that every one of them that is *left of all the nations* that came against Jerusalem, shall even go up from year to year to worship the king, the Lord of hosts, and to keep the feast of tabernacles." Now, these are they of the Ezekiel Magogean confederacy *who shall escape* the destruction that will fall upon the main body; and will form a large portion of the nations of the Gentiles *during* and *after* the millennial era, *out of whom* will spring the apocalyptic

Magogean confederacy.[1] The vast dimensions of this latter confederacy compared with that of Ezekiel; and also the difference in the agents and the method employed in effecting the destruction of each,—the former by the conquering hand of the RIDER on His white horse and His *white-robed* cavalry;[2] and the latter by *fire from heaven*,[3] —may be adduced as further proof on this point.

But, passing from this momentary digression, we now proceed to remark, that *before* the great battle for which this Ezekiel Gog and Magog confederacy are summoned together, the eighth head and his army, flushed with the pride and success of their unchecked career, resolve to invade the Holy Land, and, besieging its capital, JERUSALEM, " the city is taken, the houses are rifled, the women are ravished, and half of the city is led forth into captivity."[4]

These calamities, therefore,—which is that very "furnace of fire" in which the prophet Ezekiel declared that the Lord would "blow upon them and melt them, even as silver is melted,"[5]—taken in connection with all that they will have suffered since the formation of their unholy "league" with the false Christ, will *exceed in severity* any other that has ever befallen them since they have been a nation!

---

[1] If it be asked, But how is this? seeing that it is said of the subjects of the millennial era, that "*all* shall be righteous, from the least of them even unto the greatest of them," (Jer. xxxi. 34), the answer is, that this to the contrary notwithstanding, the millennial era *is not* a state of indefutable grace. Isaiah says, that "*the child that is a sinner*, being an hundred years old, *shall die and be accursed*." (Isa. lxv. 20.) And Zechariah states that "some *will not come up* of all the families of the earth unto Jerusalem, to worship the king," etc. (Zech. xiv. 17.) And so, *at the close* of the millennial era, when Satan is "loosed for a little season to *deceive these nations*," it is easy to account for that great apostate Magogean confederacy described in Rev. xx. 9.

[2] Rev. xix. 11-16; and 17-21.   [3] Ib. xx. 9.
[4] Zech. xiv. 1, 2.   [5] Ezek. xxii. 17-22.

There is, however, another scene, which speedily follows the apparently unchecked triumphs of this false Christ and his confederates, over the afflicted but " still beloved "[1] covenant people of God. Their assault upon the Holy City, Jerusalem, eventuates,

IV. In "*the battle of that great day of God Almighty*" spoken of Rev. xvi. 14. The *result* of this battle, however, in their boastful, self-reliant spirit, as we shall see, formed no part of their reckoning. Yes, at this point, it will be found that the ordinary far-reaching military tactics and diplomatic sagacity of their leader is at fault. This "man of destiny" will then find that the attribute of prescience forms no part of his endowments. The Devil incarnated in his person will not be omniscient!

But before passing on to this "battle," we must introduce you to *the locality of the "field"* selected for this mighty conflict. And here observe, the words are, not "*a* place, which *may be* called," etc., but it is—τὸν τόπον τὸν καλούμενον—*i. e.*, "*the* place which *is* called in the Hebrew tongue, ARMAGEDDON." The meaning of which is, that this is here actually applied in the Hebrew Scriptures, not to some vague, but to a definite and ascertainable *locality*. Allow us then to premise, that names applied by one prophet as a comparison or figure, are used by a subsequent prophet as an appellation or proper name. Thus, the figurative phrase, the " BRANCH," as used by the earlier prophets Isaiah and Jeremiah to denote Christ,[2] is applied to Him by Zechariah as *a proper name*.[3] Precisely the same principle is here applied by St. John. The *name* of " Armageddon," is a combi-

---

[1] Rom. xi. 11.
[2] See Isa. xi. 1; Jer. xxiii. 5.
[3] Zech. iii. 8.

nation of two passages in Zechariah, the one in chap. xii. 10, 11, where the prophet uses the great mourning occasioned by the death of the good king Josiah,—who was a type of Christ,—and the scene of which was in the *valley of Megiddo*,—to illustrate the general mourning of the Jews, when "the spirit of grace and of supplication being poured out upon them, they shall look upon Him whom they pierced, and mourn."[1] "In that day there shall be great mourning in Jerusalem, as the mourning of Hadadrimmon in the valley of Megiddo." But, *the place* where this mourning of the Jews shall occur, is called by the same prophet a *mountain*, not a valley. "And His (*i. e.* Christ's) feet shall stand in that day,"— the day of the overthrow of the Antichrist and his confederates—"upon the *mount of Olives* which is before Jerusalem on the east,"[2] etc. Hence these passages, combining the two parts, AR (a *mount*), and MEGIDDO, form the name "ARMAGEDDON," which signifies mount Megeddon, the "*place*" alluded to by St. John as "so called in the Hebrew Scriptures." We submit, therefore, that by a comparison of Zech. xii. 9–11, with chap. xiv. 1, 2, and verse 4, the future "battle" between the Antichrist and his Magogean confederacy, and the true Christ and His army, takes place *on the same spot* designated by Zechariah as the place for the future mourning of the Jews over their sins.

The former of these two events, THE BATTLE OF THAT GREAT DAY OF GOD ALMIGHTY, is that to which we now turn our thoughts. The prophecies which foretell the *certain destruction* of the last Antichrist and his Magogean army under the cover of those types by which they were pre-figured in the Old Testament,—the Canaanites,

---

[1] Zech. xii. 9, 10.   [2] Ib. xiv. 4, 5.

Moabites, Ammonites, Philistines, Edomites, etc., and those of Assyria, Tyre, and Sidon, and also the four great monarchies of Gentilism, the Babylonian, Medo-Persian, Grecian, and Roman—these prophecies being too numerous for quotation, we must be content to refer you to the following passages as inserted in the margin below.[1] It must suffice to observe that Antichrist and his confederates, exulting in having "planted themselves between the seas in the glorious holy mountain,"[2]—that is, "in the place called in the Hebrew tongue, ARMAGEDDON,"—and elate with the pride of victory, will little dream that they are madly rushing upon the terrible doom which soon awaits them, by provoking the God of Israel to bring upon them swift destruction. For, *in the midst* of that unparalleled "tribulation" brought upon the Jewish nation at their hand, and just at the point of time of those *unchronological*[3] events of "that generation which is not to pass away till *all* the things spoken of shall be fulfilled,"[4] lo! like "the *lightning*" that flashes athwart the heavens,[5] that VISIBLE MANIFESTATION of the Rider whom St. John saw "seated upon His white horse," and upon whose thigh a name was written, KING OF KINGS AND LORD OF LORDS," now takes place, when "*every eye shall see Him, and they also which pierced Him, and when all the kindreds of the earth,*"—*i. e.*, the Gentile antichristian confederated nationalities aforesaid,—"*shall wail because of Him.*"[6] Aye, and the same also with that

[1] Isa. xxvi. 19-21; xlvii. 1-15; xlix. 24-26; Jeremiah xii. 14-17; xxxiii. 1-7; Ezekiel xxi. 28-32; xxv. 1-17; xxvii. 1-19; xxviii. 1-17; xxxi. 1-17; xxxii. 17-22; xxxiv. 16-23; xxxv. xxxvi. 1-7; xxxviii. 1-17; xxxix. 1-24; Micah vii. Zechariah xii. 1-5; xiv. 1-6.

[2] Dan. xi. 45.

[3] See on "Short Unchronological Period," etc., "Our Bible Chron.," pp. 80, 166, 182.

[4] Matt. xxiv. 34.   [5] Ib. 27.   [6] Rev. i. 7.

APPEARING of the Lord Jesus Christ described by the prophet Zechariah, chap. xiv. 5: "And THE LORD MY GOD SHALL COME, AND ALL THE SAINTS WITH HIM," *i. e.*, His white-robed cavalry riders of " the FIRST RESURRECTION:"—which event transpires at the first or *invisible manifestation* of Christ, as described in 1 Thess. iv. 13-18 —" and *His feet*," the prophet continues, " shall stand in that day *upon the mount of Olives*, which is before Jerusalem on the east," etc. (verse 4).

But the momentous question here is, *For what* comes He and His risen and glorified saints? First, let the prophet Zechariah answer. Referring to the invasion of the Holy City, etc. by the last Antichrist and his Magogian confederates, he says, chap. xiv. 3, "And THE LORD shall then go forth, *and fight against those nations*, as when He fought in the day of battle." With this exactly corresponds St. Paul's prophecy of the overthrow of " the man of sin and son of perdition," etc. : " And then shall that *wicked* be revealed, whom the LORD shall *consume* with the spirit of His mouth, and *destroy* with the brightness of his (παρουσία, *i. e.*, His personal) coming." (2 Thess. ii. 3, 4, and verse 8.)

Yes, we repeat : τῇ ἐπιφανείᾳ τῆς παρουσίας αὐτοῦ— "with the brightness of His (PERSONAL) coming." Now, when the apostle is speaking of "that wicked " (ἄνομος), who is to " be revealed," verse 8, he uses the word ἀποκαλυφθήσεται, *apokalypse:* and to show what he means by the apocalypse or revelation of " that wicked one," he says, verse 9, οὗ ἐστιν ἡ παρουσία κατ' ἐνεργείαν τοῦ Σατανᾶ, etc. ; " whose coming is after the working of Satan ; " which " *coming*," as we have already shown,[1] and all Protestant commentators admit, is to be a *personal* coming

---

[1] See pages 121-122.

of the LAST ANTICHRIST. But, with an inconsistency which defies all comparison, these same commentators, when they come to apply this identical word παρουσία to the LORD JESUS CHRIST, insist that it denotes a *spiritual* coming!

Let us however look at this matter. Zechariah says: "Then shall THE LORD go forth, and fight against those nations, *as when He fought in the day of battle.*" Allusion is here made to the overthrow of the Egyptian army in the Red Sea, when they were pursuing the Israelites. And *how* did the Lord then fight against the Egyptians? Was it by His *spiritual* presence? To determine this point, we have but to turn to the book of Exodus, chap. xiv, 24, 25. "And it came to pass that in the morning watch, *the Lord looked* unto the host of the Egyptians, through the pillar of fire and of the cloud, and troubled the host of the Egyptians, and took off their chariot wheels, that they drave them heavily: so that the Egyptians said, Let us flee from the face of Israel, for THE LORD fighteth for them against the Egyptians." Now, whatever may be said of this passage by that class of modern expositors who, if they do not fully adopt, yet to an alarming extent are copying after such theological models as Bp. Colenso, who denies the truth of the Pentateuch; of Renan of France, who impugns the divinity of Jesus; and of Strauss of Germany, with his captivating poetical infidelity: still, "the Lord who looked upon the Egyptians" in the midst of the sea through that "pillar of cloud and of fire," was none other than "the angel of God," or that DIVINE "MESSENGER OF THE COVENANT," mentioned in the 19th verse of this chapter, and who so often *visibly* manifested Himself to his people under the Old Testament dispensation. Yes. He was none other than the MANIFESTED JEHOVAH-ELOHIM, whose "*voice*

Adam *heard* in the garden in the cool of the day;"[1] who *spake* to Moses out of the midst of the burning but unconsumed bush;[2] who *visited* Abraham in the plains of Mamre and *ate* of his cakes, butter and milk, and the calf which he had dressed;[3] who *wrestled* with Jacob at Penuel;[4] aye, and besides numerous other instances of similar manifestations, who took up His permanent abode as THE SHEKINAH,—and which St. Paul styles "THE GLORY,"[5] or *visible presence* of the JEHOVAH-ELOHIM,— first in the Tabernacle in the wilderness, and then in the Temple at Jerusalem, beneath the outstretched wings of the cherubim over the mercy-seat in the Holy of Holies; but more especially when "in the fulness of time," as "the promised seed of the woman who was to bruise the serpent's head,"[6] HE took upon Himself the limitations of creaturehood as the son of Mary in Bethlehem's manger![7] Indeed, we can know nothing of God, except as a *revealed* and *manifested* God in the Person of His son Jesus Christ! Look at the conflict of Jesus with His satanic tempter in the wilderness. Was He not *personally* present with His arch foe during that conflict? Look at the cross. Was it not a *real victim* who expired thereon? Follow Him to the rocky tomb of Joseph of Arimathea, and watch there as did Mary till the morning of the third day. Was not the *resurrection* of Jesus from the dead a *literal* resurrection? Then join the " men of Galilee forty days after," to whom, as they stood " gazing up into heaven" at the receding resurrected and glorified body of the ascending Saviour, the "two men in white apparel" said unto them, " *This same Jesus*, which is

---

[1] Gen. iii. 8-10. [2] Exod. iii. 3-5. [3] Gen. xviii. 1-3.
[4] Ib. xxii.-24-30. [5] Rom. ix. 4. [6] Gen. iii. 15.
[7] Matt. ii. 1, 2; Luke ii. 7.

taken up from you into heaven, *shall so come in like manner as ye have seen him go into heaven.*"[1]

We have thus entered into these plain Scriptural details on this subject in order to demonstrate, that when the time shall have come that "THE LORD shall go forth to fight against these antichristian nations as in the day of battle," it will be a *personal* face-to-face conflict between THE ANTICHRIST and his Magogean hosts, and the Lord Jesus Christ as the "KING OF KINGS AND THE LORD OF LORDS," whose divine title is the "Faithful and True."[2] Yes, in that day, "His *feet* shall stand upon the Mount of Olives which is before Jerusalem on the east."[3]

And mark: when Daniel and Jeremiah predicted of *the time* of "Jacob's trouble" already alluded to, they also foretold that "he should be *saved out of it.*"[4] And so, this is the time predicted by St. Paul, 2 Thess. i. 7–9: "When the Lord Jesus shall be revealed from heaven with his mighty angels in flaming fire,"—because, as saith the prophet Isaiah, "*by fire*, and *by his sword*, will the Lord plead with all flesh, and *the slain of the Lord shall be many*,"[5]—thus "taking vengeance on them that know not God, and that obey not the gospel of our Lord Jesus Christ;"—*i. e.*, these living antichristian nations—"who shall be punished with everlasting destruction from the presence of the Lord, and from the glory of his power,"[6] etc. The phrase in the above passage—"And the *slain* of the Lord shall be *many*"—requires a passing remark. These words imply that *some shall escape* those judgments that shall fall upon the main body of the anti-

---

[1] Acts i. 9–11. For a full exposition of the scriptural doctrine of the Second Personal Pre-Millennial coming of Christ, see our work on "The Second Coming of Christ, the Great Question of the day, is it *Pre* or *Post*-Millennial," etc.

[2] Rev. xix. 11–16. [3] Zech. xiv. 4. [4] 2 Jer. xxxi. 7; Dan. xii. 1.
[5] Isa. lxvi. 16. [6] 2 Thess. i. 7–9.

christian hosts. These will be, first, that portion of the *Jewish* nation, constituting "the *residue* of the people that *shall not be cut off* from the city"—Jerusalem—at the time of its last invasion by Antichrist, as described Zech. xiv. 1, 2. And second, those of the *Gentiles* that shall be "*left* of all the nations which came against Jerusalem," verse 16. These, therefore, are those parts of "the inhabitants of the world," Jewish and Gentile, which, "when the judgments of God," as above described, "are abroad in the earth, *will learn righteousness*." (Isa. xxvi. 9). And so, while of the "residue" of the escaped *Jewish* nation, it is declared, "and it shall come to pass *in that day*, that I will pour upon the house of David and the inhabitants of Jerusalem the spirit of grace and of supplications: *and they shall look upon* ME *whom they have pierced, and shall mourn*," etc. (Zech. xii. 9, 10); those of "the land of overshadowing wings," though having formed *an alliance* with the Antichrist for the purpose already specified,[1] shall constitute a large portion of that *Gentile* retinue of whom it is said, Zech. xiv. 16, that they "shall even go up from year to year to *worship* the King, the Lord of hosts, and to *keep the feast* of tabernacles." And this brings us to our concluding remarks on the subject in hand, namely:

V. *The final doom of the last Antichrist and his Magogean confederacy.* Marshalled in hostile array on the battle-field of "ARMAGEDDON," you behold the antagonistic hosts. On the one side, you descry the apocalyptic eighth head, with his antichristian confederates, engaged in their assault against Jerusalem, the Holy City. On the other side, "*the house of Judah*," a mere handful compared with the "all nations" arrayed against them, and as yet *without* a visible and efficient Head to lead them.

[1] See pages 185–189 of this work.

He is, however, *nigh at hand,* even HE who has said, that He would " make the house of Judah as His *goodly horse* in the day of battle; yea, that they shall *be as mighty men* which tread down their enemies in the mire of the streets in the battle: and they shall fight *because* THE LORD *is with them,* and the riders on horses shall be confounded."[1] We are here to bear in mind, that these are " *the residue* of the Jewish people that were not cut off from the city,"[2] when first invaded by the enemy. Their arms, however, are nerved to the conflict with a *supernatural* energy, for "the Lord is with them," leading them on to victory " *by the spirit of His mouth!* "[3]

But, as the battle advances, and the Magogean hosts have *their personal* leader, the EIGHTH HEAD of the apocalypse, so at length " the house of Judah." Thus St. John: " And I saw heaven opened, and behold a white horse: and He that sat on Him was called FAITHFUL AND TRUE, and in righteousness doth He judge and make war. His eyes were as a flame of fire, and on his head were many crowns: and He had a name written which no man knew, but He himself. And He was clothed in a vesture dipt in blood:[4] and His name is called, THE WORD OF GOD."[5] Then, too, He has *his army.* We must not here forget the statement of Zechariah: " And the Lord my God shall come, *and all His saints with Him:* "[6] *i. e.,* His risen and raptured saints of THE FIRST RESURRECTION. And so St. John, " And the armies which were in heaven "— for they had all been previously " caught up to meet the

---

[1] Zech. x. 3-5.   [2] Zech. xiv. 2.   [3] 2 Thess. ii. 8.
[4] By comparing Isa. ix. 5, and 1. 17, with chap. lxiii. 1-3, it will be seen that the latter verse refers, not to the first, but to the second coming of Christ.
[5] Rev. xix. 11-13.   [6] Zech. xiv. 5.

Lord *in the air*"[1]—followed him upon white horses, clothed in linen white and clean.[2]

And now for *the battle!* St. John says: "And I saw *the Beast*,"—that is, the Beast who came to the Jews with the " mark, or name, or number of his name " (" 666 "), and who had been " received " by them as their Messiah, *alias* Louis Napoleon III.,—" and *the kings of the earth and their armies*," or his Magogean confederates, " gathered together to *make war* against Him that sat on the horse, and his armies." On the other hand, says Zechariah, " Then shall THE LORD go forth and fight against those nations, as when He fought in the day of battle."

Finally, *the result* of the battle. St. Paul says: " Whom the Lord *shall consume* with the spirit of His mouth, and *destroy* with the brightness of his coming."[3] And St. John says of the " eighth " head, that he " *goeth into perdition*."[4] First then: Of the Lord Jesus Christ it is declared, that " out of His mouth, as the King of kings and Lord of lords, goeth a sharp sword, that with it He should *smite the nations and rule them with a rod of iron*," and that " He treadeth the winepress of the fierceness and wrath of Almighty God."[5]

In the next place St. John adds: "And I saw an angel standing in the sun: and he cried with a loud voice, saying to *all the fowls* that fly in the midst of heaven, Come and gather yourselves together *unto the supper* of the Great God."[6] . . . "And the Beast was taken, and with him the false prophet that wrought miracles before him, with which he deceived them that had received the mark of the Beast, and them that worshipped his image. These both were cast alive into a lake of fire burning with

---

[1] 1 Thess. iv. 13-17.   [2] Rev. xix. 14, 16.   [3] 2 Thess. ii. 8.
[4] Rev. xvii. 11.   [5] Ib. xix. 15.   [6] Ib. xix. 17.

brimstone." Thus, they together "*go into perdition.*" And the *remnant were slain* with the sword of Him that sat upon the horse, which sword proceeded out of his mouth: and the *fowls* were filled with their flesh."[1]

It will doubtless be interesting, in drawing these remarks to a close, to advert to Ezekiel's description of the *magnitude* of this Magogean army, and of the *number of* weapons used by them in this "battle of the great day of God Almighty."

First: Of the *army*. "And it shall come to pass in that day, saith the Lord, that I will give unto Gog a place there of graves in Israel, the valley of the passengers on the east of the sea;"—*i. e.,* between the Dead Sea and the Mediterranean,—"and it shall stop the noses (marg., mouths) of the passengers: and there shall they bury Gog and all his multitude: and they shall call it 'the valley of Hamon-gog,' or *the multitude of Gog*. And SEVEN MONTHS shall the house of Israel be in burying of them, that they may cleanse the land." . . . "And it shall be to them a renown, the day that I shall be glorified, saith the Lord."[2]

Second. Of their *weapons*. "Behold, it is come, and it is done, saith the Lord God: This is the day whereof I have spoken. And they that dwell in the cities of Israel shall go forth, *and shall set on fire and burn the weapons,* both the shields, and bucklers, and the bows and arrows, and the handstaves, and the spears, and they shall burn them with fire SEVEN YEARS: so that they shall take no wood out of the field, neither cut down any out of the forests; for they shall burn the weapons with fire; and they *shall spoil those that spoiled them, and rob those that robbed them,* saith the Lord."[3]

---

[1] Rev. xix. 20, 21.   [2] Ezek. xxxix. 11-13.
[3] Ezek. xxxix. 9, 10.

It is in place here to remark, by way of explanation, that the difference between the "seven months" in burying the slain carcasses of the Magogean army, and the "seven years" devoted to the burning of their weapons, is accounted for by the fact that the "weapons" will be substituted in the place of "wood," for purposes of *ordinary fuel*, which will supply the want of that commodity among the Jews for "seven years." Whereas, if consumed by the process of a general bonfire, it would require a comparatively short period to reduce them to ashes.

And now, we bring to a close these somewhat extended prophetico-historic expositions of Rev. chap. xvii. 9-17, together with those prophecies which form integral parts of it. We deem a general recapitulation of the subjects treated of unnecessary, the table of contents furnishing a complete synopsis of them. But in dropping the curtain at the conclusion of the tragical scenes that have been introduced upon the prophetical platform, whether as relating to the *past*, the *present*, or the *future*, it is due to ourself to say, that we have been actuated by *one single motive*—that of leading the reader's mind to imbibe correct views of THAT SYSTEM OF POLITICAL ECONOMY which Almighty God, as the "Governor among the nations" and "the head of the church," has revealed in Holy Scripture for our "instruction in righteousness," and to prepare him for "all those things which are coming upon the earth," as foreshadowed in the *present* portentous "SIGNS OF THE TIMES." What we have said is open to criticism. If wrong, let it be exposed and corrected. If right, all we ask is, that you admit it. A word more, and I have done.

The prophecy before us, as we have seen, closes this sublimely terrific scene with the *total overthrow* of Daniel's "vile person" or "wilful king" with whom the

Jews entered into an *unholy* "*league,*" and whom they "received" as their Messiah, and who is the same with St. John's eighth head and St. Paul's "Man of sin and Son of perdition"—the last Antichrist—Louis Napoleon III. And also, with the *total extermination* of his Magogean confederacy, on the battle-field of "Armageddon," in Palestine.

With this "battle," therefore, *terminates for ever* the season of that "GREAT TRIBULATION" to the Jews, called by Jeremiah and Daniel "*the time of Jacob's trouble.*"

And now, this event consummated, the "more sure word of prophecy" opens to the enraptured eye of faith "the GLORY that shall follow the *sufferings* of Christ" and of the Abrahamic covenant seed of Israel, who St. Paul declares are "*still beloved* for their father's sake;"[1] together with the Lord's redeemed "bride," the Gentile church, "taken out of (or from among) the Gentiles, to the praise of his name."[2] The former, together with the converted of the Gentile nationalities, to constitute the SAVED NATIONS IN THE FLESH ON EARTH;[3] the latter to REIGN CONJOINTLY WITH CHRIST[4] OVER them,[5] seated on their thrones[6] "*in the air,*"[7] during the MILLENNIAL ERA OF "A THOUSAND YEARS."[8]

"And I heard a loud voice in heaven, saying, NOW IS COME SALVATION, AND STRENGTH, AND THE KINGDOM OF OUR GOD, AND THE POWER OF HIS CHRIST; for the accuser of the brethren is cast down, which accused them before our God day and night."[9]

---

[1] Rom. xi.　　[2] Acts xv. 14.　　[3] Isa. lx. 1-7
[4] Rev. iii. 21.　　[5] Rev. v. 10.　　[6] Rev. xx. 4
[7] 1 Thess. iv. 13-17.　　[8] Rev. xx. 4.　　[9] Rev. xii. 10.

APPENDIX.

PROPHECIES RELATING TO

POPE PIUS IX. AND THE SULTAN OF TURKEY,

ON THE SPEEDY OVERTHROW

OF THE

PAPACY AND MOHAMEDISM:

VIEWED IN CONNECTION WITH

THE TWO FAMOUS MANIFESTOES,

THE ENCYCLICAL LETTER OF POPE PIUS IX.,

AND

THE FIRMAN OF THE SULTAN OF TURKEY.

The following article was originally written at the special request of the Rev. A. E. Campbell, D. D., Corresponding Secretary of "The American and Foreign Christian Union," and was first inserted in the April number of "The Christian World," published by that society. It is now added as a suitable appendix to the preceding exposition of the prophecy founded on Rev. chap. xvii., and others connected with it.

R. C. S.

POPE PIUS IX., AND THE SULTAN OF TURKEY.

In harmony with the preceding prophetical expositions, and particularly those connected with the PAPACY and MOHAMMEDANISM, we observe, that it is conceded by every reflecting mind, that the times we live in are pregnant with events of unparalleled interest and significance. Among all classes there is a general though undefined *presentiment*, that they forebode *great changes* in the national, political, and ecclesiastical or religious order of things as at present constituted. Diplomatists, legislators, warriors, naval and military, and the learned of all departments and grades in the church and in the state, are on the tip-toe of expectation of a HALCYON ERA, as speedily to take the place of the *existing* revolutionary tendencies of the times, as seen in the disorganizing and ruinous results thence arising.

It is proper here to observe, that this expectation, which shares largely in the sympathies of the learned in the nominal Christian church, both clerical and lay, is founded upon what may be termed the *levelling-up* process of human progress as following in the track of civilization, and the evangelizing of all nations by *ordinary* instrumentalities—the march of mind as developed in the progress of the sciences, philosophy, and the various religious and benevolent agencies of the day.

There is, however, a large and increasing class of thinking men in the church of Christ, who, while they concede our near proximity to the fulfilment of the prophecies—when " the Lord shall come out of his place to punish the inhabitants of the earth for their iniquity; when the earth also shall disclose her blood, and shall no more cover her slain;"[1] and when shall be verified the promise—" then the moon shall be confounded, and the sun ashamed, when the Lord shall reign in Mount Zion, and in Jerusalem, and before his ancients gloriously;"[2] yet have no sympathy with the prevailing view regarding those *agencies* by which this great moral revolution is to be effected. A realization of their hope of this event as *imminent*, is founded upon those prophetic " SIGNS OF THE TIMES," which are to immediately precede and inaugurate it. They maintain that both the ecclesiastical and political heavens and earth are now being thronged with these very " signs," numerous as the stars in the firmament. The prophecy of St. Paul, Heb. xii. 26, 27,— " Yet once more I shake not only the earth, but heaven; which word, yet once more, signifieth the *removal* of those things that *are* shaken, as of things that are made, that those things which *cannot* be shaken may *remain* " —they claim *now* is in course of fulfilment before the eyes of men. Hence their amazement at the " slowness of heart " of those who, with the plea, " show us a sign from heaven, that we may believe," *do not* discern these " SIGNS."

We, on this point, however, would submit, whether,

---

[1] Isa. xxvi. 21.   [2] Ib. xxiv. 23.

in this plea, we have not the evidence demonstrative of the *fallacy* of the pretence, that when a " sign " appears, we cannot but recognize and understand its import. Such a recognition of " the signs of the times " as the divinely appointed forerunners of the *events* to which they point, depends solely upon our having " inquired and searched diligently as to *what*, or *what manner of time*, the spirit of Christ which was in the old prophets did signify, when they testified" of them. Neglecting to do this, the Jewish nation, notwithstanding the numerous "*signs*" which immediately preceded, accompanied, and followed the FIRST COMING of our Lord, involved them in the sin and guilt of "*not knowing* the time of their visitation," and so resulted in their crucifixion of Jesus, and the consequent judgments of God that have since rested upon them. And, for the same reason, even *after the resurrection*, our Lord pronounced against his own disciples the scathing reproof—" O fools ! and slow of heart to believe all that the prophets have spoken " concerning me.[1] And does not the same hold true of all those who, in these " last days " or " perilous times " predicted by St. Peter and St. Paul,[2] neglect to " take heed to that more sure word of prophecy which shineth in a dark place,"[3] in regard to those " signs " which are to immediately precede, accompany, and follow the SECOND COMING of Christ, and the " setting up of that kingdom of the God of heaven which is to break down and consume all others ? "[4]

Now, of this class of " SIGNS," we affirm, and shall proceed to prove from the prophetic Scriptures, that the ENCYCLICAL LETTER OF POPE PIUS IX., issued from the Vatican of Rome, December 8th, 1864, to all the patri-

---

[1] Luke xxiv. 25, and verse 44. [2] 2 Tim. iii. 1 ; iv. 4 ; 2 Pet. iii. 3, 4.
[3] 2 Pet. i. 19. [4] Dan. ii. 43, 44.

archs, primates, archbishops, bishops, and faithful of the so-called Holy Catholic Church throughout the world, on the one hand; and the contemporaneous FIRMAN OF THE SULTAN OF TURKEY in reference to the improvements to be made in the Holy City, Jerusalem, on the other; *are the two most significant and portentous "signs of the times" that have transpired during the present century.* Pass we, then,

I. TO THE ENCYCLICAL LETTER OF POPE PIUS IX.

In order to understand the bearing of this notable manifesto on the subject in hand, it will be necessary to furnish a brief outline of the *prophetico-historic* rise, career, and final destiny of the "LITTLE HORN," which was to "come up among the ten horns" of Daniel's fourth or Roman beast, chap. viii. 8, and which all Protestant expositors admit to symbolize the PAPAL POWER. Now of this "little horn," the prophet says:—"I beheld, and the same horn made war with the saints, and prevailed against them *until the ancient of days came*," etc., verses 21, 22. He also "beheld, because of the voice of the great words which he spake against the Most High; even until the beast was slain, and his body destroyed, and given to the burning flame," verse 11. And he then adds:—"as concerning the rest of the beasts, they had their *dominion* taken away, yet their *lives* were prolonged for a season and a time," etc., verse 12.

It is here to be specially noted, by the way, that the "little horn" in the above prophecy is the *eleventh*, as coming up "among," and is consequently distinct from, the "*ten horns*" of the fourth or Roman nondescript beast.

To proceed: History attests that the Roman empire, in its civil or political aspect, as denoted by the "fourth beast" of Daniel, chap. vii. 7, was divided into *two parts*, the West and the East, as symbolized by the *two legs* of iron of the metallic colossal image, Dan. ii. 33, between A. D. 337 and 395. Its subdivision into *ten principalities*, as denoted by the "*ten toes*" of the image and the "ten horns" of the beast, did not transpire till A. D. 532. The next year, A. D. 533, the "little horn" made his appearance "among the ten horns," by the edict of Justinian, which constituted John II., the then Patriarch of Rome, the universal bishop of all the churches throughout Christendom, as the so-called VICEGERENT of Christ on earth." [1]

But, superadded to the spiritual prerogatives of this "little horn" power, was that of a *temporal sovereignty* as well. This is symbolically indicated by the words of the prophet, that "before him there were *three of the first horns plucked up by the roots*," chap. vii. 8, which was verified, as all prophetical expositors agree, when the exarchate of Ravenna in A. D, 730, Lombardy in A. D. 755, and the state of Rome in A. D. 774, fell into the hands of the Papal see, the emperor Pepin, meanwhile, having constituted the Pope in a manner KING of Rome, by which the above three, not only, but the *remaining seven* horns of the ten were subjugated to, and ultimately terminated in, him. And so, as depicted in the synchronic imagery of the apocalypse, the *crowns* which were at first placed upon the *seven heads* of the beast,—denotive of the seven forms of government through which the empire was to pass [2]—were transferred to the "*ten horns*," as symbolic of the ECCLESIASTICO-POLITICAL sove-

---

[1] See pages 124–129 of this work.
[2] See pages 51–53 of this work.

reignty of the "little horn" over the *entire Roman earth*, in token of which, after the example of his predecessors from A. D. 774, Pope Pius IX. still claims to wear the TRIPLE CROWN.

Nor is the inspired prophet less explicit in marking out the *period* assigned to the career of this "little horn" power. The saints were to be "given into his hand for *a time, times, and the dividing of time,*" Dan. vii. 25, at the expiration of which, the JUDGMENT SHOULD SIT, "to take away his *dominion*, and to consume and destroy it *unto the end,*" verse 26. This prophetical number, which, in accordance with the year-day theory of interpretation, is to be reckoned as 1,260 prophetical years, as nearly all expositors admit, is to be dated from the edict of Justinian in A. D. 533, as stated above, and which, when added thereto, brings us down to A. D. 1793. Accordingly, it was during the revolutionary reign of terror in France, which resulted in the decapitation of Louis XVI. in A. D. 1793, that the "*dominion*" which more immediately belonged to and depended upon the Roman see, at the "pouring out of the Vth apocalyptic vial on the seat of the beast," (Rev. xvi. 10, 11), "*was taken away*" from the "ten horns" or "the rest of the beasts."

Still, the *power* of the Papacy, though then exceedingly weakened, was not totally destroyed. "The *lives* of the kings were prolonged for *a season and a time.*" Hence Daniel's addition to the 1,260 years of two other numbers—the 1,290 and the 1,335 days (or years) of chap. xii. 11, 12—which, all having a common commencement from A. D. 533, gives to the prolonged "*season,*" the period of 30 years, and to the "*time,*" of 45 years, or a total of 75 years *beyond* A. D. 1793.

This introduces us to that notice of the *encyclical letter* of Pope Pius IX., which, as occurring at this particular juncture of affairs, forms, as we have said, one of the two most significant and portentous "signs of the times" that have marked the history of this century. It is quite superfluous to say, that it furnishes the evidence of the continued lives of the "ten horns." Yes, THE PAPACY STILL LIVES!

Nor can the history of that stupendous antichristian power since A. D. 533 furnish evidence of the putting forth of more arrogant and blasphemous claims to supreme and unlimited sway, *spiritual* and *temporal*, as alleged to to have been "entrusted to Pius IX. and his successors by our Lord Jesus Christ himself, in the person of the blessed St. Peter, chief of the apostles," "not only in regard to each individual man, but with regard to nations, peoples, and their rulers," *against* those who affirm what his holiness calls, "*the impious and absurd principle of naturalism*," to wit—that "liberty of conscience and of worship is the right of every man—a right which ought to be proclaimed and established by law in every well-constituted state," etc. These extracts, as indicating the general character and purport of the Pope's manifesto, must suffice. We would only add, that it is followed by an "Appendix," setting forth *ten classes of errors*, commencing with "Pantheism, naturalism, and absolute rationalism," and ending with those of "modern liberalism," in which is included "Protestantism." Against one and all of the authors and promoters of these "errors," the Pontiff thunders out his anathemas, in every form which an exasperated mind and hot words can command, on account of "the very great grief" which their combined assaults upon the holy Catholic church have occasioned his pious soul!

We shall now proceed to show, in the light of the GREAT CALENDAR OF PROPHECY, that this encyclical letter of Pope Pius IX., as the representative head of the great western Antichrist, analogous to the application of a galvanic battery to a diseased and decayed body, is indicative of *its speedy dissolution*. In other words, we mean to say, that the very force by which this antichristian system is attempted to be galvanized into renewed vitality, being counteracted by an *inherent* process of dissolution, will soon expend itself, when *death* will ensue. It will be well here briefly to recapitulate the *chronological standpoints* connected with the rise, career, etc., of this stupendous power.

We have already shown that the whole period assigned to the career of the " little horn " of Papacy and his " ten " vassal " kings," was 1,335 years ; which period, *commencing* with the rise of the Popedom in A. D. 533, *ends* in A. D. 1868.[1] We have also shown that " the dominion of the ten kings " was taken away in A. D. 1793, at the end of the 1,260 years during which he was to " make war with the saints and prevail against them." The " season" and "time," or the 75 years *beyond* the 1,260, therefore, during which their " lives were to be prolonged," reckoning from A. D. 1793, also *runs out* in A. D. 1868. Hence, from the present year, A. D. 1866, only two years remain for their survival, down to A. D. 1868.

A short time, this, the reader will say, for the *accomplishment* of what remains, in effecting the overthrow of this stupendous power. But, let us see. A due consideration of what is indicated in the prophetic pages as to the *process* of this consummation, will, we opine, settle this point. In the first place, Daniel says, chap. vii. 26, that " the judgment that should sit," to " take away the *dominion* of the little horn," was " to consume and to

---

[1] See pages 124–132 of this work.

destroy it *unto the end*, *i. e.*, of the 1,335 days or years of chap. xii. 12. History abundantly shows that, despite the extraordinary efforts put forth by the Papacy to recover from the blow which the "*ten horns*" as "the seat of the beast" received during the FRENCH REVOLUTION in A. D. 1793, the *temporal power of the Popedom* has been on the wane. And Louis Napoleon III., since his accession to power as the *revived* VIIth Head of the Franco-Roman empire, has nearly swept away the last remaining vestiges of that power. Hence the moanings over, and the protestations and anathemas against, the interference of the *civil* powers of the state with the arrogant *ecclesiastico-political* claims of the "LITTLE HORN," as fulminated from the chair of the Vatican, in his recently published "encyclical."

Let us now pass to a notice of the *effects* of this notable manifesto of Pope Pius IX. True, his holiness "has received the members of the sacred college, and addressed to them an *allocution*, in which he said that in the present day robbery was committed under the pretext of nationality, but that the *triumph* of the church was certain, the day only of that triumph being uncertain. His holiness added, that after witnessing the destruction of the enemies of the Holy See, and the triumph of truth and virtue, he would exclaim with Simeon— "Lord, now lettest thou thy servant depart in peace."

But we may say to him, as Ahab, king of Israel, said to the messenger of Benhadad, the boastful king of Syria:—"Tell him, let not him that girdeth on his harness, boast himself as he that putteth it off" (1 Kings xx. 11). It is here to be borne in mind, that the *originators, abettors,* and *promoters* of the *ten classes of* "*errors,*" from the atheistic "pantheism of absolute rationalism," down to the most diluted form of "modern liberalism," constitute the IDENTICAL "TEN HORNS" of the Roman principalities or kingdoms, over which this "little horn" of the Papacy has for so many centuries swayed his gigantic ecclesiastico-political sceptre. Who, therefore, can be surprised, that the journals of the day already announce, that "the Pope's encyclical letter had produced an *extraordinary sensation* in Europe. It is regarded as a formal repudiation of the convention between France and Italy for the settlement of the Roman question, and a refusal to compromise existing differences. The English, French, and Italian newspapers discuss it at great length, and generally condemn it. The FRENCH GOVERNMENT is said to be greatly annoyed by it, and it was expected that it would lead to a *complete revision* of the relations between the Pope and the Catholic hierarchy and clergy in France."

Furthermore. "A circular of the French minister of Justice, dated the 1st instant, addressed to the bishops, announces that the council of state is occupied in examining the project of a decree for authorizing the publication of that part of the Pope's encyclical letter, which *grants a jubilee*." The minister says:—"As regards the *first part* of the letter and the appendix, your eminence will understand that the reception and publication of these documents, which contain propositions contrary to the principles on which is based the constitution of the empire, *could not be authorized*." The French clergy had also held a meeting, to arrange preliminary measures for a gathering of all the prelates, chief priests, and deacons of the church in France, to concert measures for informing the Pope of *the unpleasant effect* produced by the letter throughout France." And, besides, "A French imperial decree appoints PRINCE NAPOLEON Vice-President of the Privy Council."

Again. In speaking of the recent action of MAXIMILIAN, in regard to the confiscation of the estates of the Church in Mexico, and the restoration of the property of the church as an impossibility, etc., the writer says:— "The assumption of the Emperor to invest prelates, pay the clergy, and regulate their property, is of special importance, in view of the *recent bull* issued by the Pope against any interference of the state in ecclesiastical affairs. This action of the emperor of Mexico, was no doubt *instigated* by the astute emperor of France, who is supposed to meditate *a still larger* assumption of authority, to the extent of declaring the French Catholic church *absolutely independent*. The result of this Mexican movement will therefore be regarded with great interest, as involving the *religious*, as well as the *political*, destinies of the people."

Aye. And not only of the Mexican empire, as a *limb* of the French, as one of the "ten horns" of the Roman earth. Louis Napoleon III., as the eldest son of the church, has only *commenced* the work of despoiling the "little horn" of his arrogant ecclesiastico-political assumptions in these "last times." In the Apocalypse, chap. xvii. 1–5 and verse 15, the Holy Spirit, under the *revived* VIIth head of the beast—which is that of the reigning emperor of the Franco-Roman empire—the symbol denoting the Papacy is changed to that of a "woman" called "the great whore, upon whose forehead is written, MYSTERY, BABYLON THE GREAT, THE MOTHER OF HARLOTS AND ABOMINATIONS OF THE EARTH," who "sitteth upon many waters," symbolic of the "*peoples*, and *multitudes*, and *nations*, and *tongues*," over whom she has so long reigned, and still continues to reign, as also "over *the kings* of the earth," verse 18.

Now, this is revealed in immediate connection with

the "*judgment*" which is to overtake her; while the agents who are to inflict this "judgment" are those very vassal "kings" or "*ten horns*" of the "peoples," etc. (verse 16), who are *now* being so incensed at the audacity of the Pope's encyclical letter. We have only to turn to verses 15–17, as already stated, in evidence of this, and of the *mode* or *manner* in which this "judgment" is to be inflicted. "And the ten horns which thou sawest upon the beast, these shall *hate* the whore, and shall make her *desolate and naked*, and shall *eat her flesh*, and *burn her with fire*. FOR GOD HATH PUT IT INTO THEIR HEARTS TO FULFIL HIS WILL, AND TO AGREE, and give their power *unto the beast*"—*i. e.*, "the beast from the *earth*, having two horns like a lamb, but who speaks as a dragon" (Rev. xiii. 11)—"*until the words of God shall be fulfilled.*"

The inevitable conclusion, therefore, is this: that unless our interpretations of the prophecies in reference to the rise, career, and final doom which awaits *the "woman"* whom St. John saw "drunken with the blood of the saints, and with the blood of the martyrs of Jesus" (Rev. xvii. 6), can be shown to be fallacious, the above act of the ten horns or kings in destroying her, " root and branch," cannot be postponed beyond the *close* of the 1,335 years allotted to her, which period ends in A. D. 1868.

But, let us now pass,

II. TO THE CONTEMPORANEOUS FIRMAN OF THE SULTAN OF TURKEY, ON THE SUBJECT OF THE IMPROVEMENTS ORDERED TO BE MADE IN THE HOLY CITY, JERUSALEM.

Here, again, we must turn back to the prophet Daniel, for information regarding the *prophetico-historic* rise, career, and final destiny of the TURCO-MOHAMMEDAN power. It must suffice here to state, that though there are several striking marks of resemblance between the characteristics of this power and that of the Papacy, yet that they are not *identical*, as some writers contend, is evident from the facts following: Unlike the Papal "little horn," which appears among the "ten horns" of the *Roman* beast, the Turkish "little horn" springs out of one of the "four notable horns" of the *Grecian* he-goat (chap. viii. 8, 9, and verse 21). This was the *Arabian* horn, which, with other provinces, fell to Ptolemy, one of the four generals among whom Alexander's empire was divided after his death.[1] The prophet tells us that *this* "little horn" was to "wax exceeding great toward the *south*, and toward the *east*, and toward the *pleasant land*," i. e. PALESTINE (verse 9).

Again. The *period* assigned to the empire, the Medo-Persian, out of the *conquest* of which by the Grecian, when divided into four kingdoms, this "little horn" was to arise, instead of 1,260 years, was 2,300 *days, or years* (Dan. viii. 14). We submit the following, as the historic verification of the commencement and close of this remarkable and much-controverted period, only remarking by the way, that in the interpretation of the above prophecy, the records of *ancient* history must answer to the prophetic description of the *commencement* of the vision; and the records of *modern* history, AFTER 2,300 years intervening, that of the *termination* of the vision. Also that these periods, if rightly fixed, will prove strongly-marked and well-defined epochs, thus furnishing us with a double argument and a double test to the determination of the *exact epoch* required.

[1] See pages 122-124 of this work.

This period, then, it is to be remembered, comprehends the duration of the *whole period of events* predicted in the vision; of them, and of no more. For, the question of the one angel to the other angel is not, How long shall be *a part* of the vision? But, "How long shall be *the vision?*"—called a vision, to distinguish it from that which is its principal subject,—"the vision concerning the daily sacrifice." Nor, again, is it said, How long shall be the vision from some era (as of Daniel's seeing it,[1] for example) *antecedent* to the commencement of the vision; or, from some era (as of Alexander's victories[2]) *subsequent* to its commencement: but simply, "How long shall be the vision?"[3] *i. e.*, of what *duration*, from its commencement to its close.

What, then, marks the date of its *commencement?* "I saw in a vision," says the prophet, "and behold, there stood before the river a ram which had two horns"— "the kings of *Media* and *Persia*"—(verse 20): "and the two horns were high; but one was higher than the other, and the *higher* came [or had come] up *last*. I saw the ram pushing westward, and northward, and southward, so that no beast might stand before him; neither was there any that could deliver out of his hand,"[4] etc.

Let it here be observed, that as with the taking of Babylon by Cyrus *began* the renown of the Medo-Persian empire, and that its supremacy continued to the time of Xerxes, *and no longer;* so the commencement of the vision *must* be dated either from Cyrus' taking Babylon, B. C. 536 or 538; or Xerxes' defeat in Greece, B. C. 480. The interval, as history attests (if we except a few isolated defeats, as in Scythia and Marathon), was marked by

---

[1] Dan. viii. 1-4.
[2] Ib. verse 4.
[3] Ib. verse 13.
[4] Ib. verses 3, 4.

the unchecked victorious pushing of the *two-horned ram*, " so that no beast could stand before it ; " and so continued down to the time of Xerxes' expedition against the Greeks, when, at the battles of Salamis, Platæa, and Mycale, *Persian preëminence received a mortal blow*, from which it never recovered. Henceforward, the two-horned ram was no longer enabled to " do according to his will." It is clear, therefore, that the " vision " cannot be dated *earlier* than b. c. 536 or 538, nor *later* than b. c. 480. This, it will be perceived, leaves a space of only 56 years, within which to fix the exact epoch. In either case, the 2,300 years, if reckoned from the former dates, must have *ended* in a. d. 1762 or 1764 ; and if from the latter, in a. d. 1820.

It requires, however, but an impartial glance at the history of the Persian empire during the above interval of 56 years, to determine the point in question. For, first, though the successes of the two-horned ram (Cyrus), would seem to verify the commencement of the 2,300 years with b. c. 536 or 538, so far as ancient history is concerned ; yet the *modern* era at which this number would have expired, furnishes *no* corresponding event to that indicated by the prophecy, viz., the *overthrow* of the Turkish power, or the cleansing of the Christian countries or the Jewish sanctuary from the Mohammedan yoke. The same remarks will apply, second, to the *first* Persian expedition into Greece, that ended with the battle of Marathon, b. c. 490, there being *no* corresponding event in modern history, to the *close* of the 2,300 years, if reckoned from that date, to indicate the *overthrow*, etc., of the Turkish power. There remains, therefore, third, the era of Xerxes' expedition, of which the setting out from Susa is determined by a famous eclipse of the sun to the year b. c. 481, and which arrived at Thermopylæ soon after the summer solstice, in the year following. That this event *fully meets the terms* of the prophecy in every essential particular, will, we opine, appear from what follows.

The epoch in question is expressly set forth by Daniel himself, chap. xi. 2, as one prominent, and to be *noted* in the history of Persian greatness. "Behold, there shall stand up *three kings* in Persia (Cambyses, Smerdis, and Darius); and the *fourth* (Xerxes) shall be far richer than they all: and by his strength, through his riches, he shall stir up all against the realm of *Grecia*," etc. Now, mark: It was at the above-named date, B. C. 481, that the two-horned ram, eager for conquest, collected his *whole strength* in preparation for a conflict with the united forces of the Grecian he-goat: and, so general was the impression "that none could deliver out of the *ram's* hand," that, as a matter of self-preservation, many of the smaller republics of Greece itself succumbed to the demanded acknowledgment of subjection to the *Persian* monarch, by the delivery of earth and water. And yet, Xerxes, with his waving banners of twenty-nine tributary nations accompanying (as Herodotus describes it), collected from Scythia north to Ethiopia south, and from India east to Thrace and Libya west, having advanced " westward " across Asia Minor to Sardis, " northward " across the Hellespont into Thrace and Macedon, and " southward " from Macedon to his conflict with the Greeks in the passes of Thessaly, was there humbled by the much smaller force, yet superior valor of the latter, and Persian supremacy *ended*, by the emancipation of the *Asiatic Greeks* from a foreign yoke. Thus, we have the testimony of *ancient* history to verify the commencement of the 2,300 years with 480 B. C. Then, next,

Counting from this era, the 2,300 years *ended* in A. D.

1820. Accordingly, *in this year*, as modern history attests, the Greek insurrection broke out, from which *began* that dismemberment of the provinces of the TURKISH EMPIRE, which has ever since been going on; and by which, from Greece, from Moldavia and Wallachia, from Algiers, Egypt, and the Holy Land, taken in connection with the events of recent date, is clearly indicated a RECESSION, to an immense extent, of the overflowing waters of this mystical Euphratean power.[1] But more on this subject anon.

In this connection, there is a need-be to enter a little more into detail in regard to the TURCO-MOHAMMEDAN POWER. The "little horn" which denotes it, you will observe, was not to appear upon the prophetical stage until "the last end of the indignation," *i. e.*, in "*the latter time*" of the ARABIAN kingdom out of which it was to arise. (Dan. viii. 19, 23.) To determine this point, we must repair to the Apocalypse, where, in chap. ix. 1–11, we have depicted the symbolic rise of the SARACENIC POWER, denoted by the symbolic "*locusts*," the followers of the great Arabian impostor, MOHAMMED, whose name in the Hebrew tongue is *Abaddon*, but in the Greek tongue hath his name *Apollyon, i. e., the destroyer;* and whose *hegira* or *era* is dated from his flight from Mecca in A. D. 622.

Now, these Saracens were introduced upon the prophetic platform as a *scourge* to the apostate devotees of the Roman beast in the *eastern* or *Greek* branch of the united empire, whom they were empowered to "torment for the space of *five months*" (verse 5), or 150 years of prophetical time, *i. e.*, "each day for a year." This period, it is to be observed, is to be dated, not from the

---

[1] See Rev. ix. 14, and xvi. 12.

hegira in A. D. 622, but from the Arabian impostor's *first proclamation* of his sanguinary mission in A. D. 612, when Mohammed demanded,—"Who will be my vizier?" To which Ali replied, "O prophet, I am the man. Whoever rises up against thee, I will dash out his teeth, tear out his eyes, break his legs, and rip him up!" Accordingly, *from this year*, the Saracenic hordes issued forth in propagandist swarms like "locusts," swift as horses, firm as lions, and cruel as the sting of scorpions, to make *proselytes* to their faith, and to *punish* the eastern provinces of Christendom. Hence, after having desolated Damascus and Jerusalem, in A. D. 630, THEY ERECTED THE MOHAMMEDAN MOSQUE OF OMAR ON MOUNT MORIAH,—the very spot on which once stood the glorious temple of Solomon,—and proclaimed to the helpless subjects of their wrath: "Ye Christian dogs, ye know your option—the *Koran*, the *tribute*, or the *sword*." Thus this "little horn waxed exceeding great toward the pleasant land," PALESTINE. (See Dan. viii. 9-12.) Suffice it to say, that the Saracenic empire continued to extend itself almost unchecked from A. D. 612, till at length it began to decay, and so continued down to A. D. 762,—*a period of exactly* 150 *years*, according to the above prophecy—when its once united power was rent in twain, and the *eastern* dynasty of the Abyssides became the antagonist of the *west*. Its last remaining vestiges, however, disappeared in A. D. 1057, when Tangrolipix, the TURK, put an end to it by the conquest of the caliph of Persia.

Hence the rise of the TURCO-MOHAMMEDAN or ISLAMIC POWER, which was *another scourge* in God's hand, for the punishment of the unfaithful of his professed followers, both *Christian* and *Jewish*. These Turks, as warriors, differed from the Saracens as *infantry* differs from *cavalry*. The Saracenic locust army were "*like unto* horses prepared for battle " (verse 7) ; whereas the Turks *mounted* " horses " (verse 17). In Rev. ix. 13-15, they are introduced upon the stage of the Roman earth under the symbol of " four angels," or messengers of judgment, which, for a time, are represented as being "*bound*" on the other side of " the great river Euphrates," but are now " *let loose* " to pass that river, to make inroads into the *eastern* or Grecian branch of the ROMAN EMPIRE, and to erect themselves into a monarchy upon the ruins thereof. They are called " four angels," for the reason that, at the time of their remarkable passage over the river Euphrates, they were under the command of *Solymun Shahum*, and his *three sons;* and, upon the father being drowned in crossing, they brought themselves under " four other captains," viz., *Otrogulus*, and his *three sons*,[1] of whom one was the famous Othmun, who, a little after, established on a firm basis that great empire, the OTTOMAN, over which his family sways the sceptre to this day.

Again: That the phrase, " *the great river Euphrates* " (Rev. ix. 14), symbolizes the TURCO-OTTOMAN EMPIRE, will appear from the fact that, as the term Euphrates in Isa. viii. 7, was symbolically employed to denote the territory of the *Assyrian* army which bordered upon that river, so, by analogy, the twice-repeated phrase as a symbol in Rev. ix. 14 and xvi. 12 under this VIth trumpet and the VIth vial, as all the best expositors admit, cannot represent any other than the *Turkish power*, they being no less borderers upon the *Euphratean* territory, or the

---

[1] As early as A. D. 507, a deputation of ambassadors from Turkey told the emperor Justinian, that their empire was divided into FOUR SULTANIES, viz., *Bagdad, Aleppo, Antioch,* and *Iconium,* as is related by one of the Byzantine historians, and noticed by all their writers. (See Pocock's Researches, ad Abul-phar. pp. 106, 108, and Launday, Hist. p. 86.)

inhabitants of the same tract, than were the Assyrians. Their being "*bound* on the great river Euphrates," indicates a pause, or *season of repose*, during which those judgments which had been inflicted upon the eastern or Greek church by the Saracens under the VIth apocalyptic trumpet were suspended. Not that there was a total cessation of the *Saracenic* power as a scourge to the apostate Christians of the east; for, although their empire was ruptured in A. D. 762, yet their sceptre was not completely broken, until, as already stated, Tangrolipix snapped it asunder by the overthrow of the caliph of Persia in A. D. 1057.

We now observe, that *the period* assigned to the mission of this Turco-Ottoman or Mohammedan power, was for "*an hour, and a day, and a month, and a year*, for to slay the third part of men,"[1] etc. As the phrase "*an hour*" is uniformly used in the Apocalypse to signify an *indefinite* period of time, it will be so applied in this place. The sense then is, that the Turks were loosed from their confinement on the borders of the Euphrates as the predestined instruments of God, to inflict ruin upon the eastern or Grecian empire, *even* " for a day, a month, a year," etc., which, as a *definite* prophetical period, computing "each day for a year," stands thus:—a *day*, 1 year; a *month*, 30 years; a *year*, 360 years, of sacred lunar time. This period, therefore,—(1 + 30 + 360 = 391 years)—reckoning from A. D. 1057, when Tangrolipix erected the Turkish empire upon the ruins of the Saracenic, brings us down to A. D. 1453. Accordingly, *on this very year* (the interval from A. D. 1057 having been filled up by a series of the sorest judgments ever inflicted upon Christendom, first, by the hand of Togrel-Beg, and sub-

[1] Rev. xix. 15.

sequently by that of Alp Arslan,) the Turks, with the sultan Hinemar as their leader, *besieged the capital of Constantinople*, that city which for centuries had held before the world the position of " the queen and mistress of the east," and which, by conquest, has been retained by them down to this day.

Aye. This Turco-Mohammedan "little horn," like that of the Papal, STILL LIVES. The Turkish crescent still surmounts the dome of the Mosque of Omar on the Mount Moriah in the Holy City, JERUSALEM, and the Sultan of Turkey, like the Pope of Rome, Pius IX., has just issued the following firman, which appears in "The Christian Advocate and Journal," published by "the Methodist Book Concern" in this city, bearing date Jan. 12, 1865, under the head of—

"SIGNS OF THE TIMES."

"The 'Jewish Intelligencer' (published in Constantinople), gives the following passage of a recent letter from Jerusalem, by the Rev. W. Bailey:

"Jerusalem, which is generally so quiet at this season, has been all astir this week in consequence of an order from the *Porte*, that all the streets should be levelled and paved, and that all obstructions should be removed. This order has been executed in true Turkish style, and many a tale of loss and oppression can probably be told by the poor store-keepers and some houseowners; but the *improvement* to the city and the *public benefit* will be great. We shall now have broad and airy streets, where before we could scarcely move. When the work is completed, it will, indeed, be an advance in civilized effort, and quite an achievement for Turkey. *The Jews are very much concerned about this gathering up of the stones, and making broad the ways of Jerusalem:* they say, 'NOW WE ARE CERTAIN MESSIAH'S COMING IS VERY NEAR.'"

We must here observe, by the way—*and well they may say so*. For, reference is here made by them to the following prophecy of Isaiah, chap. lxii. 10-12 : "*Go through, go through the gates; prepare ye the way of the people; cast up, cast up the highway;* GATHER OUT THE STONES; LIFT UP A STANDARD FOR THE PEOPLE. BEHOLD, THE LORD HATH PROCLAIMED UNTO THE END OF THE WORLD,"—that is, by this very FIRMAN of the Sultan of Turkey, though undesigned on his part—"Say ye to the daughter of Zion, Behold, *thy salvation cometh;* behold, his reward is with him, and his work before him. And *they*" (*i. e.*, "the world," all nations) "shall call them, *the holy people, the redeemed of the Lord:* and *thou*" (*i. e.*, Jerusalem) "shalt be called, *Sought out, a city not forsaken.*" With the eyes of the Jews, therefore, fixed upon this prophecy of Isaiah, it is no marvel that they recognize in the above Firman of the Sublime Porte in reference to the Holy City, *a clear and explicit* "SIGN" that their "Messiah's coming is very near." It is nothing less than the "*lifting up of that standard*" before all the nations of "the world," which betokens one of the principal steps in preparing the way for the NATIONAL RESTORATION of the Jews to their own land, Palestine, and the bringing to them of that "SALVATION" which is to immediately follow, by the PERSONAL APPEARANCE to them of their Messiah.¹ But, to return to the letter. It continues thus:

"You have, perhaps, heard that there is a telegraph at *Jaffa*, which connects *Egypt* with *Beyrout*. It is now decided, I believe, that a branch line is to be made *to this city*. I also find it is very probable we shall ere long have a *carriage-road* to Jaffa, as two engineers, one English, the other Turkish, report says, are to arrive here in a few days to make preparations for it. A survey for a *railway* has already been completed, and a plan, sixty-five feet long, to lay before the Sultan, left here about a month ago." The writer adds—"I do not think, however,

¹ See Zech. xii. 9, 10; compared with chap. xiv. 1-6.

that the time for a railroad in these parts has yet arrived." But we must deferentially differ with him on that point. He then goes on to say—" Jaffa is now undergoing a *similar change* to Jerusalem. A number of coffee and other unsightly shops, outside the gate on the Jerusalem road, are to be removed, and the land sold, with the condition that it shall be *built upon;* another *gate* is also to be made. Our Pasha went three days ago to see that these important changes and improvements are properly done. A *better landing place* from the sea was nearly completed last week, and it is just possible that ere long a *lighthouse* may be built near it. Soon there is to be a lighthouse on *Mount Carmel,* and two or three others, it is said, will soon be placed on the *Syrian coast.* We have now *two lines of English steamers* touching monthly at Jaffa, in addition to the usual foreign ones, and the *French* will henceforth come oftener than formerly. THUS JERUSALEM AND THE HOLY LAND WILL NECESSARILY BE BROUGHT MORE THAN EVER INTO NOTICE. Surely these, and many like changes which are taking place around us, *have much meaning* in them. I must believe they have."

With this evidence, then, before us, that the " sick old man," as the Czar of Russia styled the Turco-Mohammedan power, like that of the Papacy, *still lives*, it now only remains that we furnish the evidence that the above manifesto of the Sultan of Turkey in regard to Jerusalem, as the representative head of the EASTERN ANTICHRIST, is the sure precursor of *its* final and speedy extinction from the list of nations.

The prophet Daniel, when speaking of the " king of fierce countenance, and understanding dark sentences," who was to " stand up " or appear " in the *latter time* of the kingdom,"—*i. e.*, the ARABIAN branch of " one of the four notable horns " of Alexander's divided empire which fell to Ptolemy—he says : " *But he shall be broken without hand.*"

We have now only to turn back to our historic verification of the *commencement* of the prophetic period of the 2,300 days or years of Dan. viii. 14, in the year B. C.

480, and of its *close* in A. D. 1820, and at the breaking out of the Greek insurrection against the Sublime Porte; and to mark the *historic waning* of the Turco-Mohammedan power from the *latter date,* for an illustration of its predicted doom in accordance with the above prophecy.

It has been God's plan all along, to *punish* those very powers, the Babylonian, Medo-Persian, Grecian, and Roman, and especially the last, that have been engaged in *persecuting* his saints, both Jewish and Christian; and also *those powers*—the Saracenic and the Ottoman—that have been used as "rods" in His hand to scourge the apostate nations of Christendom. Hence, as the *Saracenic empire* was subjugated by the Turks; so now this *latter power* is destined TO BE BLOTTED OUT FROM THE LIST OF NATIONS. On this subject, I submit what follows:—

Of the Jews who escaped the edge of the sword at the destruction of their national polity and temple by Titus in A. D. 70, our Lord predicted, that they "*should be led captive into all nations, and that Jerusalem should be trodden down of the Gentiles,* UNTIL THE TIMES OF THE GENTILES BE FULFILLED," (Luke xxi. 24.) Now, that this period, for the wisest of purposes left *indefinite* in the above prophecy, was nevertheless to embrace *a long period,* is evident from the fact, that *the Jews still remain captives* among all the Gentile nations of Christendom, while "*Jerusalem*" continues to this day to be "*trodden down*" by the proud foot of the Ottoman power. Indeed, that power constitutes *the only remaining impediment* to the national restoration of the Jews to their own long alienated "land." But, the Holy Spirit has revealed the *removal* of that impediment, in exact harmony with the prophecy of Daniel, that "it shall be *broken without hand.*" It is to transpire under and during the "pouring out of the VIth apocalyptic vial upon THE GREAT RIVER EUPHRATES," which, as has been shown, symbolizes the Turco-Mohammedan power; the effect of which is to " *dry up* the waters thereof; " while the *final* result is, "THAT THE WAY OF THE KINGS OF THE EAST MAY BE PREPARED," etc. (Rev. xvi. 12), *i. e.*, the "*kings of peoples*," or the multitudinous seed of Abraham, that was to come forth of "Sarah" as "the mother of nations," (Gen. xviii. 15-19).

Well. And what is the record of history on this subject? The answer is, that during the wars that grew out of the French Revolution in A. D. 1793, while the armies of France desolated Spain, Portugal, Germany, Holland, Russia, Prussia, Italy, and Austria, down to A. D. 1820, the *Ottoman empire*, peaceful within and without, appeared to the world, and was respected, as a powerful and mighty nation. But it was that calm which *presaged* a terrific storm. For, *commencing with this very year* A. D. 1820, was the effusion of the VIth vial upon this "great river Euphrates," by the act of Ali Pasha of Albania, in declaring his *independence* of the Sublime Porte. And, from that period down to the present time, *judgment* has been wonderfully poured out upon him from this "vial" of the Almighty's wrath, whether it has been effected by the hand of *man*, or more directly by the hand of *God*. Yes, we repeat; she has been made to suffer alike from internal commotions and foreign invasions; from plague and pestilence; from conflagrations and inundations; from storms and earthquakes; and though last, not least, from the ruinous effects of exorbitant taxations, exactions, and despotic robberies to such an extent, as to draw from the lips of that renowned historian, orator, and poet, M. de Lamartine, when speaking of the "drying up" or *progressive wasting away* of the

Ottoman empire, in the Chamber of Deputies in Paris, the following:

"The Ottoman empire," says he, "*is no empire at all;* it is a misshapen conglomeration of different races without cohesion between them, with mingled interests, without a language, without laws, without religion, without unity or stability of power. You see that *the breath of life* which animated it, namely, religious fanaticism, *is extinct.* You see that its fatal and blinded administration has devoured the race of conquerors, AND THAT TURKEY IS PERISHING FOR WANT OF TURKS."

With this statement accords the fact, that *at this present hour*, the last streamlet is scarcely discoverable in the once full and overflowing channel of the great mystical Euphrates; and though, at this moment, the ANGLO-FRENCH ALLIANCE, by a strange combination of the *Papacy* with *Protestantism*, is still spreading over it the shadow of its protecting wings, in the hope to prevent its entire evaporation, they will not succeed. God has pronounced the *doom* of that temporarily galvanized body; *and no power on earth can prevent its speedy accomplishment.* It will be found that, while man proposes, God disposes. And now mark: the very *firman* just promulgated by the Sultan of Turkey in regard to the improvements now going on in the Holy City, JERUSALEM, by stirring up the *jealousies* of the crowned heads of Europe, Roman, Greek, and Protestant, will only tend to *precipitate* that consummation. The time has now fully come "for RUSSIA to commence a movement so long thirsted for—so long imposed upon her rulers by their predecessors —*the conquest of Turkey and the possession of Constantinople.* Peter the Great first declared that "*Nature had but one Russia and she should have no rival.*" The efforts of every successive sovereign, from Catherine down, were directed to extend the empire to the Mediterranean, to drive the Turks out of Europe, construct a new Byzantine empire, and make *Constantinople* the southern capital of the Russian empire, and the centre of the Greek church." . . Accordingly, "true to the traditionary policy of his family," Nicholas I. did not abandon his designs on Constantinople, although he was unwise in the selection of *the time* for the attempt in A. D. 1854. He did not foresee that France and England were then free to form an *alliance*, in conjunction with Sardinia, and force him into the *Crimean war*, which lost him a large portion of his army, and a good deal of his military prestige. But the times are different now. The opportunity which had not arrived then, *is at hand.* Hence, Alexander II., having been "convinced of his father's error," terminated the Crimean war immediately upon his accession to the throne. But, urged on by "the hereditary policy of his race," he is reported to have recently sent a large invading army into the frontiers of the *Turkish empire*, with a resolve to push on to its very centre, and that with a view to the *accomplishment* of the grand project which originated with Peter the Great; and that, too, with the assurance of *no further interference* on the part of any of the allied powers of Europe.

We repeat, therefore, that the *total evaporation* of this symbolic Euphratean power, as the only obstacle in the "preparation of the way of the kings of the east," or *the national return of the Jews to Palestine*, cannot be extended beyond A. D. 1868, that being the utmost limit of the period called "THE TIMES OF THE GENTILES."[1]

On the other hand, as we have seen, the fall of the

---

[1] See pages 39-41 of this work. Also "Our Bible Chronology," chap. ix. sec. iii. pp. 145-147.

Papacy takes place *coetaneously* with it; and that, immediately thereupon, the agents of *its* destruction—the "ten horns," or "kings" of the Roman earth—"GIVE THEIR POWER UNTO THE BEAST HAVING TWO HORNS LIKE A LAMB, BUT WHO SPEAKS AS A DRAGON."

On this momentous subject, beyond what has been affirmed in the preceding pages, we cannot now enlarge. Suffice it, therefore, to say, that the *simultaneous* destruction of these two long-lived scourges of mankind, opens the way for the introduction upon the prophetical platform of other scenes, national, political, and moral, of a nature, character, and extent, such as the world has never known—scenes of grace and of mercy, on the one hand; scenes of justice and of judgment, on the other. Let us, in few words, present a summary view of

"THE CONCLUSION OF THE WHOLE MATTER."

We once more reiterate, what we have so often affirmed as a Millenarian, namely, that there is no MILLERISM in our expositions of God's prophetic word. By this we mean to say, that there is *no connection* between the second personal coming of the Lord as *pre*-millennial, and the subjection of the globe we inhabit *to the fire of* the universal conflagration, as alleged by that theory.[1] So far from it, TIME WILL RUN ON, AND NATIONS WILL CONTINUE TO EXIST, though under a *total change* in the physical, political, moral, and social constitution of things as they now are, and so will continue onward to the *close* of the seventh millenary of the world from the creation and fall of man. The *opening* of that NEW DISPENSATION,

---

[1] See our work—"The Second Coming of Christ," etc., chap. iv. pp. 204-216, on this subject.

which is to immediately follow the termination of the Papal and Mohammedan powers in A. D. 1868, will be signalized,

I. *By the first resurrection and rapture of the living saints.* That momentous event is indicated by the words of the angelic visitant to the prophet Daniel, "But go thy way *till the end be:* for thou shalt rest, *and stand in thy lot at the end of the* (1,335) *days.*" (Dan. xii. 12, 13). The words, "*Blessed is he that waiteth,*"—that is, in the exercise of patient faith and hope, like the martyr-" souls" whom St. John saw in his vision "*under the altar*" at the opening of the fifth seal (Rev. vi. 9–11)—"*and cometh* to the thousand three hundred and five and thirty days," —"each day for a year,"[1]—undeniably refers to Daniel's standing in his lot in RESURRECTION "praise, and honor, and glory, AT THE APPEARING OF JESUS CHRIST."[2] Indeed, this Danielic prophecy is THE KEY to the import of the scriptural doctrine of the FIRST RESURRECTION, as described by St. Paul in 1 Thess. iv. 13–18, and by St. John, Rev. xx. 4, and verse 5, last clause; and is the same "*in*" which the former apostle so ardently desired to have "a part," as expressed in those notable words, Philipp. iii. 10, 11 : "That I may know Him, and the power of His resurrection, and the fellowship of His sufferings, being made conformable unto His death ; if by any means I might attain unto *the resurrection* of (Gr. ἐξανάστασιν, or from among) the dead." These are the "*some*" among the "*many* sleepers in the dust of the earth" spoken of, Dan. xii. 2, who "shall awake to *everlasting life,*" in contrast with those who shall awake "to *shame and everlasting contempt,*" these latter being "the rest of the dead" (*i. e.*, the *wicked* dead) whom St. John

---

[1] Ezek. iv. 4–6.   [2] 1 Pet. i. 3–9.

declares, Rev. xx. 5, "LIVED NOT AGAIN UNTIL *the thousand years were finished.*" But, as we have already demonstrated, this prophetical period of 1,335 years, coetaneously with *all* the other longer dates—the shorter forming *integral parts* of them—run out in A. D. 1868.[1] It follows, therefore, that the resurrection of both is not, and cannot be, *simultaneous.* Instead, as the prophet David declares, that "*precious* in the sight of the Lord is the death of his saints,"[2] so he also says that " the *upright* shall have *dominion over them* "—*i. e.*, the wicked —" *in the morning*"[3] of the great millennial day. Further. This *first great event* attendant upon the second *pre*millennial coming of the Lord to " make up His jewels,"[4] (or, which is the same thing, to raise the dead who " sleep in Him " and change and translate " the living who remain unto His coming,") WILL NOT BE OPENLY AND VISIBLY recognized by the ungodly world in or out of the nominal church. No. He now comes as " *a thief in the night,*" to gather together His elect Gentile bride from among both the living and the dead, when, "*in that night,* there shall be two in one bed; the one shall be taken, and the other left. Two women shall be grinding together; the one shall be taken, and the other left. Two men shall be in the field; the one shall be taken, and the other left."[5] St. Paul, having spoken of " the whole creation " as " groaning and travailing in pain together until now; " and also of " the earnest expectation of the creature as *waiting for the manifestation of the Son of God,*" adds: " And not only they, but we ourselves also, which have the first-fruits of the Spirit, even

---

[1] See pages 39–41 of this work. Also more fully, " Our Bible Chronology," etc., chap. ix. pp. 129-183.
[2] Ps. cxvi. 15.   [3] Ib. xlix. 14.   [4] Mal. iii. 17.
[5] Luke xvii. 34-36.

we ourselves groan within ourselves, *waiting for the adoption*, to wit, THE REDEMPTION OF OUR BODY."[1] Thus gloriously, in a way of *grace* and of *mercy*, will be ushered in the new millennial era of the world. It will constitute the *commencement* of that "RESTITUTION OF ALL THINGS which God hath spoken by the mouth of all His holy prophets since the world began,"[2] to be followed,

II. *By the political reconstruction of present earthly governments under one human head.* The world has now tried every form of government but ONE. It has failed under all, from Adam to the last anointed king. It has failed, like Israel, even under a THEOCRACY. There is, therefore, but one form of government of human device to be tried—the government of *a man* exalted to the rank of A GOD, worshipped by all the world except those "who are written in the book of life" as "the Bride, the Lamb's wife." Such a government will be the climax of blasphemy, and it will, deservedly, sink the world into the depths of misery. It will inaugurate that UNPARALLELED TRIBULATION predicted by our Lord, Matt. xxiv. 21, Mark xiii. 19, "Such as was not from the beginning of the creation which God created unto this time, neither shall be," "which shall come on all the world" of nominal Christendom.

Let us then suppose, for the sake of illustration, that the ingathering of the redeemed Gentile Bride of the Lamb had *already* transpired. This would indicate that the *first step* had been taken toward the restoration of the ORIGINAL THEOCRACY to Israel. All heaven is in commotion. The parabolic "nobleman" has been invested by the Father with His KINGLY PREROGATIVES, and He

[1] Rom. viii. 19-23. [2] Acts iii. 21.

comes forth to " set up," upon the overthrow of *all rival dynasties*, that " kingdom which shall never be destroyed." Then, too, of those who have *overcome* by the blood of the Lamb, and to whom He has given the promise—" Ye shall sit with Me in My throne "—" I will give you power over the nations "—" Ye shall bruise them with a rod of iron, and dash them to pieces as a potter's vessel "—also, that " the saints of the Most High shall take the kingdom, and possess the kingdom for ever and ever "—yea, that " the kingdom and dominion and greatness of the kingdom under the whole heaven, shall be given to the people of the saints of the Most High "—yea more, who has said of them, " All things are yours, and ye are Christ's, and Christ is God's : " we repeat, having lavished upon them all these " exceeding great and precious promises," now that they are gathered to Him " IN THE AIR," He admits them to be COPARTNERS with Himself in the exercise of that RESTORED THEOCRACY of which HE, as the divinely constituted " heir of all things," is " THE HEAD."

But, " everything in its order." *Not yet* has Christ and His " co-heir " reigning saints commenced the extermination of His and of their enemies. That work, for a short space, is held in abeyance. " The mystery of iniquity " under its EIGHTH HEAD, must have its *full scope* of development. *Immediately*, therefore, upon the ascent of Christ and his saints " in the air," " the wickedness of man," like its antediluvian type " in the days of Noah," having " become great in the earth, and every imagination and thought of his heart only evil continually," as an act of just retribution, " He whose name is Holy " having declared, " My spirit shall not always strive with man, for that he also is flesh," now leaves the guilty nations of earth and an apostate church to their own devices. And now, behold: goaded on by the same godless principle which actuated the Israelites, in the time of Samuel, to abjure the theocratic government of GOD as their king; and which led the same nation to declare of their Messiah AT HIS FIRST COMING—"Not this man, but Cæsar"—"We will not have this man to reign over us"—so now, when the "midnight cry" is being heard throughout the length and breadth of Christendom, "BEHOLD THE BRIDEGROOM COMETH, GO YE OUT TO MEET HIM!" in view of the *signal failures* of all the experiments of the nations of earth, Jewish and Gentile, for 6,000 years, to provide a *system of government* adapted to the necessities of mankind; instead of learning a lesson from the fate of the antediluvian world which perished by water—of the builders of Babel—of the Jewish nation in their rejection of the original theocracy, and in their final crucifixion of their Messiah—we repeat: instead of this, like the first great progenitors of the race, who yielded to "the desire to be *as gods*, to know good and evil," human madness to this day continues the same; and all the policy and genius of man are set to work to make himself *independent* of all DIVINE rule, and to rest the sovereignty of universal empire IN HIMSELF.

And, strange to say, just at this juncture in the political affairs of the world, their eyes are directed toward a guiding GENIUS in every way adapted to the AGE. In illustration of this, we ask the reader to look at the following facts: The age of frantic revolution found its master-spirit in one exactly like itself—in the first Napoleon—fiery, vehement, and headlong. The age was frantic, and so its master-spirit. The *new age*, half warlike, half mechanical, has found a third Napoleon exactly like itself; fond of military splendor, thirsting for conquest, yet as firm, as exact, as impassive, as one of the machines of his own age. The headlong fury of the first Napoleon has been worked off, and cold, impassive calculation has filled its place, yet resting on the very same substratum of iron will and stony determination. The age of frenzy had its Napoleon of fire—the present warlike and mechanical age has its Napoleon of iron. Great minds indicate the advent of great deeds; and the rise of the third Napoleon, with all the FITNESS for his age, forbodes some vast revolution. The history of England, and other Protestant nations, is a history of PRINCIPLES—the history of France is a history of PASSIONS. But we have now arrived at a period in which principles and passions are united in one impetuous torrent, ready to sweep away all effete preëxisting systems; yet, for the time, being restrained, shut in, and directed in its course, by the iron will and the indomitable thirst for the glory of universal empire of Napoleon the Third. Nor is this all. This "man of destiny," as a sovereign, a statesman, a diplomatist, and a soldier, it is now conceded on all hands, is without an equal. And, measuring his *past* with his *present* position, the conviction is more and more every hour fastening itself upon the minds of men, that, convinced by experience that the world has never had a king worthy of the name; nor any form of government that was not in their view a misgovernment; and that there never can be a *permanent* form of government except as it is vested in a ONE MAN POWER; and finally, as the true position of the world now is that they are *waiting* for the appearance of JUST SUCH A KING; the time having at length arrived for his *début* upon the stage of action, he will be HAILED as such! Aye, reader. Let me entreat you—don't argue, don't quibble, or prevaricate. All will be vain. Mankind, even from the very beginning, having preferred any form of government *except* the divine, will now be left to their own choice, not only, but "God will put it into the hearts of the ten Latin horns or kings" of western Europe "*to fulfil his will and to agree* and give their power and strength and kingdom" to this ONE MAN, who will be exalted to the rank of A GOD; while all other powers, as his *allies*, will recognize his UNIVERSAL SUPREMACY over the Latin earth.

And now, having said that the establishment of this stupendous governmental power under ONE HEAD—the eighth Apocalyptic Beast—will inaugurate that UNPARALLELED TRIBULATION predicted by our Lord, Matt. xxiv. 21, " which shall come upon all the world" of nominal Christendom, let us turn our thoughts the while,

III. *To its characteristics and its results.* The *design* of this one man power being to subject *all* to his despotic sway, first, having set up " an *image* to the Beast which had the wound by a sword, *and did live*"—*i. e.*, Louis Napoleon III.—he now issues his mandate to the subjects of the *Latin* race, " causing that as many as *would not worship* the image of the beast should be *killed.*" Nor this only. For " he causes all, both small and great, rich and poor, bond and free, to receive *a mark* in their right hands and in their foreheads: *and that no man might buy or sell*, SAVE he that had the mark, or the name of the Beast, or the number of his name."[1]

Now this last, we observe, will be THE TEST of *fidelity* or of *apostasy* to the subjects of NOMINAL PROTESTANT CHRISTENDOM. Hence, to this tribulation will those be especially exposed, who have said in their hearts, " my Lord delayeth His coming," or who have joined with the scoffers of these last days and exclaimed, " Where is the promise of His coming?" Aye. This will be that " day

[1] Rev. xiii. 15–17.

which will try every man's work, of what sort it is. If any man's work *abide,* he shall receive a *reward.* If any man's work shall be *burned,* he shall *suffer loss:* but he himself shall be saved, *yet so as by fire.*"[1] Thus, " of these inhabitants of the earth," when made to *feel* the effects of the wide-spread " judgments of God" which will constitute this season of unparalleled tribulation, and " *shall learn righteousness,*"[2] and shall refuse that act of *self-dedication* to the last Antichrist which will consist of a submission by others to receive " his mark, name, and number of his name," shall finally " *come up out of* THE *great tribulation,* having washed their robes, and made them white in the blood of the Lamb."[3]

We would only add on this subject, by the way, that the *condition* and *destiny* of the above class of Christ's professed followers of these last times, will *differ* from those who believe in and watch and pray for the Lord's speedy coming, by these latter being *preserved from* this " great tribulation." " Only with thine eyes shalt thou *behold and see* the reward of the wicked;"[4] for, as already explained, such shall have been *previously* " caught up to meet the Lord in the air, and so shall ever be with the Lord." Their *future destiny,* therefore, as being, numerically, the KING-FATHER'S " *daughter,*" who is called upon to " forget her own people, and her father's house," is at last presented to the " KING'S " SON, " who greatly desires her beauty—for He is her Lord "—as His affianced BRIDE, " all glorious within, her clothing being of wrought gold." And, when the time shall have come for the *celebration* of the marriage nuptials, and she is " brought unto the King in raiment of needle-work;"

---

[1] Cor. iii. 10–15. [2] Isa. xxvi. 9. [3] Rev. vii. 14.
[4] See Ps. xci. 8.

those saved *out of* the great tribulation, may, perhaps, though less distinguished than she, be admitted to the high honor of filling the place " in the King's palace," of " the *virgins her companions* that follow her." [1] Refraining, however, from trenching upon the but *partially revealed structure* of the heavenly hierarchy in this connection; with the remark, that in view of the *exposure* of the great mass of those in these times " who profess and call themselves Christians" to that unparalleled tribulation of which we have spoken, we can discern a MOTIVE why their hearts should be stirred up within them like "the Bearcans" of New Testament times, to "search the Scriptures daily whether these things be so," [2] compared with which every other sinks into absolute insignificance. And while we say, in the language of St. Paul, " Let every man be fully persuaded in his own mind," [3] yet we would most affectionately, but earnestly entreat one and all that, at any cost, they "buy the truth and sell it not;" [4] and, having attained it, "hold it fast till HE (Christ) come, that no man take their crown." [5] And we would the more vehemently urge upon them this reasonable duty, from the consideration of our *near proximate* position to the GREAT CRISIS before us.

And, what a crisis, this! It will consist of a HEADING UP " of all those things which God hath spoken by the mouth of all His holy prophets since the world began," as connected with that vast system of " THE POLITICAL ECONOMY OF PROPHECY " of which His inspired word is the text-book. During the interval between the RAPTURE of the resurrected and living saints, and the OPEN AND VISIBLE manifestation of Christ to the nations, when

---

[1] See Ps. xliv. 10-15.   [2] Acts xvi. 11.   [3] Rom. xiv. 5.
[4] Prov. xxiii. 23.   [5] Rev. iii. 11.

"every eye shall see Him, and they also which pierced Him," and when "all the kindreds of the earth shall wail because of Him;"[1] the LAST ANTICHRIST will have run his despotic career, down to the invasion of the Holy City, Jerusalem, as described, Zech. xiv. 1, 2.

We here express it as our settled conviction, that, meanwhile, those of the Lord's chosen people who, though *left* to be exposed to the terrible sufferings of the unparalleled tribulation inaugurated by the reign of the ONE MAN power; yet, refusing to receive the impress of "the mark, or name, or number of the Beast in their right hand or in their foreheads," though prohibited by that power to "buy or sell," *they will not suffer death.* But, having "*learned righteousness*" through the judgments of God inflicted upon them, in their last extremity, they will be "*saved, yet so as by fire.*" That is, like unto the living saints *previously* "caught up to meet the Lord in the air," as the "*virgin companions*" of the Bride, "with gladness and rejoicing shall they be brought: *they shall enter into the king's palace*,"[2] by being *translated* to the heavenly domains, as were those who preceded them. And so, we submit, while "the Bride, the Lamb's wife," will be constituted of "the general assembly and church of *the first-born* which are written in heaven," who were *saved from* the great tribulation; these latter will fill the place of "*the just men made perfect*"[3] by their subjection to the fiery ordeal of that "hour of temptation which is to come on all the world, to *try* them which dwell upon the earth;"[4] and who, having "endured unto the end," shall at the last be *delivered out of it,* as above. In other words, they will form that "great multitude which no

---

[1] Rev. i. 7.
[2] Ps. xlv. 14, 15.
[3] Heb. xii. 23.
[4] Rev. iii. 10.

man could number, of all nations, and kindreds, and people, and tongues," concerning whom "one of the elders" in the vision of St. John asked him, "*What are these which are arrayed in white robes? and whence came they?* And John said unto him, Sir, thou knowest." Then the elder replied: "These are they which *came out of* THE great tribulation,"[1] etc. Accordingly, these two classes of occupants of the "King's Palace" "in the air" are thus distinguished, the one from the other. "The Bride, the Lamb's wife," is admitted to a "seat *with Him* IN *His throne:*"[2] whereas St. John saw the other "*stand before* the throne, and *before* the Lamb."[3] Of the King himself it is said: "And on his head were *many crowns.*"[4] And so, "the Bride, the Lamb's wife"—taken in the sense of a noun of multitude,—having "looked for Him" and "loved His appearing,"[5] as co-reigning "Kings"[6] with Him "in His throne," shall wear "*crowns of gold* upon their heads."[7] But of the other class, not having striven lawfully "for the crown,"[8] it is said that they "had *palms* in their hands." The collective "Bride of the Lamb" "shall *reign* with Christ," "*ruling* the nations with a rod of iron,"[9] etc. Of the other class it is said, that "they are *before* the throne of God, and *serve* Him day and night in His temple,"[10] etc.

---

[1] Rev. vii. 9, 13, 14.   [2] Rev. iii. 21.   [3] Ib. vii. 9, 15.
[4] Rev. xix. 12.   [5] 2 Heb. ix. 29; 2 Tim. iv. 8.
[6] 3 Rev. i. 6; v. 10.
[7] 2 Tim. iv. 8; Rev. iv. 4. The "elder" who spake to John, Rev. vii. 13, 14, was one of the "four and twenty elders" occupying "seats round about the throne" of the King, all of whom "had upon their heads *crowns of gold*," and who, as *representatives* of "the general assembly and church of the first-born" *already* gathered into "the King's palace," are by him distinguished, as above, from those who came *after*.
[8] 2 Tim. ii. 5.   [9] Rev. v. 10; xx. 4; ii. 27; xix. 15.
[10] Ib. vii. 15.

Return we now to that point in the impending crisis before us—the invasion of Jerusalem by the last Antichrist. This is his *last act* in that tragical scene which has already passed under review. It will form the culminating point of man's lust for KINGLY power and dominion in the earth. It commenced, as we have said, with the first created man, whom God "made to have dominion over the works of his hands, and put *all* things under his feet," with *one* exception, and that was, MAN. The earthly "dominion" of Adam was limited to "all *sheep* and *oxen*, yea, and the *beasts* of the field; the *fowls* of the air, and the *fish* of the sea, and *whatsoever* passeth through the depths of the sea."[1] That was the *utmost limit* of his power. But, not content to hold this dominion under another, he aspired to be "AS GODS," and so, to extend that "dominion" over his own species. Thus he *rejected* the Creator God as his KING. Hence, from that time to the present, the fiery passion for *human* kingly power, has rendered nothing more hateful in the eyes of worldly men than the promise and prospect of a DIVINE KING. But, after their governmental experiments of 6,000 years, and their development as matured under the reign of the LAST ANTICHRIST, it will be found that, one and all, having proved not only inefficient, but disastrous to the best interests of man; He who has said: "I will overturn, overturn, overturn IT, and it shall be no more, UNTIL HE COME whose right it is, AND I WILL GIVE IT HIM;"[2] just at the extremity of "the time of Jacob's trouble" by the Antichrist's invasion of Jerusalem, he is "saved out of it," by the coming forth of "the lion of the tribe of Judah"—THE TRUE MESSIAH—as "the minister of the circumcision from the truth of God, to *confirm* the

---

[1] Ps. viii. 6–8. Gen. i. 27, 28. [2] Ezek. xxi. 27.

promises made unto the fathers." Yea, now comes he forth "out of His place," the "highest heavens," into which He passed at His ascension as an exiled king driven from His throne, to fulfil that prophecy,—" He that leadeth into captivity shall *go into* captivity; and he that killeth with the sword shall be *killed by* the sword." [1] In a word, He comes forth to assert His exclusive right to reign as " THE PRINCE OF THE KINGS OF THE EARTH," by the total overthrow of the last Antichrist and his confederated hosts, and by the *restoration* over the nations, Jewish and Gentile, of that ORIGINAL THEOCRACY abjured by Israel in the time of Samuel.

And finally. This act of retributive justice in sweeping away all earthly dynasties as now constituted, will be the *finishing blow* inflicted upon them by the MESSIANIC " stone cut out of the mountain without hands," as the legitimate offspring of the four Gentile monarchies denoted by the symbolic colossal image of Nebuchadnezzar. And so clear and convincing will be the evidence that the AGENCY by whom their destruction is effected is DIVINE, and not human merely, that all " the *escaped* of the nations which came against Jerusalem," both Jewish and Gentile, will confess, " Verily there is a God that judgeth in the earth." In the *retrospect* of the misrule and cruel tyranny of those Gentile powers which have so long destroyed the earth, and now *concentrated* into this last, it will then be said by all the world—" *You* led the ten tribes of Israel as captives into Assyria, and, after destroying the first temple, held Judah captive in Babylon for 70 years. But 'the DELIVERER' has at last 'come to Zion,' to redress them of their wrongs. Yielding to the demand of the envious but erring Jewish nation to crucify

---

[1] Rev. xiii. 10.

their Messiah, *you* first put the Son of God to death, and then burnt the third temple, destroyed the Holy City, Jerusalem, and broke up the commonwealth of Israel; and now Israel, as God's 'battle-axe,' breaks you up. And, as though this were not enough, *you* 'fill up the cup of your iniquity' by now again invading Jerusalem, and subjecting the Jewish nation to a series of unprecedented calamities; but now, HE over whose head at His crucifixion you wrote the mock inscription, 'The King of the Jews,' is 'alive for evermore,' and by His *personal presence* and those of His co-regal saints, the Pauline prophecy, 2 Thess. i. 7–9, is verified: 'for, the Lord Jesus is now revealed from heaven with His mighty angels in flaming fire'—not to raise and judge the wicked dead—but, to 'take vengeance on *you* that know not God, and that obey not the gospel of the Lord Jesus Christ;' and now you, together with your head, 'shall go into perdition,' for you 'shall be punished with everlasting destruction from the presence of the Lord, and from the glory of His power.'"

From this moment commences the world's *moral, political*, and *physical* renovation. Immediately following the Lord's fighting against and destroying these antichristian nations, the *design* of "the Deliverer in coming to Zion," is, to "*turn away ungodliness from Jacob*," that "so all Israel may be saved."[1] To this end, "standing with His feet upon the Mount of Olives which is before Jerusalem on the east," "He will pour upon the house of David, and upon the inhabitants of Jerusalem, the spirit of grace and of supplication; *and they shall look upon* HIM *whom they pierced, and mourn*,"[2] etc. Thus "a nation," (the Jewish) "shall be born *at once*;"[3]

---

[1] Rom. xi. 26. [2] Zech. xii. 9, 10. [3] Isa. lxvi. 8–10.

and this, after the manner of St. Paul's conversion, who, as a Jew of the tribe of Benjamin, was as one "*born out of due time*," was effected only by the *personal* manifestation of Christ to him.[1] And now, the work of the world's moral regeneration having been thus *begun*, like the course of a resistless torrent, it shall spread far and wide, until the *Gentile* nations of Christendom and of Heathendom, taking within its circuitous course the restoration to Canaan of the lost ten tribes of Israel, will speedily subdue ALL NATIONS to the obedience of Christ. It must suffice on the subject, that we request the reader to turn to and carefully read Isaiah, chapters lx., lxi., lxii., and chap. lxvi. 7–21.

Then, as to the *Political* renovation of the world. As we have seen, all human governments, even the best, have been the sources of tyrannical misrule, of bloody revolutions, and of moral degradation. The elevation of the rich and powerful, and oppression of the poor and helpless, have been the ruling characteristics of them all. But, under the government of the King of Kings and His co-reigning Saints, the laws and constitution of His Empire will *reverse* this order of things. "To help the fatherless and the poor to their right, that the men of the earth be no more exalted against them." "He shall keep the simple folk by their right; defend the children of the poor, and punish the wrong-doer." "He shall deliver the poor when he crieth; the needy also, and him that hath no helper." "He shall be favorable to the simple and needy; and shall preserve the souls of the poor." "With righteousness shall he judge the poor, and reprove with equity for the meek of the earth. . . And righteousness shall be the girdle of His loins, and faithful-

---

[1] 1 Cor. xv. 5–3; Acts ix. 3–6.

ness the girdle of his reins." Such shall be the principles which shall pervade the newly inaugurated POLITICAL ECONOMY of the Millennial earth, under and during the reign of the only PRE-ORDAINED "MONARCH OF THE WORLD." Then, "The LORD shall be King over all the earth: in that day shall there be ONE LORD, and his NAME ONE." Then, "He shall judge among the nations, and shall rebuke many people; and they shall beat their swords into ploughshares, and their spears into pruning hooks: nation shall not lift up sword against nation, neither shall they learn war any more." And then, too, "Many people shall go and say, come ye, and let us go up to the mountain of the Lord; to the house of the God of Jacob: *for He will teach us of* His *ways, and we shall walk in* His *paths:* FOR OUT OF ZION SHALL GO FORTH THE LAW, AND THE WORD OF THE LORD FROM JERUSALEM." And finally, "It shall come to pass that *every one that is left* of the nations which came against Jerusalem, *shall go up from year to year to worship* THE KING, *the Lord of hosts, and to keep the feast of tabernacles.*" Not that all shall go up together, but at different times, so that within each year *all* shall go up. And those nations which *will not* go up, the terrible judgments of "no rain," and the infliction of "plagues" shall be visited upon them.[1]

Our space will only allow of reference to one additional point in this connection. The question is, Will the SEAT OR THRONE *of Christ's Universal Empire be located on earth* during the Millennial Era? We unhesitatingly answer, that it will not. However Judah and Israel might otherwise have constituted "the Bride of the Lamb," yet, by long continued rebellion against their covenant

---

[1] Zech. xiv. 16-19.

God, and which was finally headed up by their rejection and crucifixion of "the Lord of life and glory," as the King-father's Son, they *forfeited* that right, and was consequently *divorced* from their position as such. Hence, "the Kingdom of God was taken from them, and given to a nation bringing forth the fruits thereof."[1] Hence, the "taking out of (or from among) the *Gentiles*, a people for his name,"[2] who were to constitute that "BRIDE." With the above facts kept in view, therefore, let us remember that the promises of "the kingdom" belong neither to the restored Jews, nor to the Millennial Saints; for they will be the SUBJECTS of that kingdom. What the world has always wanted has been a PERFECT government—perfect in wisdom and perfect in strength. And, inasmuch as, since the abjuration of the THEOCRACY of Israel,—which was founded upon the basis of an ABSOLUTE MONARCHY,—no such a government has obtained among the nations, that theocracy must be RESTORED. And *when* restored, its *seat* or *throne* of Empire will be located, not on earth, but in HEAVEN. True, the Great King, as formerly under the Theocracy of Israel, will doubtless appoint such officials as the exigencies of the restored *Jewish* commonwealth shall require. And others of the Millennial *Gentile* nations gathered in with the Jews, may have their parliaments, etc. But, one and all, will be subordinate to the government of HEAVEN. The sources, both of law and of power, will be no longer on earth, but altogether in the HEAVENLY "Palace of the King." To this end, all the "joint-heirs with Christ," who have *no* promises of mere *earthly* inheritance, will have been raised and translated at the *first* manifestation of the Lord's second coming, to meet Him, *not* on the earth,

---

[1] Matt. xxi. 43. [2] Acts xv. 14.

but "IN THE AIR," and there "*ever to be with Him.*" Nor as co-partners *with* the Lord, will they be shut in within a single planet; but, being endowed with the faculties of *locomotion*, like unto the resurrected and glorified body of their King,—for their vile "bodies shall be *changed* and fashioned *like unto* His own glorious body"[1]—they will traverse the universe of "principalities and powers in the heavenly places." Nor will they pass by our own planet, between the inhabitants of whom and themselves, with their King, an *intercourse* will be kept up, of which, the ladder of Jacob's vision, reaching from earth to heaven, with the angels of God descending and ascending upon it, while the LORD stood at the top of it,[2] was a significant type. And, being aided by the indwelling of the DIVINITY, all their thoughts, all their achievments, and the duration and splendor of their reign, will move on co-ordinate with that of their Lord, throughout eternal ages.

Say, then, reader, is there anything in this prophetico-Scriptural view of the near future reign of Christ and His redeemed Saints over the saved nations in the flesh, on earth, during the Millennium, to indicate that it is carnal, gross, and sensual? Ah! those who now affirm that we thus teach, will think differently, when the "great voices in HEAVEN," which shall accompany the loud blast of "the *seventh* angelic trumpet" shall proclaim to the nations,

"THE KINGDOMS OF THIS WORLD ARE BECOME THE KINGDOMS OF OUR LORD, AND OF HIS CHRIST, AND HE SHALL REIGN FOREVER AND EVER."[3]

We repeat, therefore, once more. The THRONE of Christ's empire will be in HEAVEN. The "KINGS" who "possess the kingdom, and dominion, and greatness of the

---

[1] Philip. iii, 21.   [2] Gen. xxviii. 12–17.   [3] Rev. xi. 15.

kingdom under the whole heaven," are in HEAVEN; but the SUBJECTS of that kingdom, Jewish and Gentile, are upon EARTH. Nor can it be a *spiritual* reign of Christ on earth. The *idea*, that the state of the redeemed in heaven will consist of their being seated on clouds, in some remote corner of infinite space, singing psalms and hymns, throughout eternal ages, can, to say the least, find no support in the Word of God. The same holds true of Christ's reign over the earth. The reign of grace *by the Spirit* in the hearts of men, while Christ is *personally absent* from the Church, during *this* dispensation, will continue to hold its seat in the hearts of men during the *Millennial* era. But, to this latter state, will be superadded the *personal return* of Christ to his long bereaved Church, according to His promise: "I WILL COME AGAIN,"[1] when *both* will be conjoined, as explained above, never again to be separated. Then will the united voice of the Church on earth exclaim: "LO! THIS IS OUR GOD; WE HAVE WAITED FOR HIM, AND HE WILL SAVE US: THIS IS THE LORD; WE HAVE WAITED FOR HIM: WE WILL BE GLAD AND REJOICE IN HIS SALVATION."[2] Yes, then will be verified the prophetic announcement, that "the MOON SHALL BE CONFOUNDED, AND THE SUN ASHAMED, WHEN THE LORD SHALL REIGN IN MOUNT ZION, AND IN JERUSALEM, AND BEFORE HIS ANCIENTS GLORIOUSLY."[3]

And now, to close. A few words on the subject of the *physical* renovation of the Millennial Earth must suffice. We need not doubt, that the benefits conferred by the newly inaugurated government of heaven, will soon reconcile the world at large to the once unwelcome change. High above Jerusalem will be seen the HEAVENLY

[1] John xiv. 1-5. [2] Isa. xxv. 9. [3] Isa. xxiv. 23.

"Palace of the King," glowing with celestial light, and immortalizing heat. The light will be uncreated light, by means of which, in connection with such other physical agencies as God may please to employ, the climates of the earth will be gradually changed, rendering the atmosphere salubrious, and the earth fruitful, and investing both with all the healthful and delightful characteristics of the pristine Eden. Then, too, the human body will feel the change, cheering the heart, as well as gratifying the eyes and all the other senses, thus imparting new life and vigor to man's physical powers, and restoring to him that longevity peculiar to the patriarchal age. "There shall be no more thence an infant of days, nor an old man that hath not filled his days. * * * For as the days of a tree *are* the days of my people: and mine elect shall *long enjoy* the work of their hands."[1] Along with these blessings, will be an augmentation of man's intellectual powers, qualifying him for mental improvement, the acquisition of knowledge, and the extension of his resources for usefulness, before unknown. Yea, "he shall walk in the light of God's countenance; in His name shall he rejoice all the day, and in His righteousness shall he be exalted." And the earth, and man, and even the animal creation, being recovered from the curse of the fall, "In that day, shall there be upon the bells of the horses, HOLINESS UNTO THE LORD."[2]

For a more enlarged view of the physical state of the Millennial "New Earth and Heavens," as contrasted with the *post*-Millennial "New Earth and heavens," as predicted by St. Peter and in the Apocalypse, together with the other characteristics of that state under the benign rule of "THE PEACEABLE KINGDOM OF THE BRANCH"—

---

[1] Isa. lxv. 20, 23. [2] Isa. lxvi. 20.

the Lord Jesus Christ—we must refer the reader to our recently published work on "the Second Coming of Christ."

And, may every professing disciple of the Saviour, in these last days, find it in his heart to exclaim: "COME, LORD JESUS, COME QUICKLY!"

With the present and impending events of these last times in view, we close, with the following words of JESUS, to every true believer: "WHEN THESE THINGS BEGIN TO COME TO PASS, THEN LOOK UP, AND LIFT UP YOUR HEADS, FOR YOUR REDEMPTION DRAWETH NIGH." (Luke xxi. 28.) Yea, verily—

> "The world appears
> To toll the death-bell of its own decease—
> *   *   *   *   The old
> And crazy earth has had her shaking fits
> More frequent, and forgone her usual rest;
> And nature seems with dim and sickly eye
> To wait the close of all.
>
> *   *   *   *   *   *
>
> Six thousand years of sorrow have well nigh
> Fulfilled their tardy and disastrous course
> Over a sinful world; and what remains
> Of this tempestuous state of human things,
> Is merely as the rocking of a sea
> Before a calm that rocks itself to rest.
>
> *   *   *   *   *   *
>
> Behold the measure of the promise filled;
> See Salem built, the labor of a God!
> Bright as a sun the Sacred City shines:
> All kingdoms and all princes of the earth
> Flock to that light: the glory of all lands
> Flows into her; unbounded is her joy,
> And endless her increase.
>
> *   *   *   *   *   *

Come, then, and added to Thy many crowns,
Receive yet one, the crown of all the earth,
For Thou alone art worthy.

 * * * * * *

Thy saints proclaim Thee King; and Thy delay
Gives courage to their foes, who, could they see
The dawn of Thy last advent, long desired,
Would flee for safety to the falling rocks."

COWPER.

NOTES.

N. B.—The reader will please turn to the pages in the body of the work for the *subjects* to which these Notes refer.

NOTE I, page 26. (Introduction). Of our Lord's prophecy respecting THE TIME of His second coming, etc. :—" *Of that day and that hour* NO MAN MAKETH KNOWN, *no, not the angels in heaven, neither the Son, but the Father only.*" (Matt. xxiv. 36; Mark xiii. 32.)

This passage, in the *popular* theological nomenclature of the day, is triumphantly quoted as *decisive* against any attempt to determine whether THE SECOND PERSONAL COMING OF CHRIST is *pre* or *post*-millennial. Quoting the passage as it reads in our English version : " Of that day and hour *knoweth no man*," etc., all attempts to settle the question as to *the time* of that event, as *near* or *remote*, is denounced as fanatical. Hence the prevalent indifference to, and prejudice against, all *chronologico-prophetical* expositions of the subject. But we deferentially submit,—

First. Even admitting that neither man, nor angels, nor Christ Himself knoweth anything of this matter, it is undeniable that there is *one* who knoweth—even "THE FATHER," "*who hath put the times and seasons* IN HIS OWN *power.*" (Acts i. 7). Accordingly, *if* He please, and *when* and *as* He pleases, HE can make them known. That He *has* done so, we maintain is fully and clearly revealed in His word. But what now concerns us is,

Second. The *correctness* of the rendering of the above passage in our English version of the phrase, " *knoweth no man,*" etc. And here we must premise, by the way, that while in the corresponding prophecy of our Lord, as given by Luke, chap. xxi., that Evangelist *omits* this passage altogether, Mark *only* uses the phrase, "*neither the Son*," etc. (chap. xiii. 32). That the above passage in Mark, however, is not an interpolation introduced into the text after the Apostolic age, as some allege, is evident from the fact, that Matthew uses the expression, " but my Father *only*," which is equivalent to the expression, "neither the Son," for the word " only," by implication, *includes* the Son. We now pass to the phrase, " *knoweth no man*, no, not the angels in heaven, *neither the Son*," etc.

We shall here adopt in place of this rendering, the translation of Macknight: "But of that day and that hour *no man maketh known;* not even the angels who are in heaven, neither the Son, but the Father." Now, this rendering has at least the merit of consistency, when compared with King James's translation, as it regards the possession, by CHRIST, of the attribute of *omniscience;* for while this latter rendering contradicts the express declaration of St. Peter concerning Christ: " LORD, *Thou knowest all things*" (John xxi. 17), the former fully recognizes it as HE in whom "dwelleth all the fulness of the Godhead bodily" (Col. ii. 9). It is not, it *cannot,* therefore, be true, that Christ *does not know* the day or hour of His second coming. In proof of the correctness of Macknight's translation as above, all expositors unite in rendering the corresponding word in Num. xvi. 5, not "To-morrow the Lord will *know* who are His," etc., but, " The Lord will *show,* or the Lord *will make known,*" etc. And so, where the Apostle Paul uses the same word (2 Cor. ii. 2), Macknight renders the passage, " I determined to *make known nothing* among you, SAVE Jesus Christ, and Him crucified." The above, therefore, we must insist is more than sufficient to justify the rendering of the phrase in Mark—" *no man maketh known.*" Nor this only. For it follows, that although Christ *does not* reveal "the day or the hour" of His second coming, the "FATHER" does make it known. Hence, though our Lord said to His disciples, " It is not for *you* (*i. e.*, THEN, or at that particular time) to know the times or the seasons which the Father hath put in His own power," yet He predicted of them, " ye shall receive power," *i. e.*, to understand these things, " after that the Holy

Ghost is come upon you," etc. (Acts i. 8). Accordingly, St. Paul, in his Epistle to the Thessalonians, says, 1 Thess. v. 4: "Ye, brethren, *are not in darkness*, that that day should overtake *you* as a thief;" while of the *ungodly* "men who shall say, peace and safety; then sudden destruction shall come upon them, as travail upon a woman with child, and they shall not escape" (v. 5). This corresponds exactly with Daniel's prophecy, chap. xii. 9: "But the wicked shall do wickedly; and *the wicked shall not* understand; but *the wise shall* understand." St. Peter also, when speaking of that salvation which is come unto us, says of the Old Testament prophets, that they "inquired and searched diligently as to *what* (*i. e.*, of the events predicted), and *what manner of time* the Spirit of Christ which was in them did signify, when it testified beforehand the *sufferings* of Christ, and the *glory that should follow*" (1 Pet. i. 9–11). And the same Apostle assures us, that "we have a more sure word of prophecy,"—which prophecy relates, according to the preceding passage, not only to *events*, but to "*times and seasons*,"—"to which *we all do well that we take heed*, as unto a light which shineth in a dark place, UNTIL the *day* dawn, and the DAY-STAR arise in our hearts." May God of His infinite mercy incline all our hearts so to do for Christ's sake.

NOTE II, page 166. "*That no man may buy or sell*, SAVE *he that hath the mark, or name of the Beast, or number of his name.*" (Rev. xiii. 17).

This passage refers to the last great Antichristian Confederacy, or UNIVERSAL LATIN EMPIRE, which, after A. D. 1868, will embrace "all, both small and great, rich and poor, free and bond," who *swear allegiance to* the *last Antichrist*, by *receiving* his "mark," etc. "in their right hands, or in their foreheads." Those, therefore, throughout Christendom who *refuse* to dedicate themselves to him by receiving said "mark," etc., shall be permitted neither to "*buy or sell.*"

Now this prophecy has a most fearfully portentous import, in regard to all those nationalities throughout nominal Christendom, who shall be exposed to the fiery ordeal of that "*hour of temptation*, which shall come upon *all the world*, to TRY those that dwell upon the earth" (Rev. iii. 10). It will be on this wise. Of the last Antichrist, or that "*vile person*," spoken of by Daniel, chap. xi. 21, it is predicted that "*he shall have power over the treasures of gold and silver, and over all the precious things of Egypt*," etc. (ver. 43). That is, he shall have unlimited control over all the *monetary* interests and operations of the nations throughout the world. And, clothed with this "power," he will use it AS A TEST of obedience to his mandate to *receive* "his mark, or name, or number of his name in their right hands, or in their foreheads;" in other words, to *swear allegiance* to him. "Those who refuse shall be permitted neither to *buy or sell.*"

It hence results, that the TURNING-POINT of this "hour of temptation that is to come upon all the world, to *try* them that dwell upon the earth," will involve either *a final and total apostasy from* THE TRUE CHRIST, or an *adherence to* HIM, in the midst of this fiery ordeal. In the case of the *former*, they "shall be punished with everlasting destruction from the *presence* of the Lord and the *glory* of His power" (2 Thess. ii. 8, 9). In that of the *latter*, "they shall be *saved*, yet so *as by fire.*" (1 Cor. iii. 14, 15).

And mark, reader. The nature of the TEST of apostasy from, or of fidelity to, THE TRUE CHRIST, will be that of "*gold and silver.*" Job says, chap. xxxi. 24, 28: "If I *rejoice* because my wealth was great, and mine hand hath gotten me much; . . . this were *an iniquity* to be punished by the Judge: for I should have *denied* the God that is above." To do so, involves that sin of "*covetousness*, which is *idolatry*" in the sight of God. All those, therefore, "who profess and call themselves Christians," who have "*made haste* to be rich" (Prov. xxviii. 20), and who, having obtained them, "trust in the *uncertain riches*" instead of "the living God" (1 Tim. vi. 17); when this "hour of temptation" shall have come upon them, will find that their *salvation* or *perdition* will hang "trembling in the scale." To *cling* to them THEN, will involve their *perdition*. To relinquish them THEN, . . . alas, who among such will do it? "*The love of money*," having in life entwined its insidious grasp upon their hearts, can THEN be sundered only by that "FIRE which is to *try every man's work*, of what sort it is." And who will affirm that the sin of *avarice*, or "*covetousness*," is NOT predominant in most of those who are *within*, as well as those who are *outside of*, the pale of the visible Church of this day? And observe. This "*judgment*" of the Most High at the hand of him who will THEN " have power over the treasures of silver and gold," "*must begin at the house of God!*" Alas, "*who shall live*, when God doth this?" Only those, we reply, who "*shall be saved* AS BY FIRE." Better, O, infinitely better for all such, that they *now* " kiss the Son, lest He be angry, and they perish in the way, when His wrath is kindled *but a little*." Let them *now* " come out from the world, and touch not, taste not, nor handle the unclean thing," by a sincere and hearty *dedication* of themselves and their worldly substance to HIM "whose is the silver and the gold," that they may "lay hold on eternal life," and be prepared to "meet," " stand before," and " not be ashamed of Christ AT HIS COMING."

NOTE III, page 206. " *The Jews, when restored in their unconverted state, will hail the Eighth Head* (Louis Napoleon III.), AS THEIR MESSIAH," etc.

To this it is objected that it cannot be, for the reason that this false Messiah must be of *Jewish descent*, which is affirmed not to be true of the present Emperor of the French. To this we reply, first, that even admitting this to be so, yet, keeping in view the singular characteristics of this wonderful man, it is not impossible but that he may *pretend* to be of *Jewish genealogy*, and as the prophecies concerning the last Antichrist do not mention the *precise tribe* out of which he, as the false Messiah, is to arise, the Jews may not be able to *confute* the imposture; and thus, by tampering with that genealogy, he may succeed in that way to palm himself upon them as their Messiah. A very little evidence will turn the scale with the then infatuated *Jewish* nation, provided the claimant has *power enough* to advance their worldly interests. But we observe, in the second place, that as " the great Antichristian Monarch who is to bring back the Jews, is, evidently, the person who will be set up as the JEWISH MESSIAH, in opposition to the Son of David, we have only to bear in mind the fact, that, as we have seen, the *name* of the present Emperor of the French contains the numerals which, when counted as figures, gives the mystical number of 666 (Rev. xiii. 18), not only in *Latin* and *Greek*, but in *Hebrew* also. Hence, we submit, that this circumstance will go far to *confirm* any claim on his part to be of *Jewish* origin. Besides, he has this additional resemblance to the character of the last Antichrist—his features are *Jewish*, exactly those of a *Jew;* and, as so many distinguished public men who have professed to be *Gentiles*, while they have turned out to be of *Israelitish origin*,—such as Massena, Suchet, and others—so it may be with Napoleon III. His family *may* be traced up to a *Jewish* ancestor, which his features render more than probable. It is only, however, "*a little while*" that we are to await the solution of this interesting problem.

NOTE IV, page 218. "*And he (i. e.,* the last Antichrist) *shall plant the tabernacle of his palaces between the seas, in the glorious holy mountain,*" etc. (Dan. xi. 45).

That Louis Napoleon III. has already *virtually* accomplished this part of his destined mission, will appear from the following: "In the English *Morning Chronicle* of Nov. 2d, 1855, wa scontained the first or only announcement of what may be the most momentous occurence of the age, namely:

"On Sunday, Sep. 30, 1855, the French flag was hoisted at JERUSALEM. The French Emperor was made the *Patron* of the Holy Places—and *prayers* were offered up for him by all the clergy—as if Jerusalem was a part of his own Empire. This seizure of the Holy Places, which, in fact, is a seizure of *Jerusalem* itself, is among the greatest of the great events which have occurred within the nineteenth century. The rest of his acts are great only *politically*. This event is great *Scripturally*. It points to the '*beginning* of the end.'" We repeat that it is a *virtual occupation* of the Holy City, and an *actual assertion* of FRENCH SUPREMACY over the Holy Land. Let it also be remembered, that wherever Napoleon III. has planted his foot, it has never yet in any instance been *dislodged*. And the seizure of the Holy City, Jerusalem, as above, he will hold as *the gate*, for the advancement of his ambitious projects in the East.

NOTE V, page 213. This mighty confederacy of the antichristian nations . . . will also embrace as its *allies*, those nations enumerated in Ezek. xxxviii. 1-7; " *Gog, of the land of Magog, the Prince of Rosh, Meshech, and Tubal; and Persia, Ethiopia or Cush, Libya or Phut, Gomer, and Togarmah,*" etc.

The word "*chief*," in the English version of the 2d verse of the above passage, in the *Hebrew* is "Rosh," and is the name of a *place;* so that the passage should read—"The Prince of Rosh, Meshech, and Tubal." Now, Rosh, Meshech, and Tubal, very much resemble in sound Russia, Moscow, and Tobolsk: the last-named place being the capital of Asiatic Russia. . . . We find similar changes in many other names transferred from the Hebrew language: as Tarshish for Tartassus, or Tarsus; and again, the original Hebrew word, "Javan," is in the Greek "Ionia." And so, MAGOG, from whose country "GOG" is to spring, is also the ancestor of the Northern or Scythian nations, now subject to the crown of Russia. Gog is used in Ezekiel as the name of an *individual;* and Rosh, Meshech, and Tubal, as names of *nations*. *Rosh* indicates a nation descended from one of the principal *great-grandchildren* of Noah (not mentioned in Gen. x.); but *Magog, Meshech,* and *Tubal,* are the *grandchildren* of Noah, being all of them the sons of Japheth. (See Gen. x.) In the Ethnographic map of the world, Meshech and Tubal are placed *far up north* of the present Empire of Russia—Tubal on the shores of the Baltic Sea, and Meshech farther east, on the confines of Europe and Asia. Magog, at the same time, is placed in a more *southern* and *central* position, and occupies the district anciently called Scythia, and now Tartary; and embraces that portion of it now subject to Russia, and from whence are drawn so many of those stubborn troops which the *English* formerly said that they could mow down at a shilling an acre! The race of Gomer inhabited the *Northwest*, from Muscovy to Britain; while the races of Magog, Meshech, and Tubal occupied the *Northeast*, from Germany to the Yellow Sea. Gomer, therefore, must contribute very largely to swell the *antichristian* forces of the last Antichrist, the nations of *Europe* being many of them *Gomeric*. And, as this antichristian confederacy are to be destroyed *at the time* of the invasion of Jerusalem, described in Zech. xiv. 1-5; and those of them who "*escape* of the nations who went up against Jerusalem, are to go up from year to year to worship the King, the Lord of Hosts, and to keep the Feast of Tabernacles" (ver. 13), we see not how there can be, as some pretend, a *second* invasion, etc., of the Holy City by the Gomerians.

NOTE VI, page 274. The question is, *Will the* SEAT *or* THRONE *of Christ's universal Empire be located on earth*, during the Millennium?

The answer is, No. We are not to imagine that the Lord will act as an ordinary commander, placing Himself *personally* at the head of His armies. This idea seems to be purposely provided against in the 10th chap. of Zechariah, where it is said: "and the Lord shall be seen *over* them," etc. (ver. 14), but it is not said that He shall be *among* them. The Messiah, as Head of the redeemed Churches *in heaven*, as well as of Israel *upon earth*, certainly will not degrade Himself or His co-reigning Saints by dwelling upon earth, or even by mixing Himself up with earthly affairs, except in the high character of a Sovereign and Supreme Director, or Lawgiver, issuing His mandates from the Capital of the Universe enthroned "*in the air*." This, however, will not interfere to prevent an *occasional* personal intercourse between the celestial Rulers and terrestrial ruled, or between the heavenly capital and the earthly metropolis, in analogy to the things denoted by the typical ladder in the vision of Jacob, and as is indicated by the Prophet Ezekiel, chap. xliii. 1-9, and xliv. 1-3, which see.

TESTIMONIALS

FROM THE

RELIGIOUS AND SECULAR PRESS,

OF THE

REV. R. C. SHIMEALL'S TWO WORKS,

ON

CHRIST'S SECOND COMING:

THE GREAT QUESTION OF THE DAY.

Is it Pre- or Post-Millennial?

SCRIPTURALLY, HISTORICALLY, & PHILOSOPHICALLY CONSIDERED.

OUR BIBLE CHRONOLOGY,

HISTORIC AND PROPHETIC,

Harmonized with the Chronology of Profane Writers, etc.,

DEMONSTRATED.

NEW YORK:
PUBLISHED BY JOHN F. TROW & CO.
—
PHILADELPHIA: POST OFFICE BOX 1199.

THE POLITICAL ECONOMY

OF

PROPHECY,

WITH

SPECIAL REFERENCE TO THE CIVIL, MILITARY, AND ECCLESIASTICAL

RISE AND CAREER

OF

THE ROMAN EMPIRE,

AND OF ITS LAST EMPERORS,

THE THREE NAPOLEONS.

WITH AN APPENDIX ON

THE POPE'S LATE ENCYCLICAL,

AND

THE FIRMAN OF THE SULTAN OF TURKEY.

PROPHETICALLY AND HISTORICALLY DEMONSTRATED.

ILLUSTRATED BY PORTRAITS OF THE NAPOLEONIC FAMILY; A CHART OF THE COURSE OF EMPIRE; MAPS OF THE HOLY LAND, ETC.

ONE VOLUME DUODECIMO. PRICE $1 75.

JOHN F. TROW & CO., 50 Greene Street.

PHILADELPHIA: POST OFFICE BOX 1199.

[PUBLISHERS' CIRCULAR.]

JOHN F. TROW & CO., 50 GREENE ST.

SHIMEALL'S *NEW WORK*

ON

CHRIST'S SECOND COMING:

THE GREAT QUESTION OF THE DAY.

IS IT PRE- OR POST-MILLENNIAL?

WITH A REPLY TO PROF. SHEDD ON

"ESCHATOLOGY,"

ETC., ETC.

TESTIMONIALS FROM THE RELIGIOUS AND SECULAR PRESS.

In presenting this work before the public, the author does so on the simple ground that, despite the indifference, prejudice, or hostility arrayed against the subject of which it treats from its past perversion and abuse, it is nevertheless, from its intrinsic importance as a matter of Divine Revelation, *fairly entitled to inquiry and discussion* as "the Great Question of the day." All that he asks of any person into whose hands this volume may fall, is a careful perusal of it, and a candid decision as to the merits of the two main points involved: "IS THE SECOND COMING OF CHRIST PRE- OR POST-MILLENNIAL?" It is a subject that has employed the devout thoughts and earnest pens of the most profoundly learned and eminently pious and distinguished in the Christian Church of every age,— ancient, mediaeval, and modern. But still the Church continues to be divided on the great question involved, both as to the *manner* and *time* of that stupendous event. This volume presents a view of *both sides* of the question at issue, on the grounds both of the *scriptural* arguments and the *historical* developments of the doctrine; and hence will be found to furnish a *complete exhibit* of all that is essential to a thorough knowledge of the subject.

The publishers can also supply those who desire it with the author's other elaborate work, "*Our Bible Chronology, Sacred and Profane, Historic and Prophetic, Critically Examined and Demonstrated, and Harmonized with the Chronology of Profane Writers,*" etc. This work has been critically examined by a number of our ripest scholars at home and abroad, and has been decided as entitled to the rank of a *standard work* on the subject.

JOHN F. TROW & CO.

TESTIMONIALS.

"From the New York Observer."

"This is a laborious treatise upon a subject that has occupied much of the time and attention of the Church. It professes to be free from all extraneous matter, and to exhibit *all the theories* that have obtained in the Christian Church, from the early post-apostolic age to the present times. The abstract testimony of the Holy Scriptures respecting the second coming of Christ is first presented. This is followed by an examination of the question whether this coming is *past, present,* or *future.* Under this head the various theories of MILLER, GROTIUS, BUSH, and others, are discussed with much patience and learning. The fifth chapter is devoted to the consideration of *sacred philosophy*, to the Scriptural doctrine of the RESURRECTION of Christ, of the righteous, and of the wicked, *as these depend upon, and are connected with,* His second coming. A *complete synopsis* of the Millennarian Scheme is given in the closing chapter. *The whole work evinces great sincerity and devotion, and is an interesting and important presentation* of millennarian views."

"The Christian Times and Episcopal Register."

"This work is based upon the author's 'BIBLE CHRONOLOGY,' a work that has gained *high commendation* both in this country and in England, and which stands among the most valuable works relating to the subject. The preface contains a concise account of the *different theories* that have been entertained on this subject at different times, and is followed by an *appeal*, addressed to Bishop Potter and the other prominent clergymen of this city, who entertain what is called the post-millennial view. He invites them in the most pointed manner to give a reason for the hope that is in them, and challenges them to refute his own view, which is the pre-millennial. . . . *This work is the result of a lifetime of thought and study.* It is very full in all its details; it is written in an impartial Christian spirit, and is distinguished by much ability; and, when taken in connection with the previous volume, furnishes what will generally be desired for the study of this great question."

"**The Christian Advocate and Journal.**" (Meth. Episc.)

"The writer of this volume is a venerable minister of the Presbyterian Church, and a writer of good reputation for candor and research. In composing this volume, he has evidently written from the impulses of his heart, no less than at the dictates of his judgment, maintaining his own theory with an affectionate earnestness. He holds that Christ's second coming will be PRE-MILLENNIAL, or that the great period in the progress of the ages of Christ's kingdom designated by that term—which he does not slavishly limit to a thousand of our solar years—will *follow* the resurrection and the general judgment. *Of the conclusiveness of his arguments we confess our inability to decide confidently,* THOUGH WE INCLINE TO COINCIDE WITH HIS VIEWS ON THAT POINT. We are also quite willing to concede that the subject is one of *deep interest* to the believer in Christ; and we can, in all sincerity, recommend this volume to any who may desire to examine the subject, which is here discussed *exhaustively*, though not *tediously*. Though necessarily somewhat controversial, it is written in a kindly tone, and carries with it a devout and reverential faith."

"**The Christian Intelligencer.**" (Ref. Dutch Church.)

"The author of this elaborate treatise is a sincere and devout believer in the pre-millennial advent of our Lord. Our personal respect for Mr. Shimeall, and interest in the question he has discussed, have led us to examine this work with care. . . . Having read many books written in favor of this theory, we are free to say that we consider this *by far the ablest work* in support of the pre-millennial scheme of interpretation we have yet seen. It is unusually free from dogmatism, and is unencumbered with fanciful applications of events to suit the requirements of a theory. *The appeal is made to Scripture as the final authority,* and that, the author thinks, is plainly in favor of the system he advocates. . . . And as he has selected certain eminent divines to *sit in judgment* upon his performance, and decide whether he is *orthodox* or *heretical,* we await with patience their verdict."

"The Presbyterian." (Philadelphia.)

"The author maintains the pre-millennial views of Christ's coming, and reviews *the whole question* with a clear understanding of all that can be alleged for its correctness. He has given to the study of this question much time and attention, *and is well furnished for its defence against those of opposite views.* His book, therefore, will be found to contain all that is material for the *full exposition* of the subject, and with little of the asperity of controversy."

"The Evangelist."

"This volume is an elaborate discussion of what the author deems 'the great question of the day—Is Christ's second coming pre-millennial or post-millennial?' After a quite extended discussion, preparing the way for his conclusions, he sets forth his position, 'that there is to be no intervening millennium between the second coming of Christ and the day of judgment: in other words, that that event, when it does take place, will be pre- and not post-millennial. The second portion of the work is devoted to a reply to Professor Shedd's Eschatology in his 'History of Christian Doctrine.' Dr. Hatfield's views in his recent articles (published in the American Presbyterian and Theological Review) are also noticed. The author's views "are presented with care and candor, and evince much careful examination and an extended acquaintance with the subject."

"The Prophetic Times: A New Serial." (Philadelphia.)

"We hail this book by Mr. Shimeall with great satisfaction, as an able and seasonable contribution to the literature of this great theme. . . . It is the product of a learned and faithful explorer, and treats the various theories and aspects of the subject with comprehensiveness, judiciousness, and power. Taking the Bible as an intelligible book, which we are to interpret as we do any other serious writings meant for the enlightenment of mankind, he has reached the same conclusions to which every intelligent and honest investigator has come, or must come, who accepts the Scriptures in their plain literal import, which we claim to be the only true way of receiving them. In other words, he is a thorough *millenarian.*

"His method of treating the subject includes, First, an appeal, respectfully addressed to leading anti-millenarians, in which certain important points touching the merits of the subject, and the objectionableness of their manner of meeting them are well put; second, An abstract of the testimony of the Scriptures respecting the second coming, both as to the *substance* of the doctrine and its *practical* uses; third, An examination of the several false theories that have been put forth on the subject, show ing their unscriptural and unsatisfactory character, and utterly refuting them. This constitutes the largest part of the book, and what the author considers the *principal want* of a numerous class of clergy and laity, which he has mainly labored to supply. Various leading questions involved are then discussed separately, as also the nature of the RESURRECTION AND THE FUTURE ATTRIBUTES AND OFFICIAL DIGNITIES OF THE SAINTS; concluding with "A complete Synopsis of the Millenarian Scheme of the Second Coming." All this comprises 320 large octavo pages. Then follows a reply to Prof. Shedd's 'Eschatology,' embracing 117 pages, and setting forth the milleuarianism of the ancient, mediaeval, and modern Church. This is a valuable part of the book, in which Prof. Shedd's 'History' is completely put to shame, as it deserves to be as respects *this* subject. To all this is added some 20 pages of valuable notes, with an index to the whole.

"We thank Mr. Shimeall for this timely and able production, and heartily recommend it for its fairness, its comprehensiveness, its general soundness of exegesis, and its manly honesty, respectfulness, and just conclusions. He who values the truth on this great theme cannot fail to value this book. We shall rejoice in finding it extensively circulated and attentively studied. *The means of a large acquaintance with the whole subject may be found in it.*"

"The Evening Post."

"We have already noticed one or two works of this nature, and that before us is one of the most remarkable for its research and the care with which it is written. Mr. Shimeall has given to the subject of his work the study of many years. His treatise bears evidence, not only of the zeal with which he maintains his own view of the subject, but of the diligence with which he has explored the writings of others. In regard to the Second Advent of the Messiah, he has collected *all the different theories* which have been proposed, stated the arguments in their favor and replied to them in all instances in which he does not accept them. . . . This second coming of Christ, according to Mr. Shimeall's view, is to precede and usher in the Millennium. It will *prepare the way* for that age of innocence, peace, and love which is to succeed the present age of dissension, bloodshed, and crime, and to which millenarians look with earnest longings for its immediate arrival. Although Mr. Shimeall acknowledges himself in the *minority*, he gives the names of various eminent persons, both of *ancient* and *modern* times, who have adopted views similar to those set forth in his book.

"A part of the volume is taken up with a Reply to PROF. SHEDD, of the Union Theological Seminary in this city, who, in his "History of Christian Doctrine," affirms that Millenarianism, by which he means similar views to those held by Mr. Shimeall, has never been the recognized doctrine of the Christian Church. Mr. Shimeall takes issue with him on this point, and brings forward many examples of persons in the *early ages* of the Church, and the *middle ages*, and in *modern times*, who were MILLENARIANS. Lest the view taken by Mr. Shimeall should be confounded with what is called *Millerism*, he takes care to show wherein he differs from the Millerites. In the first place, *he denies the possibility of fixing the day and hour of Christ's Second Coming*, though he holds that there are certain symptoms from which its *near approach* is to be inferred. In the second place he maintains that *the conflagration of the world is not, as the Millerites hold, contemporaneously with this second* [pre-millennial] *advent of the Messiah*, since the promised reign of Christ on earth could not in that event take place.

"The reader may not accept Mr. Shimeall's conclusions, but he cannot look over the book without being interested in the discussion of a question which has engaged the thoughts of many eminent men in every age of the Christian Era, and which could occupy such a mind as that of (Sir Isaac) Newton."

"The Journal of Commerce."

"CHRIST'S SECOND COMING," is the title of an octavo volume by Rev. R. C. Shimeall, a member of the Presbytery of New York, who has devoted his energies and studies to the subject, and produced various works heretofore more or less related to it. In the present volume he has gathered a large amount of controversial matter on the Millenarian question, and presents with great energy his peculiar views. The author endeavors to give the reader a view of *all the theories* which have prevailed in various ages and countries on the Second Coming, and to furnish *in a clear and condensed form a great mass of information suited to answer inquiries often made*. He states that the reader will find the subject discussed 'free from all intricacy, even to the plainest mind.'"

"The New York Times."

The writer of this volume is well known for the extent and wide range of his studies, connected with the interpretation of the Prophetical Scriptures. All he asks for it *is a fair and candid examination* of his theory, in the interests, not of victory, but of truth, and he brings forward the names of some of the most venerated teachers and theologians of the day—under whose auspices the work appears—*to show that he is at least entitled to this consideration*. It will at once be seen that the subject of the book places it beyond the pale of ordinary newspaper discussion. . . . Still it is undeniable that many devout minds have found support and nourishment in the investigation of the prophetical records, and to all who indulge in this study, MR. SHIMEALL's book will be welcome."

"The World."

"It is impossible to over-estimate the importance of the subject which Mr. Shimeall discusses and exhausts in this volume of some five hundred pages. The first part of the work is devoted to the somewhat unreasonably vexed question of the SECOND COMING OF CHRIST. The author addresses an argumentative appeal to *ten clergymen of eminence*, including Bishop Potter and Mr. Henry Ward Beecher,—who will not probably answer him,— to reconsider their habitual '*post-millenarianism*,' and ascertain, while there is yet time, whether he may not be wholly in the wrong; and it is very certain that if these clergymen, failing to respond to his appeal, should eventually prove to have been in the wrong, the consequences both to themselves and to their congregations must be such as it is by no means agreeable to contemplate.

"We are standing now, according to Mr. Shimeall, within some *three years* of the most eventful period of human history. Historical chronology will close, as this devoted student of the 'Second Coming' assures us, with the year 1868. . . . It should be said that Mr. Shimeall, however, while he asserts the *pre-millennial* coming of Christ, argues earnestly against the *pre-millennial conflagration of all things*. . . . Perhaps the most interesting part of Mr. Shimeall's work, and that with which *post-millenarian* divines will find it hardest to deal, is the fourth section of the third chapter on 'ESCHATOLOGY,' in which he recites the '*authentic history of Chiliasm*' since the Reformation. In this section he confronts Professor Shedd with the illustrious and almost inspired Joseph Mede, and with Millenarian authorities of no less weight than John and Charles Wesley, Augustus Toplady, and Bishop Heber.

"Such men as these may have been utterly in the dark, mad, crude, and incompetent; but if this was the case, *why does their spirit rule in the churches*, and *why are their psalms, and hymns, and spiritual songs*, in all lands where the English tongue is known, *the delight and consolation of believers?*"

"The Commercial Advertiser."

"REV. RICHARD C. SHIMEALL has published a work entitled 'Christ's Second Coming,—Is it *Pre*-Millennial or *Post*-Millennial?' To the Scriptural, historical, and philosophical examination of this subject, Mr. Shimeall has devoted himself for many years. The subject of the Millennium, or the Second Coming of Christ, has been for ages held and exhibited in various and conflicting forms by numerous writers. We have, in the first place, the *Anti-Millenarians*, who allege that the Millennium is *past*. Then we have *Post-Millenarians*, who hold that the Second Coming of Christ will not occur till its *conclusion*.

A third School holds to a *future* Millennium *preceded* and *introduced* by, the Second Coming of the Saviour, etc. To this School the author of the present volume belongs.

"Mr. Shimeall enters into a very elaborate and extended review of the *various theories* heretofore held in regard to the Millennium, and *with much force of reasoning* endeavors to show how all systems except the last-named, fail to meet the claims of prophecy and Scripture."

"Zion's Herald." (Boston.)

"The author of the above-named work is a Presbyterian minister, who has evidently studied and thought upon his theme with a great deal of care, as 'the great question of the day.' *He writes with candor, fairly presenting both sides of the question.* His plan is, *first*, to present a view of all the principal 'theories' that have obtained in the Christian Church from the close of the Apostolic age to the present time; *secondly*, to show the scriptural and historical ground on which the different parties claim to rest their views; and, *thirdly*, to examine carefully each theory on its respective merits so as to enable the reader to decide for himself on which side the truth lies. He gives a complete view of the scriptural argument and of the history of the doctrine of Christ's Second Coming as found among the Ancients, Mediævals, and Moderns.

"The three principal theories discussed are, 1. That the Millennium is already past; those who embrace it are called *Anti-Millenarians;* 2. That it is still future, and that the second coming of Christ will not take place until after the Millennium; its advocates are called *Post-Millenarians;* 3. That the Millennium is still future, but that the second coming of Christ will take place before the Millennium—its adherents are called *Pre-Millennialists.* The author takes sides with the last. The book may be read with profit by all parties, as it contains much reliable information on the subject."

"The Israelite Indeed."

"This is a work which should be read by all who love our Lord and Saviour Jesus Christ. It enters into all the views which have been held in any portion of the Church concerning our Lord's coming again. *It is one of the ablest works we have met with* on this important and interesting subject, and will well repay for the reading. Let all who love the Lord's appearing read this work and get their souls warmed up on this delightful theme."

This work has been published by the patronage of a large number both of the *Clergy* and the *Laity*, of different denominations, among whom are the following:

Rev. THOMAS DEWITT, D. D.
" J. T. DURYEA.
" E. P. ROGERS, D. D.
" W. R. GORDON, D. D.
" A. R. THOMPSON, D. D.
" J. T. DEMAREST, D. D.
" S. R. JOHNSON, D. D.
" J. H. WESTON, D. D.
" J. COTTON SMITH, D. D.
" A. H. VINTON, D. D.
" W. R. WILLIAMS, D. D.

Rev. R. U. HOWLAND, D. D.
" J. H. HOUGHTON, D. D.
" W. A. SCOTT, D. D.
" J. M. STEPHENSON, D. D.
" A. E. CAMPBELL, D. D.
" JOSEPH SCUDDER.
" JOHN M. KREBS, D. D.
" THOMAS HASTINGS, D. D.
" S. D. ALEXANDER, D. D.
" JOHN MANNING, D. D.
" JOHN QUINCY ADAMS.

Brooklyn, REV. JAMES EELLS, D. D., REV. J. H. VAN DYKE, REV. J. E. ROCKWELL, D. D.

Jersey City, REV. C. K. IMBRIE, D. D., REV. P. D. VAN CLEEF, D. D.

Williamsburg, REV. J. D. WELLS, D. D.

PETER LORILLARD, ESQ.
S. W. BENEDICT, ESQ.
S. A. SCHIEFFELIN, ESQ.
E. S. JAFFREY, ESQ.
A. W. BRADFORD, ESQ.
PETER NAYLOR, ESQ.
DAVID OLIPHANT, ESQ.
WM. VERNON, ESQ.
CHARLES SCRIBNER, ESQ.
F. T. BETTS, ESQ.
S. A. CHURCH, ESQ.
THEODORE BOURNE, ESQ.

CHARLES G. HARMER, ESQ.
J. W. P. MORRISON, ESQ.
A. B. CONGER, ESQ.
WM. B. CROSBY, ESQ.
HOMER MORGAN, ESQ.
JON. THOMPSON, ESQ.
JOHN T. CRANE, ESQ.
W. H. H. MOORE, ESQ.
BENJ. R. WINTHROP, ESQ.
BENJ. DOUGLASS, ESQ.
JAMES SUYDAM, ESQ.
C. F. HUNTER, ESQ.

New Standard Work.

OUR BIBLE CHRONOLOGY,

HISTORIC AND PROPHETIC,

CRITICALLY EXAMINED AND DEMONSTRATED,

AND

Harmonized with the Chronology of Profane Writers, &c.

WITH A MAP OF THE ANCIENT WORLD, A CHART OF THE COURSE OF EMPIRES, AND OTHER ILLUSTRATIONS. FIFTY-FOUR PAGES OF TABULAR MATTER, CHRONOLOGICAL AND GENEALOGICAL, SACRED AND PROFANE,

BY REV. R. C. SHIMEALL.

We call your special attention to the work referred to above, which, from the importance of the subjects of which it treats, and the interest which is being daily awakened in its behalf, both in England and in this country, shows its peculiar adaptation to the present times. Several editions of the work have been disposed of, including among its patrons the clergy of all the different denominations—Presbyterian, Episcopalian, Dutch Reformed, Methodist, Baptist, etc. It is also peculiarly adapted to the use of Bible Classes, Sabbath Schools, and other institutions of learning, and forms a much-needed appendage to the Family Bible. It forms a handsome *royal octavo* volume of about 250 pages, bound in substantial cloth, and contains all the matter embraced in the author's Biblical and Ecclesiastical Charts, (originally published at $10 *each* per copy,) and in a much more convenient form for ordinary use.

The author's aim in this volume has been to reach a *reliable* result in regard to the exact chronology of the world from the commencement of human history. The work was commenced at the request and by the encouragement of several of the most distinguished clergy of New York city, who were cognizant of the fact that Mr. S. had devoted many years of indefatigable research and labor in this department of Biblical literature. His *mode* of treating the subject will be found entirely original. It embraces a thorough examination of every system and theory, historic and prophetic, sacred and profane, ancient and modern, of those who have heretofore occupied this field. It takes into account all the objections, difficulties, and discrepancies that are alleged as insuperable to a satisfactory adjustment of the world's chronology, and claims to have produced what amounts to "A SELF-DETERMINING TEST" of this long litigated and intricate subject.

The *plan* of the author—taking as his STAND-POINT the present state of the question of *sacred* chronology as involved in that of the *profane*—is, first, to vindicate the authenticity and inspiration of the Mosaic Records, against the alleged vastly greater antiquity of ancient nations, particularly that of Egypt, as advocated by the school of modern Egyptologists; second, to settle the question as to which of the two versions of Scripture, the Hebrew or the Septuagint, (between which there is a *chronological* difference of about 2,000 years,) is *authoritative* in determining the chronology of human history; and third, to produce an *exact harmony* of the profane with the sacred records, from the Creation and fall of man to the Nativity. And while the author places his work in the hands of all upon its merits, the Press, both Religious and Secular, has reviewed it with favor. It has also been critically examined and pronounced a *Standard Work*, by many eminent Scholars and Divines, among whom are

REV. THOMAS DEWITT, D. D., *Collegiate Ref. Dutch Church.*
REV. SAMUEL R. JOHNSON, D. D., *Dean of the Gen. Theol. Seminary of the P. E. C.*
REV. FRANCIS L. HAWKS, D. D., LL. D., *Late Rector of Calvary Church.*

Rev. John M. Krebs, D. D., *Presb. Church, Madison Av.*
Rev. Charles K. Imbrie, D. D., *Presb. Church, Jersey City.*
Rev. John Cumming, D. D., F. R. S. E. *Scotch National Church, London.*

Price of Single Copy - - - - - - $2 50

N. B.—The work will be forwarded to any part of the United States (postage free) on the receipt of the price ($2 50) on application to John F. Trow, 50 Greene St., or to the author, No. 371 West 35th Street.

www.ingramcontent.com/pod-product-compliance
Lightning Source LLC
Chambersburg PA
CBHW030748230426
43667CB00007B/885